PLAZA

Like Our Very Own

Adoption and the Changing Culture of
Motherhood, 1851–1950

Julie Berebitsky

University Press of Kansas

© 2000 by the University Press of Kansas
All rights reserved

Published by the University Press of Kansas (Lawrence, Kansas 66049), which
was organized by the Kansas Board of Regents and is operated and funded by
Emporia State University, Fort Hays State University, Kansas State University,
Pittsburg State University, the University of Kansas, and Wichita State
University

Library of Congress Cataloging-in-Publication Data

Berebitsky, Julie.
  Like our very own : adoption and the changing culture of motherhood,
  1851–1950 / Julie Berebitsky.
      p.   cm.
  Includes bibliographical references and index.
  ISBN 0-7006-1051-0 (cloth : alk. paper)
  1. Adoption.   2. Motherhood.   3. Adoptive parents.   I. Title.

  HV875 . B467   2001
  362.73'4—dc21   00-034952

British Library Cataloguing in Publication Data is available.

Printed in the United States of America

10 9 8 7 6 5 4 3 2 1

The paper used in this publication meets the minimum requirements of the
American National Standard for Permanence of Paper for Printed Library
Materials Z39.48-1984.

For my parents, with love

Contents

Acknowledgments

Many people helped in the production of this book, and I offer them my sincere thanks. Most especially, I am indebted to my dissertation adviser, Margaret Marsh. I first became interested in the topic of adoption when I was working as a research assistant on her book on the history of infertility, *The Empty Cradle.* Since then, she has encouraged and supported my work, both as a mentor and as a friend. I have grown both intellectually and personally from my association with her and offer her my sincerest thanks. The other members of my dissertation committee, Allen Davis, Sally Mitchell, and William Cutler, also deserve high thanks for their thoughtful and timely criticism and enthusiastic support. Thanks also to Temple University for generous financial support through a dissertation grant.

This work also benefited from the support and suggestions of a number of colleagues. At Temple, Sally Dwyer-McNulty and Christie Balka read early drafts of the chapters and made insightful suggestions. More important, their encouragement and interest sustained me, and our group deadlines kept me on track. Allison Hepler provided me with the insight of one who has survived the process and introduced me to Mazie Hough, who generously shared her research with me and arranged my access to the Good Samaritan Home records. Finally, I am indebted to Rodney Hessinger, Katie Parkin, and Chris DeRosa, who kept me connected to the outside world during the writing of the first draft. Katie's thoughtful reading of a number of chapters and, most important, enthusiastic help and enduring friendship at copy machines and elsewhere are especially appreciated. Special thanks also to Gina Dorre, who provided me with the benefits of her exceptional vocabulary.

I would also like to thank my colleagues in the History Department at the University of the South, especially Houston Roberson, whose friendship cheered me during the revisions. Sewanee's Interlibrary Loan Department deserves special recognition for its willingness and ability to track down even the most obscure of popular magazines. Thanks also to Brittany Glenn, who provided important research assistance with the small details. I would like to thank *Washington History* for permission to use material from my previously published article, " 'To Raise as Your Own': The Growth of Legal Adoption in Washington" (Vol. 6, spring/summer 1994). My editor at the

University Press of Kansas, Nancy Scott Jackson, also gets high marks for alternately pushing me and encouraging me at all the right places. Thanks also to Barbara Melosh, whose careful reading and astute criticism led me to clarify and develop a number of important points.

Life is, of course, not only about work. I thank the people who kept my mind off work or, often, listened to me complain about it. My parents, Bill and Beverly Berebitsky, and my brother, David, Lisa Hill, Pauline Robert, Judy Avila, and Lynn Gasser all provided a sympathetic ear and significant diversions. Finally, my deepest thanks to Woody Register.

Introduction

In 1940, the journalist Avis Carlson published an article in the *Atlantic Monthly* heralding the new array of scientific tests that could accurately measure the mental development of infants and possibly even predict the ultimate achievements their innate gifts would allow. These devices, Carlson contended, were especially good news for childless American couples whose only prospect for having a "family" was to follow the uncertain course of adoption. Although adoption was in "vogue," it also constituted "a real emotional upheaval for those who undertake it." These tests, Carlson believed, could allay "some of the anxiety and hesitance. . . . Foster[1] parents who have much to offer a child in the way of cultural advantages should be able to rest quietly in the knowledge that only a superior baby will be given them. And it would be a great help during the first precious months of adjustment to their new estate if they could be free from the nagging little fear that after all the baby may not come up to their expectations."

According to Carlson, to "have showered love on and centered hopes in a disappointing child is a bitter experience for any couple." Likewise, "to grow up in a home where more is expected of him than he has the capacity to be is one of the cruelest situations any child can have to meet." This disappointment was not limited to families created by adoption; as Carlson noted, this "fundamental disparity happens sometimes with the parents' own offspring." With the use of the new developmental tests, though, this situation could be avoided in adoption. In fact, Carlson maintained, "all responsible placement agencies yearn to keep it from happening in [adoptive] homes, where the fitting of child to home is not an act of God. Elimination of this element of chance should be part of the compensation of adoption."[2]

Magazine stories that assured prospective parents that reputable child-placing agencies now used scientific tests and rigorous screening of a child's background to eliminate the hereditarian "risk" of adoption began to appear in the 1920s. Given Americans' growing faith in science, these pieces possibly eased the fears some felt about taking an unrelated child into their home and contributed to the growing interest in adoption. By 1940, then, although highlighting the difference between adoptive and biological families, Carlson's article nonetheless presented adoption as a positive way to create a family that closely mirrored the biological ideal. Indeed, with the help of trained professionals, infertile couples could not only realize their dream of a family but also be ensured that their hopes and dreams for their children's future would come true.[3]

This understanding of adoption, in which new parents benefited as much as the child and "experts" took pains to "match" a child's potential to a family's expectations, was relatively new. In 1851, when Massachusetts passed the first modern adoption statute, most people would have regarded the "rescued" child as the primary benefactor and the adoptive parents as either big-hearted or foolhardy. Then, orphanage matrons placed children by chance and intuition after receiving word from neighbors and clergy that a family was of "good character." The investigation into both a child's and a prospective family's background, which occurred in many adoptions by 1940, was clearly an improvement over the cursory examination of old. Moreover, the idea that both the parents and the child profited conforms more to today's understanding of parenting and childhood. Yet it is incomplete to see these changes simply as a narrative of progress, for although changes in adoption practice reflected important shifts in Americans' conception of the value of children and the purpose of family, adoption also worked to support these shifts and to help construct the new family ideal.[4]

Today, adoption is at the center of many divisive, even rancorous debates that reflect the ever-increasing politicization of the family.[5] The controversy over adoption by gay and lesbian couples or single adults, interracial and international adoptions, and "open adoption" calls attention to the fact that when most people think of adoption, they tend to think first of the creation of a traditional nuclear family: the adoption of an infant by an infertile married couple of childbearing age and at least middle-class standing. In this view, far from pushing the boundaries of family life, adoption represents a conservative form of family, one that falls in line with the cultural ideal. This presumption, however, has not always been the case. This study examines how adoption came to mirror the nuclear biological family, a process that served to uphold that particular model of family as the ideal. Moreover, this study will show that adoption did not simply reflect the normative family but also helped define the ideal, contemporary family.

In the late nineteenth and early twentieth centuries, adoption, as many Americans understood it, was less rigid, adoptive parents more varied, and the structure of adoptive families more diverse. Although childless couples constituted the majority of adoptive parents during the period covered by this study, unmarried women (single, widowed, and divorced), older couples, and parents with biological children also commonly adopted and, more important, received public approval or even commendation for their actions.[6] As adoption gained in popularity, the public discourse surrounding adoption grew in proportion. Much of the discussion, whether carried on in popular magazines or in professional journals, centered on a key set of questions: What qualities made a parent? What configurations of adults and children counted as a family? Whose motivations entitled them to the right or privilege of parenthood? Adoption, more than a residual aspect of debates about family and parenthood, has served as a public site on which the culture at large thrashed out the meanings of *family* and *parenthood*—meanings that have dramatically changed over time.

Anthropologist Judith Modell argues in her study of contemporary adoption that adoption "not only mirrors biology but also upholds a cultural interpretation of biological, or genealogical, kinship." In Modell's assessment, adoption quite logically came to mirror biology, since "blood" and "birth" serve as the primary symbols of kinship in American culture. Yet I am arguing that adoption came to mirror the biogenetic family so closely not just because blood symbolizes "true" family but because social experts and middle-class Americans in the twentieth century increasingly focused on the nuclear, democratic family—the sexually satisfied, playfully compatible heterosexual couple with "planned for" children living in an "emotionally healthy" home—as the ideal and only legitimate family. This form, many believed, would save "the family" from the crisis of divorce and decline that seemed to threaten individual families as well as the stability of the larger society.[7]

The cultural discourse about adoption, especially since 1920, has been about the future, meaning, and social function of "the family," as much as it has been about blood. Blood served as the point of reference or standard of measurement when adoptive parents asserted that they loved their adopted children "just like their very own" or when Americans in general talked about adoption. This comparison referred not only to a blood tie but also to a specific understanding of the purpose of families. In Carlson's magazine article from 1940, for example, we read that children should replicate and ultimately replace their parents. But, as the author points out, such duplication and transfer do not always happen in biological families. With the practice of "matching," adoption "guaranteed" that families would function as many believed they should: to ensure that a child had the ability to achieve the class position and status aspirations of its parents. Here we see the growing tendency to treat children as a kind of consumer good, ranked according to their "extras." The most "loaded" were placed, both literally and figuratively, with families with the most "buying power."

Although this commodification of children is troubling, it represents the way some Americans thought about adoption. Even more people, including adoptive parents, social commentators, and child welfare professionals, talked about it in this way. As a consequence, the language of the market is used throughout this book to describe the relationship between adoptive parents and children in an attempt to represent one of the significant frames through which Americans saw adoption. For example, we see this perspective in 1924, when reformer Josephine Baker told readers of *Ladies' Home Journal* that every child-caring agency she consulted emphasized that "there are not enough children to go around, for the demand is always greater than the supply." In a slightly different vein, the *Saturday Evening Post* published "The Baby Market" in 1930, an article that used stock market metaphors to discuss the growing popularity of adoption. According to the author, it was a "big bull market," with "baby securities" promising "investors" plenty of "dividends" paid out in toothless smiles and endless giggles. In many of the cases, this usage reflects the growing consumerism and changing economy of the twentieth century and the lexicon that accompanied this new ethos. When a social worker had to justify the adoptive home studies that caused prospective parents such anxiety, she explained that "alas, we have no Dun and Bradstreet rating emotional stability."[8]

Sometimes, however, the description of children as commodities seemed to reflect a belief that children were in fact commodities to be consumed and adoption merely another way to satisfy personal needs and desires. In 1924, an Oklahoma department store featured adoption in the publicity for its sale of baby products. Two babies from a local child-placing society were displayed in bassinets; within an hour, enough shoppers had submitted applications to assure good homes for the "advertised" children and the bassinets. In 1931, the business manager of a college in Washington, D.C., who wished to adopt a child, requested a meeting with Grace Abbott, chief of the U.S. Children's Bureau. Not wishing to occupy too much of her time, he took the "liberty" of enclosing a statement "telling about the child that we want and about ourselves." "Perfect health" and an "American Protestant" background were two "essential requisites" for the child. He hoped that these qualities would be coupled with "at least some of the following: New England ancestry; an I.Q. of at least 110; a happy, lovable disposition; some social and cultural background." The couple certainly did not expect to get these things for nothing. He was Harvard educated ("being of the fourth generation to have attended that college") and intended to send the child "to a college of equal standing." The Children's Bureau received few, if any, other requests that so explicitly juxtaposed desires and purchasing power, although sentiments akin to these appeared in a number of others.[9]

Some Americans were troubled by this approach to adoption. Many prospective parents of modest means felt that the wealthy were buying children, using their financial power to move to the top of waiting lists or to wriggle around agency requirements, and they expressed outrage at this material evaluation of family life. Professional child-welfare agencies also struggled with this question. In the late 1940s, social workers vigorously debated whether they should begin to charge fees for adoption placements. On the one hand, reputable agencies feared being "faced with the charge of giving human life for money." If cash changed hands, what distinguished professional organizations from the black market? In addition, fees could imply that the agencies existed to serve the needs of adoptive parents, not those of the child.[10]

On the other hand, overseeing an adoption was a costly undertaking for child-placing agencies. Moreover, many child-welfare professionals argued that they were providing a professional service like any other; lawyers charged fees (even when they lost the case), so why shouldn't trained social workers? Some suggested that many prospective parents preferred this "businesslike" relationship that mirrored interactions in others areas of their lives. Whereas the recipient of charity was powerless, a couple paying a fee acquired the power of the consumer, which enabled them to demand better service from the agency. In some cases, payment could even overcome the feelings of "humiliation" that some felt over their childlessness. For example, a sterile man could use his "financial adequacy" to give his wife a child, thereby establishing "his competency in another vital area," which could "make up in part for loss in self-esteem." Within a short time, nominal fees became a standard part of professional adoption placement and were understood not as a child's "sticker price" but as payment for services rendered. As these many examples show, adoption is one of the many ways in which children's lives have been monetized and commercialized since the mid-nineteenth century.[11]

If adoption reveals the changes wrought by a growing consumer economy, in a similar manner, adoption practice displays changing attitudes regarding gender socialization. In the 1920s, as child-development experts began to argue that fathers needed to be actively engaged with their children in order to ensure their offspring's healthy emotional growth and successful acceptance of appropriate gender roles, child-placing experts began to exclude single women from consideration as parents. The process by which adoption came to mirror the normative family, to the exclusion of other family forms, was not necessarily natural or inevitable, but the cumulative result of a number of profound cultural transformations.

This focus on the normative family also must be seen within the context of the disarray and fears of the 1930s. As first the dislocation and uncertainties of the Great Depression and then the threat of fascism in Europe shadowed the lives of Americans, many turned inward to the family as a source of security, and many social commentators looked toward the family as a source of national strength. In the mid-1930s, for example, an educational organization argued that the family "represents the most integrated unit in our world of distracted and sundered groups, the most promising symbol, despite its difficulties, of greatly needed unification in our lives."[12]

At least one study noted this intense focus on family when explaining the seeming paradox that interest in adoption rose just as material prosperity was falling. After interviewing a cross section of those most involved with adoption (including adoptive parents, court officials, physicians, and attorneys), the author concluded that the "idea of bringing up children might . . . offer the possibility of more permanent satisfaction than a pursuit of prosperity which had proved chimerical." However, adoption was not simply a way for individuals to achieve private familial contentment. Rather, she asserted, the acceptance of adoption also distinguished and defined America. "People are ready to accept responsibility for the oncoming generation and the fact that a child is not 'stock of their stock' does not cause them undue anxiety." Adoption represented a "greater centering on the family unit" and seemed to many of those interviewed as "evidence that our citizens have indicated that this is to be 'the American way'—a way which contrasts sharply with the superguardianship which the authoritarian nations assume in the rearing of children." Interest in adoption symbolized American ideals of personal freedom and acceptance of difference, as well as hope for the future of American society.[13]

Rather than providing a historical survey of adoption practices, this work examines adoption for what it can tell us about Americans' changing understanding of family. As the producer of a socially created family, adoption changed as the dominant culture's understanding of family changed. These changes, of course, did not happen overnight or uniformly across lines of class or race. A study of adoption also exposes how Americans both resisted and encouraged those changes. In 1935, for example, an elderly couple wrote to the U.S. Children's Bureau for help in locating a girl to adopt. "Let me know what size girls you have," the letter stated. "Do you know anything about the stock. I don't want a girl whose parents are or was crimnals I want one I can be proud of. One thats inteligent & will take an education."[14] This letter reflected an overriding concern with heredity and a belief that an endless number of children were readily available for adoption. In addition, the letter's unsentimental tone harkened back to an older, utilitarian understanding of childhood and stood in stark contrast to the majority of letters the bureau received in this period.

More common were letters like that of a woman who, after thirteen years of marriage, was still childless and whose heart was "broken over this unfortunate thing." She wrote to Eleanor Roosevelt (letters to the Roosevelts were passed on to the bureau) after learning that all the child-placing agencies in her state had long waiting lists and that it "will probly take years before our turn comes." She mentioned no concerns about the child's background, but instead assured the First Lady that "we are highly recommended by everyone if you care to investigate us." Her desire was "something so deep in our hearts, for the wanting of a baby, that every carriage I stop to look at, gives me a pain around the heart, wishing it was I pushing that carriage."[15] Here we see an understanding of children as emotionally priceless and of adoption as being at least as beneficial to the parents as to the child. Yet in combination with the much different first letter, it also reminds us of the variety of concepts of family and beliefs about the purpose of family that exist at any given time.

The discourse swirling around adoption reflected larger concerns about the form, function, and significance of the family, but underneath this cultural debate were actual individuals trying to create their families. The second aim of this study is to recover the historical experience of adoptive parents during the years 1851 to 1950. It explores their thoughts and feelings, fears and frustrations as they moved from contemplating the idea of adoption to making the commitment to parent an unrelated child. This 100-year period witnessed the transformation of legal adoption (the legal transfer of all parental rights and duties from a biological parent to an adoptive parent) from an uncommon proceeding to a relatively commonplace event. It also saw the meaning of adoption solidify. With the growing frequency of legal adoption and the increasing professionalization of adoption placement, adoption came to be understood primarily as a legal process, not simply as taking a child to raise as one's own. Yet because people of varying social classes, races, ages, and sexualities adopted (or tried to), a study of adoptive parenthood also exposes the tensions between individual understandings of family and those of the dominant culture.[16]

Adoptive families who went through a child welfare agency to locate a child had to meet the agency's standards, but this requirement by no means stopped them from asserting their own beliefs about family and parenthood. Throughout this century-long history of adoption, we see battles for control over who would define the meaning of family. Adoptive parents continually struggled to maintain the integrity of their understanding of family in the face of the increasing power of outside authorities. In a society in which families were intensely private, adoptive families (at least at their formation) were public: much of the early history of adoption involved negotiating the divide between public and private.

As a private family matter, adoption was largely a woman's issue. Since at least the 1830s, not only has the care of children been women's primary responsibility, but motherhood has been the primary marker of womanhood. Consequently, as a number of scholars have shown, women seem to have experienced (and still experience) the pain and loneliness of involuntary childlessness much more intensely than men. With regard to adoption, it was almost always women who approached the orphanage doors and asked the director if there was a child to adopt. In return, the director based his or her decision whether to place a child in the home on the quality or potential quality of the woman's mothering. In granting an adoption decree, the courts made a similar decision whether the mother in the adoptive home met the standards of idealized motherhood.[17]

The woman-centeredness of adoption continued in the twentieth century. In the early years of the century, popular articles on adoption often commented that when wives first mentioned the subject, husbands often reacted coolly toward the idea. According to one author, "the first thrill" of adoption comes "when you win your husband's consent." In a slightly different vein, an authoritative text on adoption, published in 1943, noted that it would use the pronoun "she" instead of the grammatically accepted "he," since a woman would be the child's primary caregiver and the social worker who placed the child also was most often a woman. Today, adoption continues to be primarily a women's issue. In the growing genre of adoption autobiography, for example, more women—whether adoptive mothers, birth mothers, or female adoptees—tell their stories than men. Similarly, a recent article written by adoptive mothers began by noting that "mothers-to-be, rather than fathers, are often in charge of painstakingly arranging the adoption, as though it were an analogue to carrying a child." A history of adoption, then, is necessarily a history of women.[18]

Adoption may have supplied a woman with a child to mother, but it did not necessarily provide her with an identity as a "real mother." The experience of adoptive mothers brings into stark relief the cultural construction of motherhood. Nineteenth-century middle-class ideology held that all women possessed an innate maternal instinct, indeed, that this instinct was the essence of woman. A mother's love, therefore, was natural and inevitable. But was the love as natural and as inevitable for a woman who had not come to motherhood "naturally" through giving birth? Many believed it was not. An unspoken hierarchy existed (and still exists) within the ideological system of motherhood. The apex of motherhood, far from being universally attainable for all women, depended on a woman's successful passage through the perils of childbirth. Adoptive mothers occupied a place on the edges of this ideal from which they pleaded for cultural acceptance of a maternity based in nurture. Beginning in the twentieth century, however, as the authority of outside experts started to vie with the powerful claims of maternal instinct, adoptive mothers found themselves on more solid ground. Adoptive mothers could be as educated on motherhood as biological mothers, and so their experience began to converge with the ideal. Historically, then, adoptive mothers consistently have challenged and, on occasion, supported the dominant definition of motherhood.[19]

African Americans do not figure prominently in a history of legal adoption to 1950. After the Civil War, African Americans, largely excluded from public child welfare services, kept the tradition of informally adopting orphaned and needy children, a tradition that had originated in Africa and had continued and adapted in slavery. When private individuals founded the first adoption agencies in the 1910s and 1920s, they determined the scope of their work; with rare exceptions, they focused on serving white clients like themselves. As the influence of professional social workers in adoption increased after 1920, African American families found themselves further removed from the mainstream of adoption policy. The racist beliefs that African Americans always took care of their own—and preferred to do so—and that illegitimacy carried less of a stigma in the black community than among whites excused professionals from providing adoption services to African Americans.[20]

This is not to say that African Americans were uninterested in legal adoption. Of the four child-placing agencies I examined, only the Board of Children's Guardians in Washington, D.C., consistently worked with African

American children. Its records from the late nineteenth and early twentieth centuries suggest that African Americans adopted young, unrelated children at the same rate as their white counterparts. Possibly, then, more African Americans would have adopted had services been available. Moreover, such agencies would have had the potential to serve a large audience. Due to poverty, disease, and inadequate health care, the rate of involuntary childlessness among African Americans was significantly higher than among whites throughout the period of this study.[21]

Even if a childless black couple approached a child-placing agency that dealt with black children, they often failed to find a child, despite the large number of black children in institutional care. In 1943, for example, an African American woman from Chicago wrote to Eleanor Roosevelt pleading for help in locating a child. Married five years, she had "not been bless with a baby, as I had hope I would," despite repeated visits to physicians. She and her husband had finally approached their local child-placing society only to be rejected because they lived in a basement apartment. Her home, she maintained, was "very well heated, plenty of sunshine. . . . Why is it," she asked Mrs. Roosevelt, "that I who wants a baby very much, can't have one? When women who don't want them, have them and have them on door steps, in alleys. My marriage is going on the rocks because of this."[22]

This woman's experience was not unique. As numerous scholars have noted, social workers set unwavering standards for adoptive applicants on such issues as income, housing, marital history, and full-time homemaker status for the prospective mother. Many African American applicants found it impossible to meet these expectations. Discrimination persisted even after national efforts by African American organizations and concerned social workers began in the late 1940s to reform professional attitudes toward black applicants specifically and the black family more generally. In addition, many African Americans had a distaste for or a distrust of the formalities and investigations associated with legal adoption through a professional child-placing agency. All these factors contributed to a relatively low incidence of adoption.[23]

Nevertheless, race was (and still is) often an issue in adoption. In 1904, for example, racial tensions flared in an Arizona mining town when nuns from New York City placed forty Irish orphans in Mexican Catholic families. Outraged over these interracial placements, local Anglos abducted the children and distributed them to white homes. The courts interpreted the whites' actions as racial rescue, not kidnap, and allowed them to keep the children, despite the Catholic Church's passionate assertion that the children's souls needed Catholic homes. Blonde babies in "brown" homes, even middle-class brown homes, were an intolerable breach of the color hierarchy.[24]

The threat of race mixing through adoption was also a concern of those who worked in child welfare. In the years before adoption was in any way regulated, some reformers worried that white children, and especially white little girls, might fall into the hands of African American men who were married to or involved with white women. The placement of foundlings was another potentially problematic situation in those cases in which a child's skin was not unambiguously white. In September 1928, a two-week-old girl was found abandoned in the hallway of an apartment building in the Bronx and was taken to a local hospital. Doctors there initially listed her color as white, but within a few weeks, some people had begun to wonder if she might have a "slight taint." This racial limbo meant that the child could not be placed in a permanent home, since authorities would not know whether to place her with a black or white family. In December 1929, doctors were still baffled, with one noting that "she has a good body, but her color is questionable. She is well tanned but does not seem like a negress to me at present." A few months later, the state child welfare agency determined that the child "was of some other background than colored. The skin is very light; eyes, nose and mouth not typical of Negress . . . [some] people have even remarked that she looked like 'a little Mexican.' She is very hot-tempered." The child was placed in a permanent home shortly thereafter, although the record does not mention the race or ethnicity of the adoptive family. Although many Americans were increasingly willing to expand their understanding of family beyond blood ties, they still held fast to principles of racial difference in distinguishing kin from strangers.[25]

Historiography and Methodology

For all the foregoing reasons, adoption can tell us much about the history of the modern family in the United States. Until very recently, though, the practice has been the focus of surprisingly little historical research. It has received some treatment in histories of child welfare, but these works view adoption as one of the solutions to the problem of dependent children and discuss it in the general context of the development of foster care in the late nineteenth century. Conflating foster care and adoption, however, tends to blur the important distinctions between the two. Foster parents often adopted the young children placed in their homes and even more commonly treated the children as part of the family. Yet those who approached a child-placing agency with adoption specifically in mind usually had different intentions from those for whom adoption came after an association with a child. For many, adoption was not necessarily a functional response to a social problem but a meaningful and deliberate way to create a family.[26]

Some historians have approached adoption from the perspective of the policies of individual agencies engaged in adoption placement or from that of the social welfare experts who would ultimately come to control adoption to a large degree. Others have addressed such specific issues as the history of secrecy and closed records or social workers' attitudes toward placing illegitimate children for adoption. And finally, a number of historians of the legal system have provided thorough and insightful analyses of the development of and changes in adoption laws. These studies add important information to our knowledge of how adoption developed in this country.[27]

They are less useful, however, in telling us about adoption as a particular family form and exploring how adoption reflects and affects the larger culture's understanding of family. Social workers, for example, remained skeptical about the value of adoption until the 1920s and 1930s. Yet, as we shall see, their reservations and misgivings cannot be used as an accurate measure of interest in or attitudes toward adoption in the larger society. Prospective adoptive parents did not necessarily share social workers' concerns, and in fact, social workers' policies complicated the process for many of those who wanted to adopt a child. Moreover, these studies keep us from seeing and appreciating the role of adoptive parents in influencing adoption policy and defining the meaning of adoption.

A study that hopes to document the history of adoption from the perspective of adoptive parents faces an immediate and immense problem of sources. At least half of all nonrelative adoptions completed during the period of this study were privately arranged transactions in which the adoptive parents secured the child either directly from its biological parents or relatives or through an intermediary, such as a physician, attorney, civic leader, or member of the clergy. In these adoptions, it appears that there was a much greater chance that the adoptive and biological parent or parents would meet, however briefly. A follow-up study of such adoptions arranged in Florida from 1944 to 1947 found that 38 percent of the adoptive parents had met the biological parents; for middle-class adoptive parents, these contacts were quite brief.[28]

When birth mothers and adoptive parents had less than a high school education, however, contact was often much more direct. These birth mothers were more likely to arrange for the placement of their children (who most often were not newborns) without the help of an intermediary and with the assistance of relatives and friends; for example, a neighbor of the adoptive mother might have a friend whose grandchild needed a home. These arrangements could be quite impromptu. Although in many cases the adoptive parents had been considering adoption before the opportunity presented itself, at other times they responded to a birth mother's crisis even though they had not previously entertained the idea. The spontaneity and compassion that appear to have characterized at least a few of these adoptions can be seen as something of a midpoint between the new midcentury ideal of confidential adoptions and older, informal community methods of caring for dependent children. Unfortunately for the historian, these methods of transferring children leave virtually no records.[29]

A great many people, however, found children through social agencies such as orphanages or maternity homes, and these exchanges did create records. However, the files of the vast majority of these institutions are closed to researchers by tradition or state law. Even when records are available, they can be difficult to use. For example, in the years before social workers developed casework methods, information about a child in an institution's care could be found in the matron's daily log, minutes of the board, and any number of registers, ledgers, and correspondence files; often letters from both biological and adoptive parents appeared in these records. From these sources, I pieced together individual adoptions, from the circumstances that brought a child to the orphanage to a prospective parent's initial inquiry through the institution's evaluation of the adoptive parent and finally to the adoption itself. Through this stitching process, I was able to reconstruct enough transactions to create an accurate portrait of adoption in the last decades of the nineteenth century and first decade of the twentieth.

Tracing a child's history through an institution is more easily accomplished after the turn of the twentieth century, when social workers developed casework techniques that provided standardized information on a child. Yet these records are frustrating in their own right. For one, social workers kept case records for their own use. The voices of adoptive parents appear only in the caseworker's translation; they reveal as much, or more, about the social worker as they do about the adoptive parents themselves. Even with these shortcomings, these records provide us with a useful view of the relationship between a potential parent and a child's legal guardian as they struggled to reach an agreement about the nature of adoption and family. Because of both limited access to adoption records and the limited perspective of the records, historians must turn to other evidence to reconstruct the history of adoption.[30]

Mass-circulation magazines prove to be among the richest sources for examining the growing acceptance and changing understanding of adoption in America. Of course, prescriptive literature can be a problematic source, reflecting the ideal as opposed to the actual situation. Yet in the case of adoption, popular magazines played an important role in both popularizing this family form and establishing its meaning. Adoption frequently appeared as the subject of popular articles because of its connection to many of the social concerns of the time. As a means of caring for homeless children, adoption responded to the problems of child dependency that troubled many Americans in the first years of the twentieth century. From 1907 to 1911, for example, the *Delineator,* a popular women's magazine, ran a "Child-Rescue Campaign" that highlighted adoption. Articles answered how-to questions such as where to find a child, as well as addressed prospective parents' concerns and fears regarding such issues as possible hereditary taints and how family and friends might react to this new member of the family. The *Delineator* campaign, as I show in chapter 2, contributed to a growing middle-class interest in adoption and encouraged a specific perception of adoption.

As a means of forming a family, adoption also related to the "family crisis" that worried many Americans. As the birthrate declined and the divorce rate rose among the white middle class around the turn of the twentieth century, the popular press began to examine such previously taboo subjects as birth control, venereal disease, and sexual intimacy. Adoption took its place in this growing discourse about saving family life and solving family troubles. In 1923, in an article entitled "Cradles Instead of Divorces," millionaire financier and diplomat Henry Morgenthau contended that "every adoption prevents a divorce." According to Morgenthau, divorce "comes about because people have no one on whom to spend their superfluous affection." For "the average American," he maintained, a "mere husband or wife" was not enough. Childless couples had "to hunt up excitement outside the home." Boredom and surplus affection were not, however, just personal problems. This "is serious," Morgenthau argued, "because if America is to hold the moral leadership of the world, we must first get our own house in order. . . . To do that we must create proper home units, each with a child or children."[31]

In journals and at conferences, child welfare professionals readily admitted that popular magazines fueled a growing interest in adoption and that these articles critically influenced the understanding of adoption. In 1942, for example, the director of child welfare for the commonwealth of

Massachusetts noted that the volume of adoption petitions had more than doubled since 1935, a change she attributed to the "publicity given to adoptions by magazines, books and radio programs." At first, such experts expressed relatively little concern that laypeople and the mass media were directing the dialogue. In the 1920s, when the U.S. Children's Bureau received inquiries asking for information on specific questions—such as how to tell a child he or she was adopted—it often referred the inquirer to popular magazine articles.[32]

Yet already in the 1920s, some professionals were casting a more critical eye on the popular media. As they increasingly focused on gaining control over adoption practices, the control of disseminating information to the public became a matter of concern. The Children's Bureau began to monitor the press, sending praise to those whose articles put forth the standards advocated by professionals and letters of protest to those whose articles did not. By 1940, the degree of concern had grown to the point that a master's degree candidate in social work devoted her thesis to the topic. In a study of twenty-one popular articles on adoption that appeared in magazines from 1937 through 1940, the author found only eight that clearly promoted the standards held by professional social workers; the remaining articles, she believed, were excessively emotional. Her thesis concluded with a call to social workers to increase their efforts to disseminate their views to the public. Yet she was quick to point out that more scientific articles would not be enough. Even "the most widely read prospective adoptive parent may still come to [the social worker] without any real inner awareness of what adoption means." By contrast, social workers' professional training in "human relationships" gave them unique and informed insight into adoption. This social worker's concern suggests that magazines were a powerful transmitter of ideas regarding adoption, even in the face of contrary expert opinion, and were seen by many Americans as a trustworthy and authoritative voice on the subject.[33]

If magazines presented adoption in terms of sentiment, and social workers in terms of science, how did adoptive parents understand this form of family? Letters to the U.S. Children's Bureau from would-be parents seeking assistance in locating a child provide us with the opportunity to see how both popular and professional attitudes toward adoption filtered into the general public. These letters (by the late 1930s, the bureau received dozens of such letters each year, and by the mid-1940s, hundreds of letters arrived annually) allow us to hear individual Americans' thoughts on the relative importance of nature versus nurture and, especially, on the importance of family in American life.

This book stops in 1950, the beginning of the period (circa 1946–1970) in which adoption won widespread cultural legitimacy and there were more unrelated adoptions each year than ever before or since. Postwar America witnessed a celebration of marriage and domesticity, a rise in the number of births out of wedlock, and a turn toward an environmentalist view of human development. These factors came together to move adoption even further into the mainstream of American life. Yet this movement to the center of American family practices was not so much a new period in the history of adoption as it was the culmination of a long history. For decades, adoptive parents, social workers, and interested Americans had been defining (and redefining) the meaning of adoption. Moreover, as the number of placements made by social workers increased in the postwar period, the principles regarding such matters as confidentiality, standards for adoptive parents, and "matching" that professionals had developed in the 1920s, 1930s, and 1940s affected an increasing number of adoptions. In other words, the mainstreaming of adoption in the postwar period occurred because previous generations of American women and men had already struggled to build families that, in their minds, were just as good as the "real thing."[34]

1 | Fear, Fulfillment, and Defining "Family"
Becoming an Adoptive Parent, the Early Years

Washington City Orphan Asylum
Jan. 31, 1913

My husband and myself have been thinking over the matter of adopting a little *orphan girl* between 2 and 5 years of age, if it is possible to do so. We have been married nearly 17 years but no children have been born to us, which loss we feel greatly. We want to make this our lifework in giving an excellent home to some *orphan girl*, born of *good parents*. We can give the very best of references in regards to ourselves being refined, christian people, and of good surroundings. We would like very much to adopt a little girl *right away*, if possible, and very likely another a little later on.

Would your board of managers kindly advise us further on this matter and oblige.

Yours Very Truly,
Mrs. Robert Powell
Washington, D.C.[1]

When Mrs. Powell wrote this letter to the Washington City Orphan Asylum, she must have thought her loneliness was near an end. It was not. Although the asylum had almost 150 children in its care, there was no child for Mrs. Powell. Her letter and her ultimate failure to find a child, however, highlight the hopes, fears, and frustrations of adoptive parents in the late nineteenth and early twentieth centuries.

This chapter has two aims. First, it reconstructs the experience of adopting a child around the turn of the twentieth century through the records of two child-care agencies in Washington, D.C. As we can see even in a document as brief as Mrs. Powell's letter, for many people, the decision to adopt did not come quickly or easily, despite an intense longing for a child. Prevailing attitudes regarding the sanctity of blood ties and the significance of heredity, for example, played into a prospective parent's initial consideration of the idea through the actual process of locating and, for some, legally adopting a child. Although Mrs. Powell desperately sought a little girl, she also wanted one with a background and heritage she could comfortably accept—in her words, a child "born of *good parents.*"

Her ability to locate such a child, however, ran headlong into social reformers' efforts to find ways to keep poor families intact, efforts that significantly impacted the number and type of children available for adoption. The Powells desired a young child free from the threat of interference from biological parents, but there were few such children to be found. These factors, when coupled with prospective parents' unfamiliarity with the new adoption laws and the growing bureaucracy of child welfare institutions, made the adoption of an unrelated child a difficult and frustrating procedure.

This chapter also explores Americans' changing understanding of adoption and responses to the growing emphasis on adoption as a *legal* as well as a personal relationship. In the late nineteenth century, legal adoption was still uncommon enough that "adoption" did not necessarily signify a judicial decree. In many cases, families raised children like their own but, for a variety of reasons, never formalized the relationship. In fact, a few adoptive parents seemed to resist the idea that a piece of paper could create a meaningful family. For them, "family" meant emotions felt and responsibilities willingly assumed, not duties or rights juridically determined. Using the records of the Children's Aid Society of Pennsylvania, we see how legal adoption struck at the heart of some people's understanding of family, centered on mutual affections and personal commitment, and uncomfortably infused the concept with legal and economic meaning.

History of the Washington City Orphan Asylum

In 1815, Dolley Madison, wife of the fourth president, was among the founders of the Washington City Orphan Asylum (WCOA). One of the first such institutions in the country, the WCOA was created to care for children orphaned by the British raid on Washington during the War of 1812.[2] In addition to donations from citizens, a number of local Protestant congregations provided initial financial support for the asylum. A volunteer Board of Lady Managers supervised the daily activity and was responsible for all decisions regarding the admission and placement of children. Male trustees, also volunteers, administered the institution's finances. Prior to the Civil War, the institution generally cared for fewer than thirty children at a time. As Washington grew, however, so did the needs of the city's children. In 1876, a new facility opened, capable of comfortably housing 130 children, although at times the asylum cared for as many as 180.

According to the bylaws of 1878, the WCOA gave admission priority to full orphans (both parents dead); however, the institution also accepted half orphans and destitute children. In fact, these last two groups constituted the majority of the children who received care. Over the course of the nineteenth century, American reformers had come to believe that aid given too freely encouraged dependence. Accordingly, the WCOA followed a strict policy of admitting only children of the "deserving" poor. Before the WCOA would accept a child, its parent or guardian had to provide references, preferably from her or his local pastor, attesting to the person's "worthy" character. If a parent deviated from middle-class norms as far as alcohol consumption, sexual behavior, or even swearing were concerned, his or her worthiness could be questioned, and the child turned away. If the board believed that a child's parent or parents could, but simply would not, provide for it, the board rejected the application. Around 1880, for example, the board refused to admit the children of one woman on the grounds that her husband, whom the board stated was "lazy and good for nothing," should be forced to care for his children. The WCOA also refused admittance to illegitimate children, foundlings, and African Americans. WCOA directors gave admission preference to boys under the age of six and girls under ten unless a child was a full orphan.[3]

As early as the mid-1860s, the WCOA began to place children for adoption in the District of Columbia, Maryland, and Virginia. Previously, some children had been placed with families under terms of indenture, but in 1865, the first annual report noted that in addition to a number of children who had been indentured, "2 kind ladies have each adopted a little girl as her own child." Although both indenture and adoption placed a child with a family, they were fundamentally different: indenture signified an economic relationship, adoption an emotional one.[4]

Since the colonial period, dependent children had been indentured to private families from whom they received food and board in exchange for their labor. A child's indenture typically ended at the age of eighteen or twenty-one, at which time the young adult received a small sum of money, a suit of clothes, and a Bible, according to the terms of the contract. Often the indenture obligated the family to provide education or training as well. Even as it became increasingly common to care for dependents in institutions during the Jacksonian era, indenture continued, although reports of overwork and abuse caused the practice to fall out of favor in the last half of the nineteenth century.[5]

Informal adoption—that is, taking a child to raise as one's own but without any legal recognition—also existed as a means to care for orphaned or dependent children in colonial America and in the early nineteenth century, although it is impossible to determine how frequently it occurred. Orphans or half orphans commonly went to live with blood relatives or family friends who took them in as part of the family. Historian Margaret Marsh has shown that childless couples often eagerly received these children. For example, John Hancock, signer of the Declaration of Independence, was raised by his childless uncle and aunt after his father died; when they died, John inherited their property. Other childless couples who wanted the experience of parenthood or who needed an heir could take in the child of a living relative and raise that child as their own. In many cases, testamentary adoption occurred, with childless couples using their wills as a way to provide for a child they had raised. Still other forms of informal child sharing afforded those who wanted to parent the opportunity to do so. Colonial households often took in unrelated children as apprentices or servants or provided care for a child in need. These various relationships would not necessarily terminate the child's relationship with his or her biological parents.[6]

Legal adoption, however, did not exist. Adoption was not a part of English common law, which privileged the inheritance rights of blood relatives. In the late eighteenth century, a few Americans began to move away from this legal tradition by formalizing relationships through the passage of private adoption acts in the various state legislatures. The Massachusetts legislature enacted 101 such bills between 1781 and 1851. In 1804, the Vermont legislature granted the adoption petition of a childless couple who had been given an infant by a poor woman whose husband had deserted her and the baby; over the next sixty years, the state approved approximately 300 similar petitions. These individual bills generally provided for a change of the child's name and often for the child to inherit from its new parents. The acts also were expensive and time-consuming and, from the point of view of the adoptive parents, required a degree of social and political influence.[7]

In 1851, Massachusetts passed the first *modern* adoption law. This general adoption statute was more efficient and effective than passing individual acts, especially since it clarified a child's right to inheritance. It also detailed the steps by which a child's custody could be transferred to another guardian and completely severed all legal ties between a child and its biological parents. By the time Massachusetts enacted its law, a number of factors had combined to create a climate favorable to the institution of adoption. Most significantly, America had a rapidly growing number of children who were orphaned, homeless, or neglected as a result of the dislocations caused by expanding urbanization, immigration, and industrialization. Some of these children would find new families, and the adoption law gave these relationships legal security.[8]

The law also reflected new understandings of childhood, parenthood, and family life that had developed by the middle of the nineteenth century. Although most colonial households were nuclear in structure, their boundaries tended to blur, with children leaving home at some point to attend school or learn a skill in another family. These patriarchal households also were integrally linked with the surrounding community in matters of politics, social life, and trade. Distinctions between public and private life were not clearly or immutably drawn. Beginning in the late eighteenth and early nineteenth centuries, however, things began to change. The white, middle-class family, especially in northern and midwestern towns and cities, lost many of its public and productive functions and became more of a private institution.

Although it remains difficult to pinpoint the exact causes and moments of change, the middle-class family responded to profound shifts in the nation's economic, social, and political systems. As a market economy replaced a subsistence economy, the family moved from producer to consumer, and men followed production into the world outside the home. These economic changes created a more mobile and anonymous society that ultimately affected courtship and marriage patterns as children moved beyond the grasp of parental or community control; in choosing a mate, individual choice and mutual affection replaced parental suggestion. The married couple and their children—not the household—soon became the fundamental unit of society. In these families, separate from the larger community, the focus centered on the emotional rather than the economic support that members provided to one another. In private homes presided over by a loving mother and united by affection, children were a crucial element. Consequently, they began to take on a new significance, no longer valued for their productive labor but for the unique innocence and playfulness of their age. Whereas in the colonial period families and community were interdependent and intertwined, by 1830, the middle-class family existed in spatial, emotional, and functional opposition to public society. Family life, at least for the financially secure, was now largely private.[9]

Republican ideology also reached into the family, focusing attention on individual happiness, relations of power, and mutual rights and obligations. This new perspective can be seen most vividly in changes in nineteenth-century family law. The courts, in their decisions in a number of custody cases, were moving toward a legal code based on nurture, not blood. Rejecting the principles of absolute authority and patriarchal prerogatives, the judiciary began to consider the best interests of the child. No longer did a father possess complete control over the custody of his children; now, in custody disputes that ended up in court, judges decided who would provide the best care for a child. Overall, these decisions benefited women, as judges consistently gave mothers custody, especially of girls and children under the age of seven, in divorce cases and other custody battles. These decisions gave legal standing to the new emphasis on a woman's emotional domestic role that accompanied the development of private families. An idealized understanding of mother love became the standard the court used in determining custody cases.[10]

Decisions that challenged the belief that paternal authority was absolute contributed to the creation and acceptance of adoption laws. In cases in which the birth mother was dead, for example, courts sometimes gave control of a child to grandparents or other relatives rather than the father when the court deemed that these surrogates provided the child with maternal care. Although courts did not sever blood ties easily or often and generally favored the biological parent in a custody dispute with a stranger, the concept of "best interest" lent support to the idea that parenthood consisted of more than a genetic connection.[11]

The Massachusetts adoption statute reflected the new sentimental view of children and the cultural emphasis on their needs, especially for nurturance. In totally severing a child's relationship with its biological parents, the law gave adoptive parents a way to have their "own" children that was much more complete than the earlier, informal practices. Although childless couples were by no means the only people who adopted, the law provided them with a way to complete their conjugal families and achieve the new private, domestic ideal. The law also required that judges be satisfied that the applicants could provide for the child before granting the petition. In evaluating prospective parents and determining that the adoption was "fit and proper," the law focused on the welfare of the child. The Massachusetts law quickly became a model for other states. By the end of the nineteenth century, most states had enacted adoption statutes.[12]

In some cases, orphanages developed ways to acknowledge adoptions even before a state had passed a law. In 1895, Congress created an adoption statute for Washington, D.C., that allowed the legal transfer of a child's custody. It spelled out the terms by which adopted children gained inheritance rights and gave judges authority to transfer custody to "proper persons." However, in 1877, well in advance of the passage of this law, the WCOA began to keep an adoption register separate from its indenture contracts. The printed forms stated that the adoptive parents would promise to keep, protect, and treat the child "as their own" and "advance and settle [him or her] in life according as circumstance may admit." This slip of paper served as the legal transfer of custody. The brevity and generality of this document ("as circumstance may permit"), as opposed to the lengthy indenture contract that clearly spelled out the terms of the relationship, also underscored the private nature of family life. By 1895, at least seventy families had adopted unrelated children. The records of the WCOA suggest that prior to the development of the adoption form, people simply indentured children they intended to raise as their own: of the five girls indentured from 1851 to 1854, three were under the age of five.[13]

The WCOA did not actively seek either indenture or adoption situations for its children, but rather waited until an interested party approached the asylum. Mindful of the possible dangers and abuses of the indenture system, the WCOA abolished the practice for girls in 1882 and thereafter allowed them to be removed only "if there can be, by adoption, secured a home, which is one in reality, not merely in name." The monthly board minutes indicate that the WCOA actively enforced the adoption mandate. Aware that someone who really wanted a domestic servant could simply word his or her appeal in the appropriate fashion, the board vigorously questioned prospective adopters and immediately rejected any application that seemed even slightly suspicious.[14]

After 1900, the number of adoptions of WCOA children substantially decreased. At this time, the WCOA began responding to a national call to keep poor families together whenever possible. Its focus shifted from accepting permanent custody of children from families in difficult circumstances to providing temporary care until the families' situations improved. This change was first mentioned in the 1907 annual report; however, the shift was apparent as early as 1901, when the majority of relinquishment forms began to state a specific date or "until I can care for them," rather than until the child reached the age of eighteen. Although the number of available children dropped dramatically, the board minutes show that prospective adopters continued to request children.[15]

Adoption.

The Washington City Orphan Asylum hereby adopts _To Mr. George and Alice E. of New York City_

as our child*ren*_ *two*

Orphan named _Jessie, & James_ aged *13, & 10 yr. old* now

in said Asylum. And _George H. & Alice E._ covenants with

said Asylum to provide said Orphan with suitable food, clothing, lodging and medi-

cal attendance, in health and in sickness; and to instruct _them_ adequately

in usefulness, and in reading, writing and arithmetic.

WITNESS our hands and seals this _ day of _June 1878_.

Mr. George H. & Alice (SEAL)

Mrs. J. Lyman (SEAL)

In the late 1870s, the WCOA created two new contracts, of which this is one, to transfer custodianship of children to those specifically interested in adoption. The brevity of the new contracts, as compared with the much more detailed indenture form, underscores the growing emphasis on family privacy. (Library of Congress)

The Washington City Orphan Asylum placed children for adoption as early as the mid-1860s. (Library of Congress)

throughout the city. White children were cared for in the abundant special-ized institutions. Infants were immediately placed in private homes with wet nurses who were paid eight to ten dollars a month. Institutions for African American wards were not as plentiful. The situation for African American youths older than ten was especially dire; the board lacked not only a train-ing facility but also an institution in which to house them. Consequently, the BCG placed some dependent children in the local prison or reformatory. Temporary housing for African American children committed for brief peri-ods or until a foster home could be found was also a problem. In 1899, Susan Cook, an African American social worker, consulted with the BCG and estab-lished the Children's Temporary Home near Howard University to fill this need. As these examples indicate, the relationship between the BCG and Congress faltered in dealing with the needs of dependent African American children; Congress legislated the duties of the BCG but often failed to pro-vide the BCG with the autonomy, authority, or appropriations to fulfill those obligations.[20]

Although the BCG used institutional settings to care for its wards, its goal was to find homes for all children it considered suited for family life. This policy was quite progressive. Throughout the last decades of the nine-teenth century, philanthropists and charity workers vigorously debated the merits of "placing out" (similar to today's family-based foster care) versus institutional life, then the predominant method of caring for dependent chil-dren. In 1899, members of the National Conference of Charities and Correc-tion voted to advocate placing out as the preferred option. Not incidentally, placing out was significantly less expensive than institutional care.[21]

The BCG largely succeeded in finding private homes and reducing expenditures for the care of its wards; by 1905, three-fourths of both white and African American wards resided in free homes (that is, to which no board was paid). In the majority of these cases, families used indentures as a legal vehicle to transfer custody of the BCG wards, and in the cases of older children, some work was expected in return for their keep. Although the BCG originally placed black children in white homes, it discontinued the practice when it discovered that many of the black children were denied access to an education. When the BCG subsequently sought black families with whom to place the children, they had no trouble finding adequate homes. Some families took children on trial for adoption and eventually completed legal adoption proceedings. It is unclear how frequently the BCG sought prospective adoptive homes, but, as mentioned previously, adoption was not a logical alternative for the majority of children. Generally, about 5 percent of both African American and white BCG wards were on trial for adoption during a given year.[22]

"Born of Good Parents"

For prospective adoptive parents, taking an unrelated child into their home was taking a step into the unknown. During the late nineteenth and early twentieth centuries, cultural beliefs about heredity and attitudes regarding illegitimacy compounded a prospective adopter's natural fears. These concerns were so pervasive that it is not surprising that Mrs. Powell specifically requested a child "born of *good parents.*" Americans' faith in the power of heredity especially affected attitudes toward adoption. Many people, for example, assumed that characteristics such as poverty or laziness could be inherited. Some also believed that an individual's future fate lay in the moment of her or his conception; if a child had the misfortune to be conceived in the throes of drunken passion, a likely future of alcoholism or insanity awaited. In 1876, one legal commentator, referring to the new adoption laws, warned that the "fact that the subjects of adoption are so largely taken from the waifs of society, foundlings, or children whose parents are depraved and worthless; considering also the growing belief that many traits of mind are hereditary and almost irradicable; it may be questioned whether the great luxury of the American rule is for the public benefit."[23]

Eugenicists, whose influence increased in the early twentieth century, made their disapproval of adoption widely known. Henry H. Goddard, a leading eugenicist and author of the famous study *The Kallikak Family,* which claimed to prove that generation after generation inherited the social pathology of their ancestors, spoke out against adoption. Goddard told the story of a family who, moved by compassion, adopted a young girl to raise as their own alongside their biological children. Time passed, and the family's son fell in love with the girl. They married and soon began to have children. But the children were feebleminded. Although the girl had escaped her hereditary taint, it had appeared in a subsequent generation, and, Goddard warned, it always would.[24]

Beginning in the late nineteenth century, a number of progressive thinkers, social scientists, and reformers began to challenge these views. Jane Addams, John Dewey, and others whom historian Paul Boyer labels "positive environmentalists" argued that people also were creatures of their environment. An individual's poverty or immorality came about through his or her exposure to a degraded and immoral society, not because of an innately and irreparably defective character. Environmentalists actively worked to create better physical spaces—cleaner cities, safer workplaces, and purer amusements—in the belief that these changes would result in more moral citizens.[25]

Adoptive parents had to put aside their fears and join this group, which argued that an environment's influence could overcome any taint of heredity. Despite the dire predictions of eugenicists and others, many people adopted children with less than ideal family histories. For example, of the twenty-one legal, unrelated adoptions of children who entered into the BCG's custody between October 26, 1903, and January 25, 1906, six had parents with alcohol problems. The records of ten children are without information on one or both parents. Of the remaining five, one's mother had been arrested and convicted for being a "vagrant and public prostitute," another had syphilis, and yet another lived in the Government Hospital for the Insane.[26]

The troubled backgrounds of the children are not surprising. In the 1890s, many social reformers began to argue that authorities should remove children from their families under only the most egregious conditions. Consequently, the children who ended up in permanent BCG custody (and who were, therefore, eligible for adoption) usually came from families with such severe problems that social workers believed they could not be salvaged. Although it is possible that caseworkers or judges could have exaggerated the problems in light of their own standards of morality, case histories indicate that the majority of BCG wards came from deeply distressed families.[27]

These were the children available. If prospective adopters could not overcome fears about "tainted blood" or a child's previous environment, then they could not adopt. The sad case of John Hill suggests just how gripping these concerns could be. When John was one month old, his father made arrangements with a Mrs. Dwyer to care for the infant. His father had promised to pay Mrs. Dwyer board, but in seven months, he had paid her only three dollars, and it was rumored that he was now in Norfolk, Virginia. It appears that Mrs. Dwyer approached the BCG to have the child classified as dependent, entered into BCG custody, and then legally transferred back into her custody on trial for adoption. These actions would prevent John's father from returning and reclaiming the child.

These efforts to retain John imply that Mrs. Dwyer had a deep attachment to the boy. Three years later, however, when John was four, the agent noted that he was "developing transmitted vulgarity; incontinence of wine, and tainted blood inherited from father"; then the agent added, "Mrs. Dwyer [is] glad she did not adopt him." Three years later, Mrs. Dwyer returned

John because she could no longer control him. We will never know if fears about John's heredity were the primary reason Mrs. Dwyer decided not to adopt the boy, but his story shows how pervasive and credible Mrs. Dwyer's concerns were—credible enough to be accepted as justification for changing her mind.[28]

As part of their involvement in the national debate about the care of dependent children, BCG agents participated in a pioneering effort to promote family-based care sponsored by the *Delineator,* a popular, New York–based women's magazine with a national circulation of close to a million. The *Delineator's* "Child-Rescue Campaign," the subject of the next chapter, began in November 1907 and continued through February 1911. In its heartrending appeals, the magazine emphasized the importance of nurturance and environment over heredity in a child's development. Although it featured children from around the nation, two of the first children profiled in the series were BCG wards from Washington.[29]

The *Delineator* reported that James, a "sturdy" white four-year-old, entered BCG custody on his mother's request in 1904 when he was only eleven months old. His mother was a laundry worker whose husband had deserted her and their three children, and she could no longer make ends meet. After relinquishing James, his mother, too, vanished. The courts then classified his case as abandonment, according to the magazine. However, more was known of James's background than the article told. James's father was an "unstable drinking man," according to BCG records, and his mother's moral reputation was in doubt. In fact, James was illegitimate. Although his mother had a long-term relationship with his father, she had never divorced her first husband, who had left her because of her "immorality." Despite the fact that many readers would have interpreted these circumstances as alarming signs of heritable disaster, the BCG and the *Delineator* apparently did not believe that they rendered a child unfit for adoption. Or if so, they apparently did not feel obliged to pass on this information. James was quickly placed with a Massachusetts family whose only son had died five months earlier. Her heart "filled with joy" at receiving the child, James's new mother gratefully wrote to the *Delineator.* In "two years," she said, "I believe James will be as dear to us and fill the place of our own son. . . . He resembles our boy in a marked degree."[30]

Even those who adopted from the private WCOA—which screened applicants to ensure that only children of the worthy poor were accepted—expressed fears about the children's heredity. In March 1901, the Widmans took six-year-old Katie Moreland and twelve-year-old Allen Rogers from the asylum. Almost immediately, the children began "constantly giving a description of their homes & of their parents," according to a letter from Mrs. Widman to the director of the WCOA. The couple was shocked by what they heard: "Almost the first information from Allen to Mr. Widman was that his mother was dead. . . . that he had a colored brother[;] that his mother had this boy by a black man [and] he didn't seem to think there was anything wrong about it." Mrs. Widman continued, "You can imagine how I felt [—] I supposed every thing was spoiled." She had calmed her husband by telling him that "no doubt Allen has misrepresented his mother . . . I supposed she had a little colored fellow around the house and he thought it was a brother." But although she convinced her husband, Mrs. Widman had lingering doubts: "I still think perhaps that was the way of it," she wrote. Mrs. Widman also found Katie's background disturbing. According to Katie, her father was in jail "for stealing ice water." Despite her apprehensions, Mrs. Widman was determined to make a success of her new family and told the WCOA director that she had admonished the children, "if we ever heard another word we would punish them severely." But if the children's parentage left something to be desired, the Widmans were pleased to find them "perfectly honest. Nothing in the house is locked against them. . . . There is not a drawer or pantry place of any kind not even my trunk that is locked."[31] The Widmans recognized that the adoption of older children could bring problems, such as stealing. Although they seem to have been prepared for such imperfections, the Widmans' account shows just how alien and disconcerting a child's background could be to his or her new parents.

The adoption of illegitimate children was also shaped by prevailing cultural values and opinions. In the late nineteenth century, evangelical women across the nation opened maternity homes to help their less fortunate "fallen" sisters. Two of the most successful chains of homes, Florence Crittenton and the Salvation Army, required prospective residents to sign a contract promising to keep their children. These reformers believed that allowing a woman to give up her child would be the same as inviting her continued immorality. If a woman's lapse in morals went "unpunished," many felt she would continue to have children out of wedlock. By 1900, the vast majority of those involved with unmarried mothers—including the agents of the BCG—agreed that they should be encouraged, even required, to meet their maternal obligations.[32]

Professional social workers who began to investigate the problem of illegitimacy in the early twentieth century also thought that unwed mothers should keep their children. Their reasons, however, reflected their additional concerns regarding the children's health. The infant mortality rate of illegitimate children was almost three times that of children of legitimate birth. Keeping mother and child together and thereby keeping the child supplied with an abundance of mother's milk proved the most effective way to lower the death rate. In 1916, Maryland even passed a law requiring all mothers to remain with their children for six months after their birth. Shortly thereafter, Minnesota and Wisconsin passed similar "nursing laws" aimed at preventing the separation of unwed mothers and their children. These laws further reduced the already limited number of infants available for adoption.[33]

Some unwed mothers in the late nineteenth and early twentieth centuries did give up their children, but many, possibly even the majority, of these infants never found adoptive parents. A few women advertised in newspapers that they had infants available for adoption for a price; interested parties could purchase the child without any investigation into their character or any questions as to their motivations. Others paid a small fee, generally from ten to fifty dollars, to a baby farmer who promised to find a good home for the child. Baby farmers offered unwed mothers an easy way out of a difficult situation. In reality, however, few babies found good homes. Baby farming was a business whose profits came from capitalizing on the desperate plight of unwed mothers, not from locating adoptive homes, and the vast majority of infants died from lack of care. The more babies there were, the more money baby farmers made; as one late-nineteenth-century commentator noted, baby farmers wanted "to get rid of the little milk imbibers as quickly as possible." Another critic argued, "it may be taken as a fact that any person who makes a living through money obtained for the disposal of an infant does not care what becomes of that infant." Needless to say, these practices—and the growing movement to abolish them—cast adoption in an unsavory light.[34]

Other unwed mothers relinquished their infants to more reputable agencies such as foundling hospitals, which accepted children with no questions asked. Some abandoned their babies on the doorsteps of children's institutions. Even these babies, however, often failed to find adoptive homes. The national mortality rate for infants in institutions was appallingly high, on occasion reaching 85 to 90 percent. It was not uncommon for an illness to spread rapidly through a nursery, killing all the children.[35]

An abundance of evidence shows that when babies were available from reputable sources, adoptive parents quickly snapped them up. In Boston, for example, historian Jamil Zainaldin found one institution, the Temporary Home for the Destitute, that had such an easy time placing young children—including illegitimate children—that beginning in 1871 it switched its focus to finding infants for childless couples; the home soon found it impossible to meet the demand. Within a short time, however, the Temporary Home for the Destitute found itself under attack by those who argued that allowing a woman to surrender her illegitimate child freely and easily would encourage her continued sexual misbehavior and indirectly increase a city's social problems.[36]

Foundling hospitals often faced similar criticism, despite their supporters' impassioned statements that they lessened the incidence of infanticide. These institutions also easily found adoptive homes for the children in their custody. For example, the Washington (D.C.) Hospital for Foundlings, founded in 1887, placed 108 children in adoptive homes in its first ten years of operation; only one child failed to find an adoptive home. Tragically, the institution had a mortality rate of 70 percent, and 400 children died before they could be placed. Similarly, in the 1890s, the Sheltering Arms Home in Philadelphia noted that it always found plenty of homes for the illegitimate children it accepted.[37]

The records of the BCG also indicate that a child's legitimacy was not of primary concern to many adopters. In twenty-two legal adoptions of BCG wards, nine children were illegitimate, and three others were foundlings whose parentage was unknown. In addition, the *Delineator's* "Child-Rescue Campaign" easily found homes for the illegitimate children it profiled. Two of the first five children shown in the series were illegitimate, one of whom was a ward of the BCG. Requests poured in for this girl, and she was adopted by a couple who realized that their only child "needed a human companion."[38]

The policy of urging unwed mothers to keep their children helped create a baby shortage and shrank the pool of children available for adoption. As early as 1895, an agent of Washington's BCG, responding to a request for an infant, reported that there were none available and that "we have a very large number of applications" for the few infants it did receive. By 1910, one journalist reported that "for every unfortunate child that has lost its parents there are two homes that want it. There are not enough babies to go around."[39]

Given the terrible stigma of illegitimacy at this time, why were so many people willing—indeed, eager—to adopt illegitimate babies? Many adoptive parents appear to have been more concerned that a biological parent might interfere in their new family than that a child's parents were unmarried. For this group, possibly the potential return of a woman who had lost the stain of illicit sexuality when she surrendered her illegitimate child seemed less likely than the reappearance of parents who had relinquished their child only because they were too poor to care for it. It is, then, no surprise that foundlings especially had no trouble finding adoptive homes. For example, a BCG agent recorded that early one August morning in 1901, a "well dressed," white infant boy, who showed "evidence of [being] more than an ordinary deserted baby," was found abandoned in an alley. The case history also noted that, alerted by a brief notice in the newspaper that detailed the discovery of the child, several parties, "some of them wealthy," had already applied to adopt him. Three days after he entered into BCG custody, he had found a home.[40]

This child was an adoptive parent's dream. He was an infant, not an older child. Many adoptive parents expressed interest in adopting young children, since it would allow them to participate in all stages of a child's life and more fully feel they were the child's parents. This was another important reason why many adopters were willing to overlook a child's paternity (and, of course, an adoptive parent could take steps to ensure that the child's parentage remained a secret). In addition, in this particular case, the boy's fine clothes suggested that he was of good parentage, which might have eased prospective adopters' fears about the child's heredity. Most important, he, like other foundlings, appeared to be free of any relatives who might surface to reclaim the child and destroy the new family.

"No Relatives on Earth to Make Claim"

In her 1913 letter to the WCOA, Mrs. Powell emphatically requested an *"orphan girl,"* apparently fearful that sometime in the future a child with living relatives might suddenly be reclaimed. Despite the perception created by the multitude of asylums, full orphans constituted only 10 to 15 percent of the children in institutions.[41] The majority of children available for adoption had at least one living parent who, for prospective adopters, represented a possible source of disaster.

Despite the fact that it had legal custody of the children in its care, the BCG often hesitated to transfer custody to adoptive parents when a birth parent was living. This reluctance appears to have been prompted equally by the desire to help keep worthy families together and by the realization that the birth parent represented the potential for future disruption. Under the terms of its charter, the BCG was the "legal guardian of all children com-

mitted to it by the courts with full power ... to give them in adoption to foster parents." Sometimes, however, the BCG agent seemed uncomfortable
with this power.[42]

In February 1894, Robert and Angelina Simon, an African American couple, indentured two-year-old Mary Teresa James, who had been abandoned
the previous October. (The Simons took Mary into their home the year
before Washington passed an adoption law, when indenture was the only
form of custody available to them. Moreover, if an adoption statute had
existed at the time, it is unlikely that this "poor" family could have afforded
the legal fees.) Two months later, the BCG caseworker reported that Mary
was well and Mrs. Simon was "much attached" to her. Good reports continued, and the caseworker noted that although the home was poor, Mary was
"affectionately and kindly treated." A year later, Mary's birth mother
returned, stating that "she never intended to abandon it and was told at the
Foundling Asylum she could reclaim the child at any time."[43]

The BCG agent contacted the Simons, urging them to return Mary:

> I have no doubt you know how the mother feels at being separated
> from her, and that you will take into consideration the fact that a
> mother always has a moral right to her child so long as she leads a
> proper life herself, even though someone else may have the legal right
> as you & we have in this case.[44]

Apparently, the Simons did not respond, and a week later the agent sent
them another letter. This time, the agent encouraged them to return Mary,
even though, the agent acknowledged, the Simons had taken her with the
understanding that Mary "had no mother who would ever give you any
trouble."[45] The Simons did not give Mary back, and it appears that the birth
mother made no further effort to have her returned. The Simons were relatively fortunate. Others were not. And if trouble with the biological parents did arise, an adoptive family could not depend on the support of the
institution. As late as 1918, the BCG still had no policy regarding the placement of children in permanent or adoptive homes in cases in which the BCG
knew that the natal family wanted a child back.[46]

The prevailing attitudes regarding the sanctity of the blood tie help explain the Simons' story. The sentiments expressed by the BCG agent regarding the biological mother's "moral right" to her child reflected popular
beliefs. In 1902, *Harper's Weekly* related to its readers the true story of a
wealthy, childless woman who offered a poor woman $5,000 for her little boy.

The mother refused to sell her son. The commentator, echoing the sentiments of the BCG agent, determined that the mother had made the right choice:

> It was not for nothing that he was born of her and not of another.
> Their relation involved the mystery of ties, of those divine purposes by which when a being, of the myriad beings insentient in time and space, is brought to consciousness, it is assigned to a pair divinely appointed to be its father and mother, or the keepers of its earthly destiny. It does not matter who or what they are; they belong to it even more than it belongs to them.[47]

Although Americans had always respected blood ties, this reverence was new. The reform efforts of the late nineteenth century, which focused on keeping poor families intact and unwed mothers and their children together, glorified biological parenthood and especially biological motherhood. Only a few decades earlier, however, reformers had believed that working to keep poor families together was nothing more than ill-considered sentimentalism. Reformers, according to historian Michael Katz, never precisely articulated the reasons behind this profound change in philosophy, but rather vaguely and speciously argued that substitute parents could never replace biological ones. In fact, as was readily apparent in the rhetoric surrounding unwed motherhood but somewhat less clear in regard to poor families, reformers' concern centered as much on the fate of the biological parent as on that of the child. Children would serve as a civilizing influence on their wayward parents; without their children to serve as a check on their bad behavior, the poor and immoral would continue their downward spiral and ultimately threaten the stability of society. In addition, in the process of offering aid, the state or reformers could supervise and monitor the family.[48]

Before children were admitted to the WCOA, their parent or guardian had to sign a relinquishment form that gave the asylum full custody, including "the right to bind out." In addition, the parent agreed not to "in any way interfere with the views and directions of the Managers." The form, however, did not specifically mention adoption. Possibly because it did not have the legal right to transfer a child's custody through adoption, or perhaps out of concern for the rights of the biological parents, the WCOA on more than one occasion asked birth parents for permission to adopt out their child and abided by the parents' decision when they refused. The WCOA also knew that a parent could create quite a disturbance and noted in the annual report for 1877 that the half orphan was "too often subjected to the interference of a surviving parent, who is not merely injudicious, but frequently dissolute." Failure to get a parent's permission could end in an unpleasant situation.[49]

Three months after the Widmans adopted Katie Moreland and Allen Rogers, Mrs. Moreland approached the board about regaining custody of her daughter. The WCOA board insisted that Mrs. Moreland had "always wanted Katie adopted." Regardless of whether there had been a genuine misunderstanding or a change of mind on Mrs. Moreland's part, an ugly legal battle ensued. In December, an attorney for Mrs. Moreland approached the board requesting Katie's return. Board members read to the attorney what they characterized as "several insulting letters," apparently about Mrs. Moreland's character. The board minutes state that after much discussion the attorney decided that it was "best for Katie to remain where she is but to let Mrs. Moreland know of her whereabouts and visit her if possible." When Mrs. Widman refused the board's request to allow Katie's mother to visit, the board decided to "let the lawyers fight it out."[50]

On January 7, 1902, the Widmans and Katie's mother reached a legal agreement. In exchange for visitation rights of "not more than four times a year ... only at such times as may be acceptable and agreeable" and knowledge of Katie's address, her birth mother agreed to "not in any manner interfere with the control of the said Widmans ... over said child or do or say anything or cause to be done or said anything that will disturb the child ... in its present affections and happiness."[51]

The fear of relatives returning seems to have dissuaded many from adopting. The WCOA records include a number of requests specifically for orphans; when nonorphans were offered instead, these children were generally rejected.[52] Other would-be adopters took the nonorphan dependent children but developed strategies to minimize the risk of parental interference. Although some of the out-of-state, nonrelative adoptions recorded by the WCOA can be explained by the fact that a friend of the adoptive parents who lived in Washington assisted in finding the child, it is also possible that others purposely adopted a child far from home so that there would be little chance of a biological parent interfering. It is important to note that the WCOA was not unsympathetic to adopters' fears; in 1889, it added a clause to one adoption that allowed the adoptive parents to return the child if her birth mother interfered. In 1916, the WCOA board promised a couple from the West, who had recently adopted a daughter, that it would not disclose her whereabouts to anyone. When the girl's brother approached the board a few years later, it refused to tell him anything more than that she was well.[53]

BCG records also suggest that the threat of a relative's interference caused considerable anxiety for prospective adopters. In 1908, a BCG agent wrote to Dr. Cross, who had contacted the BCG as a result of the *Delineator* campaign. The agent recommended a white, eleven-month-old, foundling boy and assured Dr. Cross that the child was "beautiful . . . with no physical drawbacks and no relatives on earth to make claim upon him."[54] For Dr. Cross, and for many others interested in adoption, title free and clear rated as high as dimples and sturdy limbs; uncontested custody, not "tainted blood," was their primary concern.

"I Am Sure We Can Suit You"[55]

Neither the BCG nor the WCOA had a well-thought-out or routine adoption procedure. The BCG appropriated some of the traditions of the indenture system, such as trial periods, but the rest of its process remained undefined, and agents responded to questions as they arose. Although points of conflict between the institutions and adopters continually flared, areas of compromise and cooperation also surfaced.

The BCG required that a child remain on trial for adoption for at least a year or two before it would consent to a legal adoption. Returns were common during the trial period. An examination of twenty-one adoptions from 1903 to 1906, for example, showed that six children had been returned from an adoption trial before being placed permanently.[56] In these cases, trials lasted from as little as one day to as long as two and a half years. The BCG case histories do not usually indicate why prospective adopters returned a child; one case simply noted, "People dissatisfied."[57] In another, Alma, a white, five-year-old, full orphan who had spent only two months in BCG custody before being taken on trial for adoption, was returned by Mrs. Whitt because Alma "had eczema and scrofula." In spite of Mrs. Whitt's warnings about Alma's poor physical condition, another family quickly took her into their home and legally adopted her a year and a half later.[58] For the second family, the opportunity for full custody of a child with little threat of interference by a relative apparently superseded minor physical imperfections.

Unlike the BCG, the WCOA did not allow children to be taken on trial. The board believed that this policy safeguarded the children against the insecurity of a trial period and ensured the sincerity of the adopters. Although the policy appeared to be progressive and sensitive, it failed to consider the needs and fears of people adopting older children—realistic concerns, given that in WCOA adoptions, the average age of the child was six for girls and almost eight for boys.[59] Quite possibly, the prospective adopter viewed the trial phase as necessary to evaluate a child's heredity and to grow confident that a reciprocal bond of affection could be cultivated and any reservations overcome.

Such was the perspective of Mrs. Morrow, who in October 1899 wrote to the asylum requesting "a little girl one five or six years of age wd suit me . . . I thought a young child wd more easily become attached to me." Mrs. Morrow and her husband were an older couple who lived on a secluded farm about forty miles northwest of Washington. The board responded that Mrs. Morrow could have a little girl, but only if she would agree to adopt her. Mrs. Morrow replied, "we do not object to adopting the child after we become attached to it."[60] The board found this arrangement agreeable and sent Mrs. Morrow eight-year-old Virginia Kennedy, who had been admitted to the WCOA by her father, a widower. The placement seems to have worked out for both Virginia and Mrs. Morrow. The WCOA reached a compromise with the Morrows possibly because some years earlier the family had successfully taken a boy from the WCOA. The records show, however, that other prospective adopters who asked for a trial period were refused.[61]

The WCOA policy also failed to eliminate the return of adopted children. When faced with an adoptive parent who no longer wanted a child (especially if the only legal arrangement was the WCOA form), the WCOA had no choice but to take the child back. During the thirty years for which WCOA records are available, at least four families returned children they had adopted. In one case, the adoptive mother maintained that even after more than three years, the young girl she had adopted at age five "still remembered her own [birth] mother."[62]

The legal system provided another source of conflict and irritation. Given the trouble the Widmans endured to keep Katie Moreland, one might think that they had taken immediate steps to adopt her legally. In fact, they had specifically decided not to do so. The Widmans thought the WCOA adoption form gave them full custody of Allen and Katie and were "under the impression that all had been done that was to be done in the matter." When Mrs. Widman learned she had to adopt the children though the courts, she went to her local courthouse, only to encounter a clerk who, she wrote to the WCOA, "seemed to know nothing as business of that kind does not come before our courts once in a life time."[63]

Many prospective parents shared the Widmans' confusion. A number of people who received children from an orphanage or child-placing agency in these early years seem to have been unaware that the adoption needed to be finalized through the courts. Rural farmers and people of modest means often took children, and it is likely that these men and women had little knowledge of or experience with the law, which, by the late nineteenth century, had become increasingly forbidding. Lawyers, in their quest for professionalization, had developed a distinctive jargon and an impressive array of casebooks and other paraphernalia to intimidate clients from participating in their own cases. Law was now a science that required specialized educational training. In addition, lawyers were not held in high regard; according to one historian, in the late nineteenth century, only bankers stood in lower public favor. As late as 1924, a respected child-placing expert argued that many families who "felt that the children belonged to them in spirit and in fact" did not legally adopt because the process was so "thoroughly formidable."[64]

Adoption laws were new, and even if adoptive parents could overcome their general confusion, many still found the laws inconvenient, if not impossible, to use. When the Widmans visited their attorney, they learned that in Virginia, where they lived, the adoption laws ignored the custody claims of an orphanage and required the consent of any living parent "that is not a drunkard or an imbecile." In addition, each adoption petition cost twenty-five dollars. The Widmans bristled at such an outlay and decided "to have the matter laid before the Board & have some other arrangements made—it looks like a shame to take the child away . . . the children both think they are ours and call us Papa & Mama." The appeal to the board's desire to act in the children's best interest apparently worked; the Widmans kept the children. In fact, considering the custody dispute the Widmans later had with Katie's mother, it is unlikely that she would have signed the release necessary for the adoption of a child with a living parent. These situations obviously raised complicated moral and legal questions. Nonetheless, considering that most children available for adoption did have at least one living parent, many prospective adopters—if they were determined to have legal custody—had to weave their way through this tangle.[65]

Does a Piece of Paper Make a Family?

The Widmans' story suggests that some foster parents, in stark contrast to today's society, simply did not place a great deal of importance on a legal piece of paper. A decision not to adopt a child could also reflect a family's determination that a judicial decree in no way contributed to the legitimacy of their family. In some cases, families seem to have felt that the immediate facts of day-to-day care mattered more in establishing a true family than a legal contract. Taking a child, in this view, was a private, familial decision, not a public one, and therefore outside the purview of the law. In other cases, legal adoption seemed unnecessary. Whereas legal adoption provided parents with the assurance of permanency, it also gave to the adopted child the promise of inheritance. This was, in fact, one of the primary reasons many adoptive parents turned to the law to formalize their new relationship. Thus, families of limited means often had little reason to pursue legal adoption.

The case histories of children in the custody of the Children's Aid Society (CAS) of Pennsylvania during the period 1882 to 1900 provide a wealth of information on Americans' attitudes toward and the perceived necessity of *legal* adoption. Although few of the young children were legally adopted, a substantial number found homes in which they appear to have been accepted as full members of the family (see the appendix). These cases suggest that although many people wholeheartedly embraced the underlying principle of adoption—treating an adopted child in every way as if it had been born to you—some did not yet see adoption primarily in legal terms for philosophical or practical reasons. In other words, Americans had mixed reactions to the idea that families could be (or should be) created legally.

The CAS of Pennsylvania got its start in March 1882 when Philadelphia's Committee on the Education and Care of Children passed a resolution that dependent children should be placed with families instead of in institutions. In private homes, they "could be protected from the degrading associations of the street and the immorality born of herding children together." In 1883, the work of the CAS dramatically increased when the Pennsylvania legislature passed a law that children between the ages of two and sixteen could not be kept in poorhouses for longer than sixty days. The state's larger counties, including Philadelphia, chose the CAS and the policy of placing out to take care of the children affected by the new law.[66]

Although novel in Philadelphia, the idea of placing children in private homes instead of institutions was not new. In 1853, Charles Loring Brace, a New York City reformer, founded the first Children's Aid Society to help dependent and delinquent children. Brace felt that these children threatened the social order of the city and looked to stable Christian families to redeem them. In 1854, he began sending trainloads of needy and wayward children who were generally old enough to work west to the countryside. When the "orphan train" arrived in a town, farmers and local residents lined up to pick out a child.

Few of the children, however, were orphans. Almost half had at least one living parent, and in some cases, the CAS took children without their parents' permission. Usually the homes in which the children were placed received only the most cursory inspection and, at best, minimal supervision thereafter. Once chosen, children would receive care and moral instruction in return for their labor. Brace also hoped that the children would be treated (at least eventually) as members of the family, a goal that was often achieved and, on a few occasions, legally formalized. For the vast majority, however, legal adoption was not an option, since they had living parents. Brace's plan illustrates the varied understandings of children that existed in midcentury. In essence, it represented a blending of the old system of indenture, which saw children in terms of their labor potential, with the new cultural emphasis on the importance of nurture in ensuring a child's healthy development.[67]

The policies of the CAS of Pennsylvania differed significantly from those of the New York CAS. Although Pennsylvania's CAS placed its children in country homes, the children were close enough that they could be visited by the staff once or twice a year. In 1890, the hiring of Homer Folks greatly influenced the CAS's policies. Folks, a young, innovative, Harvard-educated reformer, would go on to become a national leader in child welfare work and was an especially vocal advocate of placing out and the benefits of home life. Under his leadership, the society thoroughly investigated the foster homes before placement.[68]

The aim of the investigation was not to find the wealthiest home for a child but rather to ensure that a child was placed safely. Prospective foster parents filled out applications that addressed their financial or "material fitness" for parenthood. Although families needed to be economically stable, the CAS did not require a minimum income, only signs that the family's future seemed secure and that it would be able to provide a child with life's necessities. In general, the CAS placed children with rural farmers of modest means. The CAS maintained that it situated many of its wards in "the best families in the neighborhood," but it did not want the children to have lives of leisure. In the tradition of Charles Loring Brace, the CAS sought homes where some labor would be demanded of the child in the hope of instilling a strong work ethic. The ideal placement was a farm home small enough that it was "self-contained and independent" and in which "the necessity for self-exertion" was both "pressing and unavoidable." The CAS ensured an applicant's "moral fitness" through a personal investigation of the home and a canvassing of neighbors. Here, the goal was to ensure that children were placed in families of good "character" and solid reputation.

Once the CAS placed a child, it required the child's pastor and school teacher to send quarterly reports to the society. Similar investigations became standard in child-placing agencies in the late nineteenth and early twentieth centuries, although reference letters from an applicant's clergyman or physician often took the place of initial interviews.[69]

Given the limited means of the majority of CAS foster families, it is possible that they did not feel compelled or obliged to protect their children's inheritance by initiating legal proceedings. As historian Lawrence Friedman notes in his discussion of the development of adoption laws, "the point of adoption, as a *legal* device, is not love, but money; nobody needs formal adoption papers or a court decree to love a child desperately; inheritance of property from a 'father' or a 'mother' is another matter. Adoption is not a requirement among the landless poor."[70]

In addition, the adoption process cost anywhere from ten to twenty-five dollars, depending on lawyer fees and court costs. Similar to the Widmans discussed earlier, a surprising number of CAS foster families balked at this expenditure. For example, Mrs. Agnew had cared for Emma for free for about two years when the CAS approached her about adopting the child. The agent noted in the case history that Mrs. Agnew responded that she would not adopt Emma "as the price is too high." Indeed, the twenty dollars was probably prohibitive for a family described by the CAS agent as "pretty poor." The home was so poor, in fact, that the agent noted that "this is not the place C.A.S. would now select for one of its wards."[71] In this case, a foster family was caring for a child—providing food, clothing, and shelter in addition to love, nurturance, and guidance—only to be asked to expend more of its limited funds for what in many ways amounted to a useless slip of paper, since they had little or nothing to bequeath.

In some cases, though, the aversion to the adoption fee seems to have been based more on a matter of principle than on economic hardship. A childless couple, the Hawkinses, took four-month-old Alma into their home, and the agent noted that she was immediately "loved and regarded as their own child." Five years later, the CAS agent suggested adoption to Mrs. Hawkins, who conferred with her husband and soon approached the CAS board about initiating proceedings. Although the board granted its approval, the effort stalled. Six months after the board's go-ahead, the case history noted that Mr. Hawkins was "standing out about the $15 adoption fee. Does not see why he should pay. Devoted to Alma and would be heartbroken to lose her." The case history indicated that a legal adoption never occurred. It is possible that Mr. Hawkins had second thoughts and used the fee to justify his refusal. Yet it is also possible that Mr. Hawkins believed that after caring for Alma for over five years, he was already her father in the ways that mattered to him. Paying a fee might have seemed too much like "buying" a child; an official decree might not have held any real meaning in terms of his individual understanding of family.[72]

The case of Lizzie Jones also is telling in this regard. In 1884, this five-year-old went to the Reillys for free, where she was "loved as their own child" and did not know she was not their daughter. In 1892, the agent again noted that the Reillys treated Lizzie as their child but also commented that they "will not adopt." The entries for the next few years continued to refer to the permanent quality of the relationship and to the Reillys' refusal to begin legal proceedings. In this case, the issue of adoption became a source of irritation and opposition between the foster parents and the caseworker. The confrontation culminated in the caseworker's notation that "The Reillys will not adopt and defy anyone trying to take Lizzie away." Here, the issue of adoption possibly symbolized a struggle for authority between the foster family's de facto right to a child they had raised for a dozen years and the legal right of the CAS. The Reillys won the conflict; the case history contained no more mention of adoption, and Lizzie remained in the home.[73]

The story of one of the first CAS wards further illustrates how a legal contract conflicted with some people's definition of family. Mary's biological mother brought her to the society in 1882. The CAS quickly placed four-year-old Mary with the Warringtons, who treated her as one of the family. In 1890, when Mary was twelve, her foster mother died. The foster mother's grown son, Dan, assumed care of Mary, and the agent reported that he treated her as a sister. Within a few years, the CAS approached Dan about signing indenture papers for Mary. He refused. Instead, he promised the agent that he would always care for her. A few years later, when Mary was about eighteen, the agent again approached Dan, this time about setting wages for Mary's work in the family store. Again Dan refused to be forced or cajoled into a contractual relationship with Mary. According to the agent, Dan stated that he would not pay her because she had "always been treated as one of the family and has money when she needs it."[74]

The possibility must be considered that Dan bought Mary a bonnet or two and let her come to Sunday dinner in exchange for an abundance of free labor in his store. But the facts speak more to an affective familial bond. Dan could have returned Mary to the CAS after the death of his mother, but did not. He did, however, pay for her to learn dressmaking. Dan's actions suggest that he saw family in personal and private terms; he had both given his word that he would care for Mary and acted in ways that showed his sincerity. Dan, therefore, might have resented the intrusion into his relationship by either a legal agreement or the values of a CAS agent.

Dan's resentment also is understandable in light of the new middle-class standard of domestic life that sanctified familial privacy and autonomy. By the end of the nineteenth century, families that failed to meet this new ideal increasingly found themselves the target of outside intervention. Reformers and the courts worked to ensure that all families met this norm, which, ironically, meant violating their privacy and autonomy. Public intrusion into the family, then, suggested failure, an inability to manage one's affairs. Dan's family, by contrast, was capable of managing its affairs. Indeed, if Dan and his family had deviated too much from the middle-class ideal, the CAS would not have placed a child with them. Yet by taking a CAS ward into their home, they introduced a public voice into what had been a private space. For individuals used to independent decision making, the unsolicited advice or demands of a CAS agent might have clashed with their sense of self or family. Moreover, the construction of middle-class families as private and affectionate, in contrast to the indifferent, public world of work, also might have affected some Americans' attitudes toward legal adoption. In this oppositional view, only relationships in the marketplace, not in the home, should be buttressed and ensured by law.[75]

Other factors, more pragmatic and far less principled than the above (possibly even malevolent or cowardly), could explain a foster family's refusal to adopt. A foster family might have been too stingy to pay the legal fee or to assume permanent financial responsibility, or too frightened of a child's heredity and cloudy background. In a number of adoption-like cases, the foster family had biological children, and the possibility exists that the parents did not want the foster child to share in their estate; in at least one instance, a foster father's adult children by a previous marriage protested the adoption of the foster child.[76]

The CAS had a responsibility to protect the best interests of its wards. To this end, the CAS pressured the state legislature to amend the law to allow for adoptions not only in cases in which a child's parents had actually deserted it but also in those in which the parents had been neglectful. In 1887, the legislature passed such a law, which greatly increased the CAS's authority to consent to a child's adoption.[77] Although the CAS had worked actively to increase its custodial powers, the case histories suggest that happenstance as much as standard policy dictated its attitude toward adoption in any specific case. Often agents initiated a discussion of adoption with the foster parents, but in apparently similar situations, they did not. It is possible that in the latter cases, legal impediments that were not noted in the case histories precluded adoption. In addition, by 1905, the CAS oversaw the well-being of over 4,000 children. CAS policy required agents to visit each child twice a year, a daunting task. The overworked agents probably did not have the time to encourage or enforce adoptions consistently in situations that were clearly familial—especially when families resisted. For harried agents, perhaps the knowledge that a family deeply cared for a child was enough. Other agencies, however, such as the CAS of Western Pennsylvania, insisted that those caring for young children in an adoption-like situation "promptly" initiate legal proceedings.[78]

Still, despite the CAS's attempts to enlarge adoption laws, in many cases it appears that the society preferred not to enter into legal arrangements with its foster families. The CAS placed its wards in foster homes without any type of legal contract. Without an indenture or other legal agreement, the CAS could remove a child to serve the child's best interests, and the foster parent could return a child at will. The CAS believed that "such elastic terms lighten the burden of present responsibility, and give opportunity to the growth of affection, which 'binds' more firmly than indenture or agreement papers." This statement highlights the tension some Americans felt over the question of whether the law could create a "real" family. It suggests that some people believed that emotional ties, not a legal commitment, created a meaningful family.[79]

The lack of a formal agreement worked in a child's best interest in cases in which a foster family mistreated a child or in which the foster family and the child simply did not get along. It also gave the CAS ultimate control over a child and the power to insist that a foster family behave in a certain way or risk losing the child. Although the CAS agent noted that young Mamie was "treated exactly as a daughter in the home" and that she "remembers no other home and has forgotten even her own name," the caseworker was not completely satisfied with the placement. The foster family was "respectable and kind," but it was also "very plain" and "poor." When the agent told the family that the home was too damp and therefore not suitable, the family quickly found a new residence in order to keep custody of Mamie. The agent was only slightly more satisfied with the new home, which was "very unattractive." Although displeased with Mamie's surroundings, the agent was sensitive to the emotional bonds that had developed between the child and the family and noted that she had been in the home too long to be moved.

The agent, however, was not so understanding with regard to the foster family's inquiry about adopting Mamie. The request came in 1892, well after the 1887 law that expanded the CAS's authority to consent to adoptions, and also after the family had cared for Mamie for a number of years. The initial request was the only notation of adoption in the case history, and it is possible that the foster family changed its mind or that there were legal impediments. But the caseworker never mentioned the subject of adoption again. Perhaps in this case, a poor family sought legal adoption as a means to ensure that Mamie could not be removed. Legal adoption would protect their newly formed family and serve as a way to assert to the caseworker that although they were poor, they were a real family.[80]

In most cases, the CAS tried to walk a fine line between protecting the financial future of its charges and safeguarding their newly formed emotional ties. But these cases also highlight the unique nature of adoptive families and the potential difficulties child welfare workers faced in establishing standards for these constructed families. Adoption, at least in the eyes of the law, was a way to ensure a stable home environment for the child; the Pennsylvania law of 1853, for example, stated that the court had to be satisfied that the "welfare of such child will be promoted by such adoption." To this end, the CAS investigated a prospective adopter's finances before consenting to an adoption. In one case in which a poor family requested adoption after caring for a child for nine years, the society concluded that consent should be granted only if a "definite arrangement" could be made that the child would receive education and training. In other cases, the CAS gave its consent to poor families if it was convinced of the family's moral worthiness and if the family persisted in pressing for adoption.[81]

Still other considerations could figure into a family's decision to formalize the relationship in this period. Although foster parents often voiced their fears that a biological parent would return to claim a child, not all initiated legal proceedings. One would think that foster parents would begin the adoption process quickly to ensure that they had some legal claim to a child in the event that its natal parents appeared. There were, however, a number of compelling reasons why these families might choose not to adopt. Some worried that the publicity surrounding the adoption might alert the biological parent to the child's location and possibly bring on a custody battle or interference. In addition, the fear of extortion was common enough that one mid-nineteenth-century commentator noted that as "almost everyone" knew, biological parents would "reclaim the child as soon as any money can be made out of it."[82]

Other families expressed concern that the public nature of the legal procedures would expose both the child and the community to the fact that the child had not been born to them. Families often did not tell children they were adopted (either legally or informally), out of a desire to spare the child the stigma of adoption and to promote more fully the child's identity as a member of the family. Some families, for example, requested that the CAS not use its stationery when corresponding and that the agent identify herself as a friend when making her twice-annual visits. In this early period of adoption history, the question of whether or when to tell a child of his or her adoption was rarely discussed. In 1905, one of the first articles on adoption to appear in a popular magazine admonished adoptive parents to follow their instincts and not to tell. Secrecy shielded a child from the taint of having been born to "unworthy" parents and from the prevalent belief that a poor child's heredity left something to be desired.[83]

Secrecy also helped protect the adoptive parents' emotional investment in a child. In over two-thirds of the cases, blood relatives had brought the children to the CAS.[84] The adoptive parents' fear that a biological parent might return and disrupt their happy home was matched by their terror that a child—especially one who was four or five years old when adopted and might have misty recollections of another mother or father—would seek out its biological relatives. In fact, as adults, some CAS children did approach the agency seeking information regarding their biological relatives and—because adoption records before World War II were not always closed—received it. In one case, a family moved from Pennsylvania to Wilmington, Delaware, to ensure that no one would find out that their daughter was adopted and to keep her biological father at bay; at the age of nineteen, the young woman contacted the CAS and within a few months located her biological father.[85]

In the spring of 1900, Mrs. Harris approached the BCG about adopting a young white girl, and the agent told her to visit one of the institutions in which BCG wards resided. She did and notified the BCG that a small child, Marie, had captured her heart. Shortly thereafter, she received the following letter from the agent:

> I have delayed answering your letter in order to have opportunity to visit the mother of the little girl upon whom your choice fell. This woman, Mrs. Locke, has suffered greatly because of the utter worthlessness of her husband and has been compelled to surrender several of her children to our care. She says she will consent to the

adoption of Marie, provided she can see and talk with the prospective foster parents. I suggest that you appoint a time to see Mrs. Locke at this office.

Did you see the little Beech Girl while at the Industrial Home School? She is the one of whom I made particular mention to you.[86]

The prospect of a command visit with Marie's birth mother, the emphasis on the questionable character of the child's father, and the opinion of the agent, a "professional" social worker, were enough to change Mrs. Harris's mind. She quickly abandoned her intention of taking Marie and turned her attention to the other child, asking if the BCG could give her "full legal control" of young Ethel Beech. In the end, though, the uncertainty and difficulty of the adoption process apparently proved to be too much; neither Ethel nor Marie ended up with Mrs. Harris, and she never received a child through the BCG.[87]

At the turn of the century, over 100,000 children made their homes in institutions, a fact social commentators and the press often lamented.[88] For people just beginning to consider adoption, finding a child was probably their least concern. Yet adopting a child proved much more difficult than going to an asylum and picking out one of the lonely waifs who resided there. It is clear that many people expressed a genuine desire to adopt. Some pushed aside their fears about heredity, risked the vagaries of an inadequate legal structure, and gambled on the chance of parental interference to create a family through adoption. Some, however, could not accept these uncertainties.

Countless others adopted in "spirit," deciding for any number of reasons not to formalize the relationship. Many families feared what a CAS agent indistinctly described as "the publicity" attached to adoption, suggesting that families wanted to keep the child's status secret from the child itself and from the community, and his or her whereabouts hidden from any biological relatives. Other factors could play into a family's decision not to initiate legal proceedings, including a lack of property to bequeath, concern over the cost of the proceedings, unfamiliarity with the law and distaste for the legal profession, and a complacency engendered by a caseworker's lack of insistence. And for a few others, the decision not to legally adopt possibly represented a larger aversion to judicial or public intrusion into what they considered to be the private realm of the family.

Yet even if a family chose not to adopt, the advent of adoption laws forced families who took children into their homes and raised them as their own to consider whether a legal decree contributed to the child's membership in the family in any meaningful way. As we saw, some families felt it did not. Even the agents of the CAS appeared conflicted about the purpose of adoption. They wavered from encouraging legal adoption to accepting families united solely by emotion to allowing families to legally adopt children only if they made definite economic arrangements for the child's future, despite years of past care. The cases discussed in this chapter suggest that the meaning of adoption was not yet fixed, the acceptance of a legally created family not yet complete. These differing views, however, found expression in private situations.

2 | Rescue a Child and Save the Nation
The Social Construction of Adoption in the *Delineator*, 1907–1911

Every morning, George Wilder, president of Butterick Publishing Company, noticed the ragged and dirty children who milled around outside his building. Where did these children live? Who were their parents? What was to become of them? How could he help? Wilder's concern sparked the creation of the "Child-Rescue Campaign" in the *Delineator*, the country's third largest women's magazine with close to a million subscribers. The campaign hoped to pair up the nation's childless homes and homeless children and end the practice of caring for dependent children in institutions. Although Wilder wanted to help, he also feared that the homes of America would not open their doors to the poor, homeless waifs. He was wrong. Hundreds of readers wrote in to adopt the first two children profiled. The series was an immediate and extended success, placing over 2,000 children in adoptive homes over the course of its three-year run from late 1907 to early 1911.[1]

The story of the "Child-Rescue Campaign" is, however, more than a simple tale of a powerful man trying to help those less fortunate. The "Child-Rescue Campaign" was the first time adoption was discussed in an ongoing public and popular forum; it gave a voice to the experience, demystified it, made it visible. The *Delineator* presented adoption as part of a woman's civic duty and as a form of rescue. These representations, because the campaign was so popular and reached such a large audience, influenced both the way the public understood adoption and the way women experienced adoptive motherhood. Ultimately, the series played an important role in popularizing adoption and promoting an expanded definition of motherhood.

The *Delineator*'s women readers responded enthusiastically to the series, but the magazine also sought to gain the respect and acclaim of national reformers and wanted to take a leading role in the larger Progressive Era child-saving movement. In its attempt to satisfy both its readers and the reformers, the *Delineator* found itself struggling to balance the interests of two very different constituencies. Although readers fully supported getting children out of institutions and into homes, they responded to the campaign in an intensely personal way that focused on helping individual children, especially those profiled. Many readers wanted the series to emphasize their needs and concerns as adoptive mothers or prospective adoptive mothers. For this group of women, adoption was not just a solution to a social problem; it was also the answer to their loneliness and maternal longings. Reformers, however, saw adoption as a fairly insignificant part of the solution to the problem of child dependency and believed that the campaign should move beyond finding homes for individual children. As the magazine increased its role in the national child-saving movement, a tension, even a conflict, developed between the interests of the women readers who looked at the *Delineator* as a type of adoption agency and the desires of the editors to expand the magazine's role in national reform efforts. In the end, the *Delineator* sacrificed the interests of these women for the allure of national influence.

Historians who have looked at the *Delineator's* "Child-Rescue Campaign" have focused on the role it played in child welfare reform and specifically its involvement in organizing the famous 1909 White House Conference on the Care of Dependent Children.[2] Meanwhile, scholars examining the growing acceptance of adoption in the late nineteenth and early twentieth centuries have focused on large-scale cultural factors such as changes in the value of children and in philosophies regarding child welfare and the modernization and expansion of the legal system.[3] As important as these social changes were, individuals also played an important role in the growing popularity of adoption. This chapter focuses on one important episode in the history of adoption when three distinct groups, each with its own interests and concerns, came together and presented to the public a new understanding of adoption. The "Child-Rescue Campaign" illuminates the realities of publishing a women's magazine in a climate of fierce competition; the difficulty of a for-profit venture taking a leading role in reform; the changing definition of motherhood; and the power of a mass-circulation magazine to popularize, legitimate, and shape the culture's understanding of a new social phenomenon.

The Campaign Begins

In October 1907, the *Delineator* published "The Child without a Home," which told of the 25,000 poor, primarily immigrant children who lived without a mother's love in institutions throughout New York. Although the article sympathetically portrayed the plight of dependent, immigrant children, it also underscored the potential threat they posed to society. The series officially began the next month in an issue that contained the article "The Home without a Child," written by Lydia Kingsmill Commander. Commander, author of numerous articles on social problems and a book on race suicide, exposed the thousands of well-to-do childless homes in New York City in which women played with teddy bears instead of babies. She went on to urge the nation's women, especially childless married women, to adopt homeless children. Adoption would not only save the children, Commander believed, but quite possibly save marriages, since she thought childless couples were especially at risk for divorce.[4]

This issue also contained the first installment of the "Child-Rescue Campaign." Theodore Dreiser had taken over the editorship of the *Delineator* in June 1907. Dreiser was a novelist, but his first book, *Sister Carrie* (1900), failed to rouse the public and riled many critics who thought it was "immoral." Discouraged, he turned to editing and the social status and financial stability it provided. Dreiser explained to the magazine's readers that each month the campaign would feature the photos and life stories of dependent children who were available to any interested reader who wanted to take them out of an institution and into her home. The issue also included the endorsements of the sixteen women, many of whom were active in the General Federation of Women's Clubs and other social reform efforts, who constituted the campaign's honorary advisory board.[5] Although the initial issue stated that the children could be taken by the placing-out system (what we refer to today as foster care), indenture, or adoption, readers showed an overwhelming willingness to adopt the children legally, and the subsequent children profiled were offered for adoption. The series was an immediate success. "The Child without a Home" article received more responses than any other story in that issue, and well over 300 readers wrote in requesting the first two children profiled.[6]

In addition to the children's profiles, each issue generally contained a story related to the series' goals of pairing up childless homes and homeless children and ending institutional care. Some warned of the dangers of institutional life and the threat posed to society by children raised without a mother's love and guidance. "Where 100,000 Children Wait" was the most famous of this type. Published on the first anniversary of the series, the article included a description of the effects of institutional life on a young boy. "At first, when nobody cares for him, he is only sad. Later, when he cares for nobody, he is unsafe." The *Delineator* reprinted this article in pamphlet form and had a difficult time keeping up with the requests. Other articles extolled the rejuvenating powers of hearth and home. First-person stories told of the joys adopted children brought into too-quiet homes or of the accomplishments of adoptees who had become famous. The magazine's writers wrote these articles to appeal to women's "maternal instinct" and also to their sense of civic responsibility.[7]

The series soon generated interest beyond the magazine's readership. The January and February 1908 issues contained letters of support from a number of public officials, such as the mayors of large cities with child-dependency problems, and from many prominent child welfare reformers, including Homer Folks, Hastings H. Hart, and Thomas Mulry. The letters from the reformers, although generally positive, noted that only a small number of children in institutions were suitable for adoption, since many had at least one living parent and others were too old to be likely candidates. The reformers added that if the *Delineator's* series was to be of any long-term benefit, it should tackle the larger issues facing the child savers, such as under what circumstances the courts should take children away from their parents or when and for how long the state should help parents who find themselves in temporary distress.[8]

The editors of *Charities and the Commons,* the leading social work periodical of the time, were less enthusiastic. They noted that profiling children for adoption was a good way of stirring up public interest in child welfare issues. But they also wondered whether the campaign itself was "a particularly necessary or particularly useful thing to do." Despite the *Delineator's* portrayal of thousands of children languishing in orphanages waiting to be rescued, the editors of *Charities and the Commons* believed that child-placing agencies had never "met with any great difficulty in securing plenty of applications" for children who were eligible for adoption. They, too, urged the *Delineator* to move beyond profiling individual children and begin educating its readers on broader issues.[9]

Others refused to endorse the campaign because of the hypocrisy they saw between the magazine's "save the family" rhetoric and the antilabor policies of Butterick Publishing Company. Butterick was a huge operation, producing not only the *Delineator* but also the *Designer* and the *New Idea,* and was battling against Typographic Union No. 6, which wanted to unionize workers in the composing room. When Dreiser approached the Women's Trade Union League about supporting the campaign, it declined. The WTUL believed that unions, not magazines, could best protect the children and asked Dreiser, "[is it] not fairer as well as wiser to protect the home of the child rather than help him find another home after his own has been taken from him?" There is no record of Dreiser's response.[10]

Appealing to a Mother's Instinct, a Citizen's Duty

Meanwhile, the campaign had struck an especially responsive chord with the *Delineator's* readers. At the time, the publication of women's magazines was an especially competitive business. To attract and hold subscribers, editors tried to develop a close, familial relationship with their readers, urging them to write letters relating their opinions, advice, and experiences, which were then published. The "Child-Rescue Campaign" generated a tremendous amount of reader response, fully 20 percent of all the correspondence the editorial department received during the period. The first letters the *Delineator* published expressed the intense longing for children felt by childless women and women whose children had died; they all hoped to adopt the children to "fill the vacancy in [their] home[s] and still the ache in [their] heart[s]." The *Delineator* had urged women to adopt the children by appealing to their sense of patriotic and civic duty, in addition to their motherly instinct. Yet these letters suggest that women responded on a personal level; they needed the children as much as the children needed them.[11]

Nonetheless, adoption at the turn of the century was uncommon enough, and fears about bad heredity prevalent enough, that many women needed assurance, encouragement, and a place to voice their fears before they could comfortably adopt a child. Writing to the *Delineator* allowed women to partake in, or at least feel as if they were partaking in, the culture's discourse on motherhood, family life, and child welfare. The *Delineator* mediated and directed this discourse through its choice of what letters to print. However, the success of the campaign—its acceptance by its women readers—still depended on women finding the *Delineator's* arguments to adopt compelling and its definitions of motherhood and family agreeable. As one women's magazine editor noted, "the women of America take the periodicals edited especially for them with great seriousness; and they will cancel subscriptions over night if they feel that the standard is dropping . . . editorial judgements must be carefully weighed and pondered." The *Delineator's* editorial policy had to reflect accurately the concerns and values of its readers, or it risked losing them.[12]

Over the course of the "Child-Rescue Campaign," the *Delineator* contained a number of articles that extolled the virtues of motherhood. Most of these articles were first-person accounts written by famous women such as Julia Ward Howe, author of "The Battle Hymn of the Republic," and philanthropist and social leader Edith Rockefeller McCormick, who was also a member of the honorary advisory board. These women asserted that motherhood was their highest achievement, a "holy task" and a "privilege." Articles suggested that mother love was higher and purer than marital love and that only through the self-sacrifice and devotion of motherhood could a woman reach her full potential or explore the "depths and heights" of her "nature." All agreed that a child's "touch" was "absolutely necessary" for women's "highest development."[13]

The series also articulated a definition of motherhood based on a woman's capacity to love and nurture a child, not on blood ties. In letters and short stories telling of their personal experiences, adoptive mothers argued against those who said that the only real mothers were women who had experienced the travails of pregnancy and birth. One adoptive mother asserted that "from the hour that she [her adopted daughter] came into our possession she has seemed really *our very own*. . . . [Her] shrill piping cry at early dawn filled me with a wonder that could not have been greater had I brought forth the little one with anguish."[14] If motherhood was a spiritual state, an attitude, and not the result of a physical experience, then a woman's marital status also bore no relation to her maternal instincts. Consequently, the *Delineator* sometimes advocated that single women adopt. Motherhood was woman's highest calling, Howe argued in her article on the joys of motherhood, so shouldn't single women also have the opportunity to experience it, especially since countless children suffered for lack of mothering?[15]

Women who adopted, including childless or unmarried women, had a "mother-consciousness"; women who abandoned their infants and children to the mercy of the city did not. The fact that a woman might give up her child to an institution did not necessarily mean that she lacked a maternal instinct: women who acknowledged that they could no longer care for their children and consciously surrendered them *for the children's best interest* were portrayed as heroes, as women who had made the supreme maternal sacrifice. By portraying adoptive mothers as women whose greatest wish was to be a mother and who believed that "there is no life for a woman without children," the series sought to elevate the value of motherhood. Adoptive mothers were mothers by choice. Their active quest for children could be positively contrasted with the "indifferent acquiescence" and "passive acceptance of a state commended by society" that the *Delineator* believed described many birth mothers' attitude toward motherhood.[16]

The *Delineator* also emphasized the importance of children's environment in their ultimate development, which helped women overcome any lingering fears about taking a child with a questionable background. The "Child-Rescue Campaign" appeared at a time when strong eugenics and temperance movements warned of the evils of the hereditary taint. One well-known eugenicist stated publicly that any offspring of adopted children "would be degenerates."[17] The *Delineator* countered by offering the opinions of both adoptive mothers and reformers such as Jacob Riis, who maintained that they had witnessed firsthand that "heredity is much, but environment is more." The *Delineator* maintained that "an atmosphere of mother-love" could overcome any child's "evil heredity" and result in "manly and womanly, honorable citizens." At the same time, the magazine also raised the alarming specter of a society terrorized by these same children if they were not rescued from the streets. As mothers, women had the future of society in their hands; women had a duty. They would determine whether these children grew up to be worthy and useful citizens or to fill the jails and almshouses.[18]

Many believed that middle-class women were already derelict in their duty. The "Child-Rescue Campaign" coincided with a drastic decline in the birthrate among white, middle-class women. Meanwhile, the "new" immigrants from eastern and southern Europe were reproducing at double the rate of their native-born counterparts. Social critics warned that the progeny of these "lusty sexual . . . foreign breeders" would soon overrun the nation. While eugenicists, sociologists, and psychologists studied and lamented, Theodore Roosevelt succinctly summed up what many feared: America's "superior stock" was committing "race suicide." To ensure the stability of the nation and the future of democracy, Roosevelt and others urged "old stock" American women to do their "duty" and procreate.[19]

If native-born, middle-class women were not going to have more children, the *Delineator* believed, they could at least raise the masses of dependent, largely immigrant children into solid American citizens. The respected women on the advisory committee agreed. Mrs. Harry Hastings, founder of the Society for Study of Child Nature and a member of the New York School Board, stated that the campaign was "really patriotic" and "of the highest value to the social fabric." Mrs. Frederick Dent Grant believed that the campaign was "vital in that it supplies God-fearing citizens for the coming generation."[20]

Again and again, the *Delineator* appealed to women's sense of civic duty, a duty that they could best fulfill through their roles as mothers. Again and again, the *Delineator* painted the stark contrast between children raised with a mother's love and those raised without: "upright men and women" or a "burden on the commonwealth," vagabonds, paupers, and criminals or honest, cleanly citizens, a "potential addition to the productive capacity . . . of the nation" or to the "destructive forces of the community."[21] In looking back on the first year of the series, George Wilder summed up the progress thus: "we found for them [the profiled children] good influences upon whom no one can tell what other influences might have come and through them on down the ages to the end of earthly things good shall be where evil might have been."[22]

The *Delineator's* editors emphatically and unquestionably trusted that placing these children with Christian, native-born, middle-class mothers was the way to save society and improve the citizenry. This belief mirrored the ideology behind the larger movement to "Americanize" new immigrants and suggested a fear of ethnic difference.[23] In 1918, James West, who had been one of the leading forces behind the "Child-Rescue Campaign" and was now chief executive of the Boy Scouts of America, wrote to Theodore Dreiser regarding one of the young boys profiled in the series. The boy, John, was now fourteen. His adoptive mother had written to West because her son had accidentally lost his Scout medal, and she hoped he could replace it. The mother, aware of West's role in the series, took two pages to update him on the boy's progress in school and in the Scouts and also mentioned the child's German ancestry. West was so pleased with this "definite evidence" of the success of the campaign that he sent a copy of the mother's letter to Dreiser.

In his cover letter, West mentioned the child's success and the joy he brought to his adoptive mother, but he especially focused on the redemptive quality of adoption. As he told Dreiser, in addition to the boy's progress in school, "there is the dramatic feature that the boy is of German parentage but in spite of this fact, is developing into a fine patriotic loyal American citizen." West's focus on the child's ethnicity can be understood within the context of the anti-German hysteria that swept the nation at the outbreak of World War I. It also reflects his (and the *Delineator's*) understanding of adoption as social conservation and a means to protect and save society.[24]

Adoption as Rescue

The *Delineator* also chose a narrative formula for the children's profiles that encouraged adoption and in many ways shaped the way adoptive parents experienced the adoption process. Seemingly, the profiles contained only the details of the children's background. But in fact the *Delineator* constructed the stories to generate enough sympathy that its middle-class readers would be motivated to adopt the children, while not offending their sensibilities or straining their understanding of children as innocents.[25] To this end, the *Delineator*'s profiles used the literary convention of the rescue, an extremely common plot device in popular fiction at the time.

The rescue of a child appeared regularly in domestic novels of the nineteenth and early twentieth centuries. The rescue plot gave readers the thrills of a tragedy, but with the comfort of a happy ending. A rescue changed the destiny of the rescued and made a hero of the rescuer, embodying the American ideal of individual action. It also involved risk: would the rescuer be rewarded for her fateful intervention, or would she ultimately regret it? In rescue fiction, the rescuer never repented her action, since saved children always grew up to be responsible, moral adults and often made exceptional contributions to society. The rescued always paid back the rescuer. In addition, these stories reflected two basic beliefs: humane, caring action will be rewarded; and a child can overcome initial adversity and rise to success through hard work and personal integrity.[26]

The rescue plot was the perfect structure for the profiles, allowing the *Delineator* to present the children's histories in an exciting yet sympathetic way that demanded the readers' action and promised an ultimate reward. Even the series' title, "The Child-Rescue Campaign," suggested drama and heroism, a grander phrase than the more commonly used conservation-oriented term "child saving." The pathetic tales of children who languished in institutions, abandoned by unfeeling parents or orphaned through tragic accidents, generated instant interest. Familiarity with the rescue convention provided readers with a clear blueprint for action: the stories described children in desperate circumstances—all that was left was for the *Delineator*'s readers to step in and rescue the children from their imminent fate. Most important, the formula provided a sense of security in the outcome: the reader would rescue the child, and he or she would grow up to be an ideal citizen, as in fiction. The rescue narrative also focused attention on the new relationship between the vulnerable child and the protective adoptive parent, effectively erasing the biological parents from view. Many prospective adopters feared that a natal parent would return to claim the child. However, the *Delineator* made it clear in the profiles that these children were free from that threat; a tragic death, a heroic surrender, or a cowardly abandonment had paved the way for their rescue.[27]

The series repeatedly stressed that by taking such children into their homes, women were rescuing them from a wretched fate and putting them on the path toward productive citizenship. Often the profiles hinted at even greater rewards, promising that these children showed exceptional potential; one four-year-old, for example, already exhibited qualities that "mark[ed] him for the future as an executive and a leader among men," and another child possessed a "sweet tenor voice which may develop into something out of the ordinary." These descriptions reflected the qualities the *Delineator's* middle-class readers most admired and desired in their children. They also subtly assured the readers that these children were filled with potential, not inherited flaws. After all, as the winning sermon in the *Delineator's* contest to raise women's interest in child-rescue work noted, wasn't Moses an adopted child?[28]

By constructing the children's stories as tragedies in which they were guiltless victims deserving of "rescue" by women who possessed both a strong "mother's consciousness" and a sense of national duty, the *Delineator* deflected attention away from any disturbing aspects of a child's background. Had the profiles been too realistic, too gritty, a child could have seemed too great a risk. Baby Marion, who was profiled in the third issue of the series, is a case in point. Marion was illegitimate and had been abandoned. The *Delineator* reported that "a well-dressed, attractive [white] woman" had stopped at the home of an African American family on the pretext of finding someone to do housework. While pretending to examine the home's "cleanliness," the woman managed to leave the baby, who was wrapped in paper, on a table unobserved. After she left, the family found the "emaciated" two-week-old, and when the child became severely ill a few days later, they turned her over to the authorities.

In fact, the case records of the Board of Children's Guardians in Washington, D.C., which had custody of Marion, told a slightly different story. Marion's mother had stopped at an African American family's home, but on the pretext of using the outhouse, not finding a housekeeper. The case record also makes no mention of Marion's mother's appearance. Most important, the *Delineator* failed to mention that, when found, Marion was "covered with sores." The image of a child covered with sores might have awakened readers' sympathy, but it also might have made them shrink back in fear. The children's stories may not have represented their subjects' actual experiences, but they no doubt promoted their adoption by moving the discourse away from troubling details. A number of people showed interest in Marion, including a "well-to-do" childless couple and a Maryland couple who adopted her as a companion for their only child.[29]

The stories were also consistent with Dreiser's editorial policy regarding the fiction that appeared in the magazine. Dreiser was "personally opposed . . . to stories which have an element of horror in them, or which are disgusting in their realism and fidelity to life." The magazine would accept realism, but "it must be tinged with sufficient idealism to make it all of a truly uplifting character." Although this might sound ironic coming from the author of *Sister Carrie*, a novel that graphically told of a country girl's seduction in the big city, Dreiser had learned firsthand from the novel's cool reception that readers found too much realism offensive.[30]

The profiles also reflected the growing influence of advertising, so vital to the success of early-twentieth-century women's magazines. The children's photos and descriptions resembled nothing so much as a catalogue offering goods for sale; indeed, when the series' text overflowed into the back pages of the magazine, the children's photos and stories were virtually indistinguishable from the advertisements that framed the edges of the page. Some readers' adoption requests even specifically referred to the "advertised" child. Advertisements from this period informed the consumer of the features and availability of the product and were beginning to associate the product with desirable qualities to encourage its purchase. The *Delineator* series did both. Boys and girls of every size and shape, with blue eyes and curls, brown hair and dimples, shy or outgoing, paraded through the magazine, promising readers what the market promised consumers: product satisfaction and choice.[31]

It would be unfair to say that the *Delineator* sold children like so much soap, but the ethic of consumerism and the tendency to look at children as a commodity—albeit a precious one—persisted throughout the series. Although the *Delineator* noted the preference for girls and devoted an entire issue to pleading the case for adopting boys, it apparently did not find a shopping list of desirable qualities antithetical to good parenthood. A few months after it urged readers to adopt boys, the magazine published a letter from a prospective adoptive mother who was having a difficult time locating "a child of the kind I want. . . . a little girl not more than three nor less than one and a half years old. . . . fair and blue eyed." In her defense, the *Delineator*'s continual admonishment that 100,000 children waited in orphanages did suggest to prospective adopters that their specific preferences could be met.[32]

A New Definition of Motherhood

Although a few women might have adopted in order to have blue-eyed, fair-haired adornments around their homes, the primary motivation for the majority of women who adopted appears to have been a desire to mother, to give care and love to a child—an understandable longing, given the culture's glorification of mothers and its valuation of women primarily as mothers. At the same time, however, their experience of adoption was shaped by the *Delineator*'s portrayal of adoption as rescue, as women's duty. To understand adoption at this point in history, it is crucial to examine women's individual experiences within the context of the prevailing narratives about adoption at that time.

The "Child-Rescue Campaign" made adoption publicly visible in a way it had never been before. This exposure made it easier for women to adopt for a number of reasons: it eased their fears about the mysteries of adoption; it provided them with the practical information necessary to find children with whom to ease their maternal longings; it supported their desire to adopt by giving them a reason—civic duty—for taking children into their homes; it made adoption seem less alien, both to them and to nosy neighbors or prying relatives; and it provided adoptive mothers or prospective adoptive mothers with a virtual community of other women like themselves.

But in naming and describing the experience, the *Delineator* also began to define it, to give it a specific form that necessarily influenced the way adoptive mothers came to conceptualize their experience. The *Delineator* gave women a context within which to understand their experience and explain it to others. Hence, a desire to mother was not incompatible with a duty to rescue. In letters to the *Delineator*, women described their experience in ways that reflected both the values of the series and their intensely personal feelings. One adoptive mother described her experience as follows: Ralph is "a beautiful child, with so much temperament and character that no one else had succeeded in handling him until I got him. . . . He was a waif, and has it in him to make a fine man, but could easily become a poor one under the wrong circumstances. . . . I never really lived until Ralph came to be my little boy."[33]

Another represented her experience in the following way: "At first we thought we would do it as a duty, now duty is no longer the thought, it is the pleasure love brings."[34] Still another explained: "We are not offering to take a child solely because we want a child in our childless home, but we feel deeply that it is God's will that we should take one in the discharge of our duty in the rescuing of helpless orphans from miserable lives and disgrace."[35]

Ultimately, in a time when adoption was not yet completely accepted, the construction of adoption as rescue might have helped women who wanted to adopt but had not done so because they feared the glare of disapproving eyes. The complete social acceptance of "sentimental adoptions," that is, taking a child solely to create a family, was still a few years away.

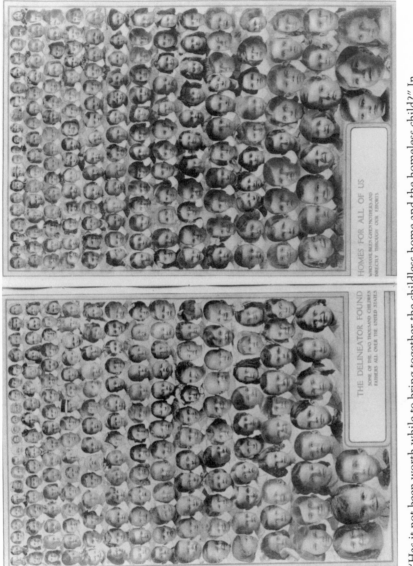

"Has it not been worth while to bring together the childless home and the homeless child?" In December 1910, the *Delineator* showed readers the "smiling" results of the "Child-Rescue Campaign." (Library of Congress)

MARION, AGED ONE YEAR AND A HALF

Little Marion Has a Strange History

BABY MARION, bright and blue-eyed and aged about one year and a half, is offered for adoption by the Board of Children's Guardians of Washington, D. C. It is desired that a home be found for her in the territory around that city.

The exact date of Marion's birth is not known, but it is assumed to have been July 21, 1906. She came into the hands of the organization on Aug. 31, 1906. She is in perfect physical condition and of unusual intelligence. The origin of this little foundling baby is shrouded in the following story:

On August 23, 1906, a well-dressed, attractive woman called at the home of a negro family in Washington and made inquiries with a view of finding some one to do housework. On the pretext of commending the cleanliness of the negro's home, she asked permission to go through the house back to the yard. As she passed through the hallway, unobserved she deposited on a table a bundle wrapped in a paper. Some time later the children of the family found the bundle and upon investigation discovered an emaciated baby girl about two weeks of age. There was nothing to furnish a clew to the little one's parentage. Six days later the child became so ill that a physician had to be summoned, and on his advice it was formally committed to the care of the

JAMES, OF WASHINGTON, D. C.

Board of Children's Guardians. Although careful search was made no trace of the mother was ever found.

Communications regarding Marion should be addressed to John W. Douglass, Agent Board of Children's Guardians, care of *The Delineator*, N.Y. City.

His Mother Could not Care for James

JAMES, a sturdy four-year-old youngster, is a little boy from Washington who wants a home. It was in that city on Nov. 14, 1903, that he entered a troublous world. When he was eleven months old, his mother with the baby James and two older children, his sister and brother, found themselves and their limited household equipment placed upon the public highway. She had been ejected for non-payment of rent. The woman, who was a worker in a steam laundry, had had a struggle with poverty to which she eventually succumbed. At this crisis in her affairs, on her own request the children were committed by the court to the Board of Children's Guardians. Her husband had before this disappeared, and since the children were taken in charge she, too, has vanished. So the case now amounts to abandonment.

During the three years that James has been a public charge he has been kept in a boardinghouse, where he is loved by all. It is desired, if possible, to secure a home for him near the District of Columbia. All communications should be addressed as in the case of Marion above.

These profiles, which appeared in the *Delineator* in January 1908, omitted some of the more disturbing details of the children's backgrounds. (Library of Congress)

head shows intelligence, and her memory is remarkable in a child of her years.

Further information about little Golden Locks may be obtained through the Child Rescue Department of THE DELINEATOR.

Virginia will Bring Sunshine into any Home that Opens to Her

HERE is a little girl who is the namesake of her own State, Virginia. Her father died a few months after she was born, leaving the mother to struggle along as best she could in the support of herself and the single child. The strain proved too severe; her health gave way, and at last she was forced to go to a hospital for treatment. While there she called upon the Society to take charge of her little one, to find her the home that she felt she no longer able to give.

That is what little Virginia is waiting for. Nearly five years old now, able and glad to bring sunshine into the family opened to her, where can she find friends who will bring what her tender life needs to make it blossom into a wonderful response of girlhood and womanhood? The only restriction is that they shall be somewhere within the confines of her native State.

Who wishes to know more of little Virginia of Virginia? Will they not inquire of the Child Rescue Department of THE DELINEATOR?

Every One Who Happens to See Him Falls in Love with Lloyd

AWAY out under the shadow of the great sheltering Rockies, as elsewhere in this wide world of ours, there are sad stories to tell of homeless children. Baby Lloyd's mother died while he was still but a few days old; and, although we never saw her, no one looking at him can doubt that she was a sweet, good woman. So winning are his baby smiles that we are very sorry that one of them failed to get into the picture.

His father seemed helpless to take care of him and his little two-year-old brother. For a while a good woman nearby boarded him; later, when his father could afford to pay his board a

This illustration from the March 1908 issue of the *Delineator* vividly shows the similarities between the children's profiles and the abundance of advertisements that appeared in women's magazines. (Library of Congress)

TWO THOUSAND HOMES FOR CHRISTMAS

THROUGH OUR EFFORTS FULLY THIS NUM-
BER OF CHILDREN WILL SPEND THE HOLI-
DAYS WITH NEW-FOUND PARENTS

AS A REMINDER of the peace and good-will that comes this holiday season to certain members of THE DELINEATOR's great family of readers and subscribers, the faces of hundreds of little boys and girls are shown on this Christmas number of the Rescue Campaign. . . . of this Christmas number of the thousands who have won love group of children. There are enough success of one of the most important faces carefully, and gradually something will come to you. The individual will have suffered from poverty in all its hideousness of foster-parents who are so eager that means to the State and the nation the products of trained minds and

We hope that all the friends of our homes east and west, north and girls who might be inmates of the...

for the dependent child. Has it not been worth while to bring together the childless home and the homeless child? Is there any movement more important than this which has given a double...

EDITOR OF THE DELINEATOR:
It is with pleasure that I send you a photograph of our little adopted daughter. As you can see by the picture, we have a real little sunbeam in our home. She is very grateful and affectionate. At first she was not especially attractive and appeared not to have a very good disposition, but was just full of fear and starved for love. When her photographs were sent home, she asked anxiously: "Did I show that I have a good papa and mama?"

She wanted so much to look happy in the picture so every one would know that she had a good home. You are all doing a grand work, and you have my heart-felt prayers.

EDITOR OF THE DELINEATOR:
We have never for one moment regretted adopting our dear little boy. He is a perfect and a continual joy; we love him as if he were bone of our bone and flesh of our flesh; and, God helping us, we mean to bring him up to be a good and worthy man.

We treat him and speak of him as if he were our very own. While many of our intimate friends know he is adopted, and while we have no great objection to this being known, yet for his sake, at present, we do not care to advertise the fact. In due season we shall tell him the truth, but by that time we hope that he will feel toward us as if we were his real parents. Until he can understand, we would spare him this knowledge.

We are greatly interested in the splendid work you are doing; we are in hearty sympathy with it and shall be glad, at any time, to do anything in our power to aid you.

EDITOR OF THE DELINEATOR:
It is with pleasure that I send you photograph of our little adopted daughter. As you can see in our home. She little sunbeam in our home. She grateful and affectionate. At first she especially attractive and appeared no a very good disposition, but was just fear and starved for love. When her graphs were sent home, she asked a "Did I show that I have a good mama?"

She wanted so much to look happy picture so every one would know that a good home. You are all doing a grand and you have my heart-felt prayers.

EDITOR OF THE DELINEATOR:
We have never for one moment adopting our dear little boy. He is and a continual joy; we love him as bone of our bone and flesh of our flesh God helping us, we mean to bring him a good and worthy man.

We treat him and speak of him were our very own. While many of timate friends know he is adopted, and have no great objection to this being yet for his sake, at present, we do not advertise the fact. In due season tell him the truth, but by that time that he will feel toward us as if we were parents. Until he can understand, spare him this knowledge.

We are greatly interested in the work you are doing; we are in hearty with it and shall be glad, at any time anything in our power to aid you.

EDITOR OF THE DELINEATOR:
The result of having a foster-child home is that I love and care for it as It brings one closer to the world's manity and makes one feel that one something for the benefit of little child

EDITOR OF THE DELINEATOR:
We are sending you a photograph tle Walter who came to our home year ago. He certainly has brought into our hearts and home. He has as one of our family from the day we. We could not possibly spare Our only regret is that we did not take child years ago.

EDITOR OF THE DELINEATOR:
I thank you very much for your kindness in us, for we have a smart, sweet years and nine months old. She is a can ask for.

She is loved by all who see her and tell you how much we love her. She a heaven out of a home for us.

EDITOR OF THE DELINEATOR:
We are sending you the picture boy, but we can't get a photograph him justice. Had we hunted the world we could not have found a brighter or more intelligent child. He has never seemed like a foster-child to us. From the moment we first saw him he has been to us like our very own.

EDITOR OF THE DELINEATOR:
My experience in having a foster-child in my home, it is this: The little boy is a delight to us. I my husband, my daughter and I have not once regretted taking him. It is two years ago this month since he came to us and we can say that he is a real comfort and joy.

father and mother are both incompetent. My one longing in life is to get out in the country on a small farm where I can devote my life to the training of my girls. If I can do anything to persuade some one else to take a homeless child, I will be glad to answer any questions.
P. S. I wish I had ten more children in my home, with plenty of money to care for them.

father or we would be a orphan asylum, too." If only some of the people that don't know the joy of two little arms around their necks and little prayers to listen to every evening would just try for a time, they would discover how much more comfort they would derive from a little child than from the dog or cat upon which a great many bestow their affection.

biographies have won Pansy. Well, we must not tell you forgotten all that was said in their ...nts are "really, truly" fathers and at comprise a series of remarkable ...ply-ever-after" story, in which the ...mpaign are heroes and heroines. ...it us to publish many—and then, ...t the practicability of our plan for ...f old-fashioned orphan asylums, you ...lity of abolishing the big institutions. ...pply for a child. Although we do ...s, applications will be gladly received

OF THE DELINEATOR:
...anted to know our experience with our ...ild. Well, we just love him as dearly ...ere our own flesh and blood. So far, ...en only joy and pleasure. We hardly ...ember that he is adopted. It would ...st kill us if anything should ever hap...ake him from us. I sincerely hope ...phan asylum will be, in a very short ...rned into a receiving and distributing ...nd that every child will find a place in ...ome.

OF THE DELINEATOR:
...the advantage of a home life in a family ...arison to that in an orphan asylum, it ...seems to speak for itself. From the ...at of our little girl it is very great. ...ht, when her prayers were said, she ...that while in the asylum (she was there ...s), every night after saying her prayers. ...ys added silently, "And I hope some ...es to-morrow to take me away from ...It seemed so pathetic to me to think of ...t after night, always looking for the ...row" that would bring her a mother ...really" home. Yet she was in a splen...tution where there were comparatively ...dren. She was well treated and the ...believe, of special care because of her ... It was her frail appearance that ...the way of her adoption until we heard ...and were willing to take her. Every ...ts a healthy child, but we felt that a ...ght-strung and delicate, needed a home ...in any other.
...sult of good care and regular living has ...aid us. When our little girl came, two ...o, she was smaller at seven than some ...e-year-old children in my primary class ...unday-school. She had a cough of at ...o years' standing and was very frail. ...Now she is large for her age, her ...as disappeared—cured by raw eggs ...ty of milk—she is full of life, and, aside ...trouble we had with the cough, she has ...ickness of any sort. I mention this be...many are afraid to take a delicate child, ...often all that is needed is just a little ...becial care and living that an institution ...many children can not give. ...e so well pleased with our little girl that ...seriously considered taking another ...boy next time. If any one feels lonely ...use in the world (and I believe there are ...ho feel that way) let her take a little ...to her heart and home. Never again ...h a woman feel of no use, and I will ...ee she will not feel lonely,

OF THE DELINEATOR:
...xperiences in having a foster-child in ...he have been and are delightful. The ...t we have with us is certainly indepen...d under no consideration could we be ...to part with her. She is the light and ...ur home, and she thinks just as much of ...we of her as if she were our own child. ...emarkably bright and is doing well in ...ork. She will not have reached eight ...til September, yet she is doing fourth-...work in part and she is very quick in vocal ...music. She sang "Luther's Cradle ...Hymn" at a Christmas entertainment. ...given in church a year ago last Christ...mas time, as a solo, and has taken part ...in similar work in school. If you should ...come and offer one thousand dollars to ...take her from our home indefinitely, ...the offer would be useless, as she is ...above and beyond price.

We are striving as well as we know to bring her up in a Christian home and as far as possible in a similar environ ment, and shall agree nothing in order to bring her to Christian womanhood.

These narratives allowed adoptive mothers to present their experience in such a way that their decision to adopt could not be challenged—they were fulfilling their civic duty—*and* their sincere desire for a child and genuine mother's love could be expressed.[36]

Abandoning Readers, Embracing Reformers

The *Delineator's* role in the national child-saving movement reflected the larger realities of publishing in the early 1900s and especially the personalities of those in charge of the magazine. According to his biographers, Theodore Dreiser understood the pathos and pain of the poor as simply a reflection of the laws of nature. He was also driven by the desire to overcome the poverty of his birth and achieve respectability. It is possible that along with his fatalistic beliefs, Dreiser possessed a sincere sympathy for and desire to help the weak. But even if Dreiser had doubts about the ultimate efficacy of the campaign, editing a powerful women's magazine with national influence gave him the status he craved.[37]

Publisher George Wilder had his own set of beliefs and concerns. Wilder was a man with two hats: he wanted to help humanity, but he also wanted a successful magazine. Wilder's humanitarian impulse leaned toward helping individuals who en masse would create a better society, not working for large-scale reforms; he believed that changing individuals would change society, an outlook more in tune with nineteenth-century approaches to reform than twentieth. His idea to match up childless homes and homeless children reflected this philosophy. Wilder took an active hand in overseeing the magazine, and he wholeheartedly believed in the "Child-Rescue Campaign." In October 1908, he wrote to Dreiser telling him to "push, Push, PUSH" the child-rescue work "harder this year than ever." Wilder's confidence in the goodness of the campaign was so great that, as he told Dreiser, "Gabriel, keeping the book up yonder, may possibly have used the tears of joy shed by these children & their new found mothers to wipe away some of your sins & even mine recorded on his pages."[38]

While Wilder dreamed of heaven, Dreiser looked for ways to meet the criticisms of child welfare reformers and expand the series' impact. From the beginning, the series had advocated home placement over institutional care for dependent children, in addition to the more immediate goal of matching children with mothers. It was, however, becoming more and more difficult to balance the personal side of the campaign with the national reform work geared toward abolishing institutional care. Wilder seemed unable to decide which was more important. His letter to Dreiser continued:

> Confound these approvals of our work by Presidents and Secretaries of Home Finding Societies. Give me one letter from a woman's heart to whom the Joys of Motherhood have come through this campaign. Of course, I want the approval of these officials. I don't mean just what I have said. But . . . one letter telling the joy brought to some woman's heart through a little child will get more results than one hundred approvals.[39]

Wilder's reform impulse, his personal belief in the power of changing individuals, and his responsibilities as a businessman were in conflict. Wilder was keenly aware that readers found personal, emotional appeals more compelling than dry, factual admonitions from experts, but he also wanted the prestige and rewards of leading a major reform.

The *Delineator* needed to keep its subscription numbers high in order to justify its position in the reform community. Keeping readers happy meant keeping the monthly profiles of children and addressing readers' concerns as adoptive mothers. Reformers, however, wanted the magazine to abandon the profiles and focus on informational, issue-oriented child welfare stories. As James West explained to reformers, he used the stories and photos "because it guarantee[d] a direct personal interest," even though he knew "that in most cases it would be a comparatively easy matter to find good homes for the particular children . . . we have presented."[40]

The *Delineator* stated that its profiles were not meant to focus on specific children, but rather to represent the type of children available. Yet there is no evidence that readers saw the children as mere types. Indeed, women readers responded to the children as individuals; each month, hundreds of women would write in specifically for manly Bobby or adorable Sue. The story of five-year-old "little Daisy," for example, whose mother had died and whose father could no longer support her, moved over 600 readers to write in to adopt this child, "bright as the blossom whose name she bears."[41]

The evidence suggests that many women treated the *Delineator* as a sort of adoption agency. Beginning with the July 1909 issue, the *Delineator* began to accept applications not only from people interested in the profiled children but also from anyone in any part of the country interested in adopting. The *Delineator* would then forward the application to an appropriate agency or institution. Women's magazines encouraged this type of intimate, familial relationship in order to maintain consumer loyalty. In addition, it is easy to imagine that a woman who might have had a few reservations about adoption could assuage them with the knowledge that a powerful, national magazine was behind her. And it helped those readers who were still unsure about how and where to get a child.[42]

The *Delineator's* desire to lead the battle "for the best interests of the child," thereby gaining national influence, respect, and probably more subscribers, caused it to neglect—even abuse—the interests of its readers. The constant parade of adoptable children misled the readers: there was not an overabundance of children eagerly waiting to be adopted. In fact, there were relatively few children available *for adoption*. As reformers of the time knew, and as historians have shown again and again, the overwhelming number of children in institutions were there only temporarily and could not be adopted because one or both of their parents were still alive.[43]

The *Delineator* did acknowledge, even repeatedly, that there were more homes available than children, but it did so in a way that obscured the truth. In April 1910, for example, the *Delineator* published a letter from "an unusually earnest woman" who had not been able to get a child:

> Last fall I wrote you in regard to taking a little girl. The [child-placing agent] corresponded with me and was satisfied enough by her investigation, but she has been unable to get me a little girl. Now I would like to ask where are all the homeless children that *The Delineator* sends out an appeal for from month to month? What need is there of wasting so much space in your magazine, if it is such hard work to find a child when the home is waiting?

The *Delineator* responded by blaming the shortage on the policies of institutions, which, eager to continue receiving their "drafts upon the public treasury," refused to release the hundreds of children "imprisoned" within their "cold, dreary" walls. According to the *Delineator*, institutional greed, not the children's personal status, was the problem. And, consequently, the *Delineator* could admonish its readers to work even harder in their efforts to save the children and abolish institutions.[44]

To "guarantee interest," the *Delineator* had structured the "Child-Rescue Campaign" around finding individual mothers for individual children, but this emphasis conflicted with the realities of its larger reform goal. In its discussion of ending institutional care, the *Delineator* never emphasized that most children needed temporary foster care, not permanent adoptive homes. And every indication suggests that the *Delineator's* readers wanted children to raise as their own *forever*. Published letters from readers refer to issues of specific concern to adoptive parents and describe relationships based on a biological model of parenthood. One reader wrote that her adopted son "believes we are his real parents," and another stated that she and her family loved their adopted son "as if he were bone of our bone and flesh of our flesh."[45] These letters reflect fear that a birth parent would return and disrupt their new families, not pleasure that they could help a parent in temporary distress by caring for a child.

There had been a movement to care for dependent children in homes rather than in institutions as early as the 1890s—well before the *Delineator* began its "Child-Rescue Campaign." When James West joined the campaign sometime in 1908, the stage was set for the *Delineator* to take a leading role in child welfare work and the home-placement movement. West was nationally known for his work in the playground and juvenile court movements. In addition, West was a friend of President Theodore Roosevelt. West arranged for himself and Dreiser to meet with the president in October 1908, out of which came the famous January 1909 White House Conference on the Care of Dependent Children. At the same time, Dreiser announced the formation of a Child-Rescue League, which readers were urged to join to help the cause of dependent children nationwide. Membership in the league was free. The magazine vaguely defined members' duties as taking a "friendly interest" in the children in their community. Members were also occasionally urged to write letters to their congressmen regarding children's issues and the creation of a national children's bureau. The point of the league was to use the sheer numbers of the *Delineator*'s subscribers to give power and validity to the magazine's child welfare recommendations.[46]

Child welfare advocates and President Roosevelt wholeheartedly adopted the policy of home care at the 1909 White House Conference on the Care of Dependent Children. The war was won, and by all accounts, the *Delineator* had played a vital role. The victory, however, left the *Delineator* with an extremely popular campaign, but no cause. In a period of fierce competition among women's magazines, the *Delineator* naturally hesitated to abandon such a popular series, especially since the White House conference had generated so much positive press. The magazine had been able to capitalize on the campaign's success with bold, banner headlines announcing "4 More Homeless Children," compelling even more women to buy the magazine. The series was so well known that in Maryland one man ran a door-to-door scam in which he claimed to be a representative of the *Delineator* collecting money for the children.[47] Every indication showed that the profiles continued to touch the hearts of countless women. And their interest in children justified the *Delineator's* role in the national reform movement. Yet, if there were no problem, readers would not tolerate the waste of so much space or the call for so much wasted energy on their part.

After the White House conference, the *Delineator* began to stress the need for mothers' pensions in the monthly series. This represented a significant shift in focus. Now the emphasis was not solely on how to save dependent children from lives of degradation but also on how to ward off dependency in the first place. This change reflected the larger movement among reformers from a "save the child" philosophy, which had prevailed in the nineteenth century, to a "save the family" perspective in the twentieth. Whereas in the nineteenth century, reformers had quickly removed children from the corrupting influence of their immoral or poor families, now reformers believed both that poor families needed the civilizing influence of their children to keep them from falling further from grace and that nothing could replace a birth mother's love.[48]

In his report to Congress on the conference, President Roosevelt urged that the "widowed or deserted mother, if a good woman . . . should ordinarily be helped in such fashion as will enable her to bring up her children herself in their natural home." The *Delineator* seized on this challenge and urged readers to support the new cause. Possibly realizing that this new focus challenged the basic premise of the "Child-Rescue Campaign," the *Delineator* assured readers that this effort would "make none the less important the need of homes for the care of homeless children." This, of course, was blatantly untrue: the establishment of mothers' pensions, which would help widowed and deserted mothers keep their children, would further reduce the number of *adoptable* children.[49]

In addition, the ideology behind mothers' pensions—the importance of the "natural" family, the primacy of blood ties, and the irreplaceability of a birth mother's love—was at odds with the campaign's efforts to destigmatize adoption and expand the definition of "mother" to include ties of care as well as ties of blood. This is not to suggest that the *Delineator's* readers who were pro-adoption were against mothers' pensions. Rather, the *Delineator's* attempt to be all things to all people represented a potential clash of interests and often resulted in articles with misleading, contradictory, or inconsistent information. One wonders whether the many women who saw the "Child-Rescue Campaign" as a friend in their quests to find children and an ally in their efforts to create families recognized the conflict between their desires and the *Delineator*'s growing emphasis on mothers' pensions. One wonders whether adoptive mothers who seemed so grateful to have their concerns voiced, their experience named, felt betrayed by the focus on blood ties.[50]

The "Child-Rescue Campaign" ended abruptly and without explanation in February 1911, shortly after Dreiser left as editor. Although West showed that the campaign still generated a huge amount of reader response, the new editors decided against continuing the series, and West soon left to work for the Boy Scouts of America. The series reappeared once in January 1912, but the reform angle was gone. Instead, the *Delineator* urged readers to adopt the children as Christmas gifts for themselves. In August 1912, under the direction of the reform-minded journalist William Hard, the *Delineator* launched a campaign for mothers' pensions. Whereas the "Child-Rescue Campaign" had called on women to open their mothers' hearts wide enough to take in children not of their flesh, the new campaign urged women to spread their mother love by working to help other mothers keep their children. Women who took in dependent children were no longer cheered as the possessors of a strong "mother consciousness"; now they were the "strangers" who received the children "torn" from poor mothers.[51]

Nonetheless, the "Child-Rescue Campaign" had made a lasting impression in the minds of readers. In 1919, the *Delineator* announced the creation of a "Child-Helping" Department to educate women on the "science" of child placement. Editor Honore Willsie, herself an adoptive mother, introduced the series by explaining that "more and more people, recalling our earlier work, are asking this magazine to find children for them." Carolyn Conant Van Blarcom, a nurse and midwife reformer who served as the *Delineator*'s health editor, directed the series under the slogan "To find the right homes for the homeless is a sacred duty and a blessed privilege." Although child placement was the focus, the series also promised to inform readers about the "scientific method" of handling the problems of childhood. The series bore a striking resemblance to the earlier series, with portraits of children approved for adoption and references to women's patriotic duty.[52]

There were also some noticeable differences. Unlike the "Child-Rescue Campaign," which had actively sought input from women readers, this series contained the advice of child-placing experts. Leaders in the field such as Hastings H. Hart of the Russell Sage Foundation and Sophie van Senden Theis, superintendent of child placing for the State Charities Aid Association of New York, made up the advisory council. The *Delineator* promised readers that the information presented would be "vouched for" by the advisory council's executive committee. This new approach reflected the larger culture's romance with professionalization and the growing belief that medical and scientific experts should oversee the nation's mothers. Readers' voices and opinions did not appear. Their personal experience no longer gave them expert status: they were expected to listen and learn from the professionals on such issues as when and how to tell a child he or she was adopted. If they were afraid to adopt, experts, not women who had lived through those same fears, would put them "right in the matter." The mother love that had opened their hearts in the past was now deemed too sentimental to be a trustworthy guide for placing a child. Science, not sentiment, was necessary to ensure a child's healthy "adjustment."[53]

The new series lasted less than a year and, like its predecessor, vanished without a trace; apparently, explaining the need for IQ tests and home study lacked the emotional appeal of the earlier series' stories of motherless waifs.[54] In the "Child-Rescue Campaign," women's experience, energy, and intelligence were vital to the cause of reform; now their ignorance threatened the cause of science. For whatever reason, the series failed to rouse readers, and the editors, ever aware of their fierce competition, abandoned it.

The "Child-Rescue Campaign" began as a solution to a distinct problem as identified and understood by one man. George Wilder's construction of the problem reflected his (and much of the larger society's) fears about immigration, race suicide, and the social threat posed by uncontrolled, undisciplined, un-American youth. Implicit in his solution of matching up childless homes and homeless children was the belief that native-born, middle-class homes were superior not only to institutions but also to the children's natural families—at least in the social terms of providing the children with future opportunities and American values.

It is nothing new to state that adoption always includes a judgment about who will be a better parent for a child and that this assessment necessarily reflects the culture's beliefs about what qualities make a good parent *at that moment in time*. What is fascinating about the "Child-Rescue Campaign," however, is that this judgment shifted as the series moved away from Wilder's attempt to match poor, dependent children with more prosperous and stable homes and toward embracing reformers' efforts to keep birth mothers and children together. This shift highlights the social construction of motherhood and speaks to the question, Who at any given time determines who and what a mother is?

When fear was the primary motivation behind the campaign, the *Delineator* portrayed adoptive mothers as society's key to salvation and its best hope for the future. Although the "Child-Rescue Campaign" presented adoptive mothers positively throughout the series, over time, the discourse shifted in favor of birth mothers. In July 1908, the *Delineator* acknowledged that separating a birth mother from her child was sad. But the *Delineator* also believed that a birth mother "however low her lot has fallen, surrenders her baby willingly, feeling, with the remnant of mother-love that lives within her, that her child must have a better chance in life than that which has come to her."[55] As the *Delineator*'s craving for more national influence grew and the staff's involvement with child-saving reformers who now favored keeping families together increased, the magazine's understanding of the problem, and hence the solution, changed. By October 1909, the *Delineator* stated that surrendering a child was a "frightful sacrifice" and that providing a child with another home was only "the best we can do."[56] What was once a heroic sacrifice was now horrific.

If this shift compromised the interests of women who wanted to adopt, the series was nonetheless instrumental in popularizing and destigmatizing adoption, whether it intended to or not. Although most states had adoption statutes by the time of the campaign, adoption was still not publicly or candidly discussed. Although articles on adoption had appeared in popular magazines a few times before, the "Child-Rescue Campaign" was the first time the spotlight focused on adoption for an extended period. In addition to allowing women to work out some of their fears about adoption and addressing some of the issues adoptive parents faced, the series served a practical purpose by showing interested parties where and how to adopt children. The campaign's overwhelming success showed that women were ready to adopt and believed that adoption created *real* families in which children were treated not as workers but as one of their own, and mothers felt the same love and devotion as if they had given birth.

3 | Redefining "Real" Motherhood
Representations of Adoptive Mothers,
1900–1950

In 1920, a woman who had been adopted as a child wrote an article for a popular magazine in which she tried to dispel many of the misconceptions about adoption. She devoted much of her account to proving that adoptive mothers were in fact "real" mothers, despite the lack of a blood bond with their children. To make the point, she recounted the story of a friend who also had been adopted as a young child. When grown, this woman, now a mother of two, met her birth mother for the first time:

> "She kissed me; and I kissed her," my friend told me. "Then I sat down in a chair and stared at her. I could see that my features resembled hers. But, in all truth, I could not feel that she was my mother. My mother was the 'mother' of my baby days, just as real as anything can be, despite the fact of my birth. *She* was my children's grandmother— not this stranger! I tell you, I couldn't feel it any other way. It's the love and the care which make a mother a mother, more than the child-bearing does."

It is impossible to know how many readers would have agreed. However, given the focus of the article and the vehemence with which the author asserted this claim, it seems clear that she felt that most Americans still believed in the superiority of a biological maternal tie.[1]

Throughout the period covered in this study, most Americans assumed (to a greater or lesser degree at various moments) that all "normal" women were or wanted to be mothers. Motherhood and maternal sacrifice generally were glorified and romanticized and described as woman's highest and truest calling and the key to her female identity. Many people looked askance at married women (especially middle-class and elite women) who were not mothers, often labeling them selfish or immature and questioning their womanhood. These beliefs encouraged—indeed, compelled—women to understand their identity, if not to derive their identity, based on their relationships to their children. Aside from any individual maternal desire that a woman may have felt, women lived their lives within a culture filled with social incentives, encouragements, and pressures to mother. In short, motherhood conferred status, nonmotherhood only stigma.[2]

However, the dominant culture's idealization of mothers generally equated motherhood with biology, not nurturance. Because they had not given birth, adoptive mothers found themselves on the edges of the culture's ideal. Commentators often portrayed adoptive motherhood as different from, and inferior to, biological motherhood. In response, adoptive mothers (and their advocates) argued for a definition of motherhood that would legitimate their identity as "real" mothers. Adoptive mothers never completely rejected the prevailing ideology of motherhood. Rather, they made their claim by showing how their motherhood fit with certain tenets of the ideal that were not dependent on a blood tie or physical maternity. Because they defined their motherhood in relation to the ideal, representations of adoptive motherhood shifted as the dominant understanding of motherhood changed.

Before 1920, prescriptive literature emphasized the power of adoption to protect and save society and presented adoptive mothers as both "rescuers" of society's cast-off children and women with strong, even exceptional, maternal instincts. In this construction, many believed that single women had as much right to adopt as married women. During this period, adoptive mothers had few chances publicly to name their own experience. When they did have the chance, many used the rhetoric of redemption, but they also insisted that motherhood was a spiritual, not a physical, state. After 1920, responding to a changed social climate and an altered understanding of motherhood and family life, the portrayal of adoption and adoptive mothers shifted. Although representations highlighted the everyday similarities between adoptive and biological families, they also emphasized what now could be seen as the positive difference of adoption. Authors used the vocabulary of choice to underscore adoptive mothers' conscious decision to mother and their unique preparedness for motherhood.

Hopeful mothers had other opportunities to put forth a new understanding of motherhood. In order to become mothers, these women had to convince someone they would be *good* mothers. In expressing their longing, women used an emotional language of despair and loss to convey the sincerity of their desire and the centrality of motherhood to their identity. "I need a child so badly. My heart aches for one until I feel I can't bear it," a California woman wrote in a letter that echoed countless others in both its anguish and the choice of images to describe the pain.[3] Expressing desire, however, was not enough. Many women also consciously contrasted their active quests and domestic accomplishments with examples of maternal abandonment and neglect to show the advantages of motherhood by design. Blending the concepts of desire and design with the acknowledgment of failed fertility, some adoptive mothers suggested a modified understanding of "maternal instinct," which *some* women just "naturally" possessed independent of physical reproduction. Adoptive mothers often reiterated and even celebrated the idealized construction of motherhood, yet they also posed a challenge to the narrow definition of motherhood and offered an alternative to the biological family. The united voices of adoptive mothers helped expand the ideal beyond blood to include ties of care and commitment.

"Maternal Instincts of Wonderful Strength"

Although women have always borne and cared for children, both women's actual experience as mothers and the culture's understanding of the institution of motherhood have changed dramatically over the last three centuries. In the colonial period, women were valued as mothers, but they also were regarded for their roles as wives, neighbors, and Christians. However, in the early nineteenth century, the attention focused on women's role as mothers for a number of reasons. The removal of the father's place of work from the middle-class home reconfigured that space as a female place of nurture. Isolated from the sins of the world, women became society's moral guardians, most especially through their influence over husbands and children. The new republic's need for virtuous future citizens also highlighted the important task of mothers. And finally, religious leaders believed that a child's ultimate salvation depended on its mother's wholesome influence during its early years when its character was formed. Together, these factors emphasized the importance of motherhood to society at large, an importance that commanded respect and that would ultimately justify women's movement beyond the confines of their homes. By the 1830s, motherhood was enthroned as women's most important role.[4]

This model of womanhood held that all women, simply because they were women, possessed a maternal and moral sensibility. As numerous historians have noted, this ideology allowed women, even encouraged women, to move beyond the boundaries of their homes to spread their moral influence into the world at large. The mid-nineteenth-century domestic reformer and educator Catharine Beecher, who never married, was one of the first to argue that women's maternal sense necessitated their entrance into the public sphere. Beecher not only advocated that single women express their maternal instinct through teaching and nursing but also maintained that these women provided a service to society every bit as valuable (if not more valuable) as that of the mother in the home. In the early twentieth century, women continued to use the ideology of female difference and moral superiority to justify their public work in such areas as social reform, for which their gender seemed especially suited.[5]

Yet even as Americans respected the motherliness of all women, they held the biological mother–child bond apart in special reverence. In 1839, for example, the Reverend John Todd wrote that "God planted this *deep*, this *unquenchable* love for her offspring, in the mother's heart." Many commentators believed that only through bearing children could a woman realize true happiness. In 1891, a physician asserted the primacy of maternity when he noted that a woman's "inmost nature yearns to spend its treasures of love and service upon her own offspring. . . . the heart which hears no echo of love from its own child is inexpressibly sad." Even the love between a husband and wife, according to nineteenth-century advice givers, suffered in comparison to the intensity and purity of a mother's feelings for her child. Marital literature from this period continued the theme: "The mission of woman is childbearing. Women who have not married, or who have married and not borne children, do not know what happiness is. There is a void in their lives which no other experience fills."[6]

Adoptive mothers in the late nineteenth and early twentieth centuries experienced their motherhood in a culture that held these somewhat contradictory understandings of women's nature. On the one hand, given the widespread belief in women's maternal essence, many Americans could accept a woman's decision to adopt as natural, or at least understandable. On the other hand, the cultural veneration of the physical process of birth and exaltation of the blood tie meant that most people saw adoptive motherhood as a pale imitation of biological motherhood.

As late as 1924, for example, S. Josephine Baker, a well-respected physician and consultant to the U.S. Children's Bureau, wrote an article on adoption for the *Ladies' Home Journal* in which she clearly stated that she believed the adoptive relationship was qualitatively different from a relationship founded on biological parenthood. Dr. Baker told readers:

> Of course you cannot at first love just any child as well as you do your own, and I am inclined to believe that the adopted child must show a higher standard of character and "make good" in a far better way than a natural child to be accepted on anything like the same basis by any father or mother. It is very easy to forgive your own child. . . ; but, try

as you will, there is not the same readiness to understand the behavior of the boy or girl who does not belong to you by right of birth.

This assessment applied not only to adoptive families in which a birth child was present but also to those families that had only adopted children. As Baker's opinion suggests, many Americans clearly distinguished the maternal experience of women who had given birth from those who expressed their maternal potential through adoption. Although many people understood an adoptive mother's desire and might even respect her decision, they also believed that her motherhood was different. Adoption provided a woman with a child to love, but it did not necessarily provide her with a completely recognized claim to "real" motherhood.[7]

If adoptive mothers could not claim status as real mothers, they could at least receive credit as superior citizens. As the previous chapter demonstrates, articles on adoption before 1920 emphasized the redemptive aspect of adoption and encouraged women—especially childless women—to see adoption as part of their civic duty to society. This was not the first time that a woman's role as mother had been linked to her obligations as a citizen. Since the American Revolution, the ideology of motherhood had held that women could fulfill their duty to the nation by training their children to be productive and moral citizens. This construction of motherhood justified women's access to education, provided women with a political identity, and invested mothering with a power that transcended the four walls of a woman's home. The connection between motherhood and women's civic duty continued throughout the nineteenth and early twentieth centuries as women argued that their role as mothers necessitated their involvement in a wide variety of public issues.[8]

Adoption as duty, however, represented a twist on the usual understanding of civic motherhood. Here, native-born, middle-class women's duty to their country included rearing not only their own children but also orphans and children whose mothers were not up to the task. It also altered the nature of a mother's relationship to the state. Civic mothers met their public obligations in private service to the men of their households. Adoptive mothers, however, lost the intermediary of their husbands and sons and entered into a more public and direct service to their country, while still remaining in their homes.[9]

The connection between adoption and a woman's civic duty also exposes an important aspect of the relationship between motherhood and citizenship. Mothers had the power to make children into ideal citizens, but just as important, being a mother also made a woman a better citizen. Once a woman loved a child, she necessarily felt connected to—and therefore anxious about—the future. In other words, caring for a child moved a woman beyond selfish interests to broader social concerns. Native-born, middle-class women, as President Theodore Roosevelt pointed out during the race-suicide scare of the early twentieth century, had a "duty" to reproduce that was comparable to men's service in the military. But more than just providing society with the "right" kind of citizens, motherhood also made these women into the right kind of citizens. According to one commentator from 1908, it was a psychological "fact" that raising a child brought out "the sanest and best instincts and safest motives." Motherhood, then, was not only a private, individual experience. Rather, these new feelings also changed a woman's relationship to the public sphere, increasing her awareness of the world around her. This heightened perception might lead to action, thereby contributing to America's "whole program of social development." More important, this commentator believed that without a child to love, a woman could become a danger to society, her heart "the breeding place for dragons and other things unnatural."[10]

Although the *Delineator's* "Child-Rescue Campaign" was the most extended adoption appeal to emphasize women's civic obligation, others also saw adoption as a way to enhance the nation's citizenry. In 1916, Mrs. Charles Judson, a physician's wife who privately placed children out of her home in Philadelphia, stressed that adoption was a means to Americanize children and maintain Anglo-Saxon values. Judson believed that adoption gave

> to our country more of the best class of American citizens. Our forebears, through toil and struggle, often gained ideals, culture, refinement, and beliefs which have built up this nation. So many families where such inheritance obtains are childless. If a child is adopted and these ideas and beliefs passed down to it, we create another American citizen guided by the same uplifting faiths as held and helped our forefathers.[11]

An article entitled "A Plea for Adoption," which appeared in 1911 in *Good Housekeeping*, sheds light on the way adoptive mothers, as opposed to social commentators, understood adoption. The article, which was actually a lengthy letter to the editor, was written by a Kentucky woman who described her motivation to adopt as grounded in a desire to mother, not a duty to save. This woman's only biological child had died, and she was unable to have any others. When she could no longer suffer her "loneliness" and "sorrow," she adopted a child to whom she could give her mother's love. This mother was devoted to her adopted son and emphatically stated that she could not give him up, even if giving him up would bring back her dead son. It was only toward the end of the letter, as she attempted to convince readers who might be hesitant to adopt, that the woman mentioned the social aspect of adoption. "The chance that one may make a splendid man of a boy who otherwise would remain a charge upon charity," the author maintained, "is surely sufficient incentive to induce one to brave the responsibility." *Good Housekeeping,* however, chose to emphasize this point by headlining the letter "The Large Opportunity, Not to Say Duty, Which Confronts Childless Couples."[12]

Ultimately, although the construction of adoption as rescue helped legitimate adoption, for adoptive mothers who wanted an identity as real mothers, this construction created a critical distinction between their experience and that of biological mothers. The popular understanding of a mother's love encompassed feelings that went well beyond fulfilling one's civic obligations. The belief that women had a duty to civilize society propelled women into careers as reformers, educators, and health professionals. If adoption was regarded as a woman's duty, then adoptive mothers merely occupied a place on the continuum of ways nonmothers expressed their maternal feelings. Women who also had biological children may have viewed their adopting as a sign of their commitment to society, but for childless women living in a culture that at best stigmatized them, adoption was a way to join the community of mothers. These women wanted acceptance as real mothers, not praise for raising derelict children. Although women sometimes heard that motherhood was womankind's form of national service, the most consistent and pervasive message insisted that motherhood was a private and intimate experience.

Before 1920, the views of adoptive mothers rarely appeared in print. When they did, they challenged the idea that adoptive motherhood was an imitation of "real" motherhood. Some adoptive mothers presented their experience in a way that blended the concepts of duty and mother love; others avoided the issue of civic obligation. As one stated in 1908, "They say that I can never know the feeling of a real mother, of the woman whose mortal frame has endured the martyrdom of a physical maternity, but nevertheless he is my son, the son of my spiritual self, of all that is best in me." By drawing an explicit comparison between her experience and the experience of birth, this adoptive mother asserted that true motherhood was not an event of the flesh but the essence of womanhood.[13]

In 1909, Zona Gale, a popular writer who later adopted a child, published a short story, "Adoption," that presented a similar understanding of motherhood and challenged those who made a distinction between an adoptive and a birth mother's love. In the story, a childless married woman searches for a child to adopt, not to serve any "social need" but because she is "simply hungering for a child." She sacrifices for the unknown child, scrimping and saving and making do so that she can purchase clothing and furniture for the child. The woman finally locates an infant in a nearby town and eagerly shows his photo to all her women neighbors. But before she can bring the child home, he dies. The story concludes with a touching portrait of this mother's grief and the neighbors' response to her. These women try to comfort her, but, as the narrator points out, "many of them had lost little children of their own, and could not regard her loss as at all akin to theirs." The narrator, however, asserts that her loss is just as real and offers a definition of motherhood based not on a physical relationship to a child but on a woman's spiritual acceptance of maternal responsibility. In this story, the motherly emotions society prizes—self-sacrifice and eternal, inexhaustible love—have nothing to do with a blood tie, but arise out of a woman's "natural" appetite for motherhood.[14]

We Wanted Children

In the 1920s, firsthand accounts by adoptive mothers began to appear in popular magazines. These articles took advantage of a changed social climate to present adoption in a new way. This decade witnessed a return to private life and a preoccupation with pursuing individual pleasures, not solving social problems. The popular understanding of womanhood, marriage, and motherhood also underwent a profound transformation. Although sexual behaviors among some groups had changed long before, the 1920s, according to historians John D'Emilio and Estelle Freedman, marked the acceptance of modern sexual practices and values by the culture at large. Suddenly, women were erotic beings, and sex was about more than procreating. A successful marriage now depended on both partners' sexual satisfaction. And although children were as necessary as ever for a complete and happy marriage, they were to be consciously and carefully planned for so that all members of the family could reach their "highest personal happiness." To this end, by the 1920s, many middle-class women used some form of contraception to limit family size. In addition, as the twentieth century progressed, the sufficiency of maternal instinct was called into question as experts argued that women needed to supplement intuition with professional advice. Courses in parent education flourished as middle-class women (and some men) tried to absorb the latest in child-rearing techniques. Scientific information, not instinct, became the new sine qua non of ideal motherhood. Stories about adoption during the 1920s and 1930s reflect these changes, presenting adoption not as benevolent rescue but as modern American family life.[15]

Stories by adoptive mothers, filled with the minutiae of the adoption process, were realistic, not overly sentimental. These stories tried to demystify and normalize adoption by showing adoptive families experiencing the same trials, tribulations, and joys as any family. Adoptive mothers argued that their families were just ordinary families, and they wanted to be treated as such. One woman lamented that it was "an almost impossible task to raise an adopted child in a normal manner," since neighbors continually brought up the fact that her children were adopted, berated her with "much unsought advice," and zealously scrutinized the way she cared for her children. These portrayals also showed the difficulties of adoption, such as the initial troubles of adjusting to a child. When the authors did acknowledge a difference between their families and biological families, it was a positive difference. After all, their families were consciously planned. As one father explained, "We took the boy because we wanted him. This cannot always be said of own parents." In the few stories in which the "rescue" theme appeared, it was minimized or an afterthought. The message was clear: adoptive parents benefited as much from adoption as the adopted child.[16]

A few of these stories were written by women who were both adoptive and biological mothers. The fact that they had given birth gave these women the authority to speak on the subject of motherhood and to be taken seriously. These women were also in a unique position to challenge those who believed that adoptive parents could not love their children as much as biological parents did. In doing so, they posed a direct, if unconscious, challenge to the faith in the strength and inimitable quality of blood ties. In 1935, one woman confided to the readers of *Scribner's Magazine* that she had "examined her heart closely" to determine whether she loved her biological daughter more than her adopted children. She concluded that she loved each of her children differently, in a way that respected their individuality and had nothing to do with the blood that flowed in their veins. The popular novelist Kathleen Norris, also an adoptive and a biological mother, wrote an article for the *Ladies' Home Journal* in which she expressed her belief that "the miracle of bearing a living baby is no more astonishing than the companion miracle of finding a small person adrift in the world without a mother, and bringing him triumphantly home to his silver bowl and spoon." Norris "state[d] from experience" that an adoptive child rewarded a mother's love "just as richly as does the baby Mother Nature sends haphazard."[17]

These women also sought to establish a definition of motherhood and family that would provide them with cultural legitimacy. As one eloquent adoptive mother who also had biological children stated, "love-lines, not blood-lines, make motherhood . . . true parenthood is a stewardship which has no necessary relation to physical parenthood." As she told her adoptive son (and the world), "I did not give you physical birth; but that doesn't matter. Whoever did, wouldn't have been your real mother until she worked and cared for you and learned to love you as I do. For some reason that neither of us will ever know, she brought you into the world but left motherhood for me. You're my son because I wanted you and took you and raised you and loved you." In this construction of motherhood, conscious choice and conscientious care replaced instinct and intuition.[18]

Articles that appeared in popular magazines used the language of choice to underscore the planning and persistence of adoptive parents in creating their families. When "choice" appeared in articles about adoption before 1920, it usually referred to the large selection of available children from which adoptive parents could pick their favorite. (Although many articles suggested that there was an abundance of children, there were actually relatively few adoptable infants and young children from as early as 1900.) After about 1920, however, choice was used in its modern connotation to show adoptive parents' thoughtful decision to undertake parenthood. For example, the 1937 article "We Wanted Children" details a childless couple's careful preparation and committed determination in each of their three adoptions to get just the family they desired. The author refers to her adopted children as "wanted" children. This phrase placed this adoptive family squarely in the middle of the new companionate family ideal and may well have reminded readers of Margaret Sanger's favorite slogan in support of the modern family and birth control: "Every child a wanted child." A few years later, an editorial in the Ladies' Home Journal made the connection even more explicit by noting that "the most truly 'planned families' anywhere are the families with adopted children." This planning, the editor believed, gave legally adopted children "a better than normal child's chance. For they go to homes that desperately and genuinely want children."[19]

The "chosen-child" story first appeared in articles about adoption in the late 1910s; within a short time, child welfare professionals were encouraging parents to use this motif when explaining adoption to their children. Briefly, the chosen-child story tells of the adoptive parents' desire and search for a child and the child's special qualities that made them pick him or her out of a crowd of babies. The first articles that endorsed this method of telling often described how a child would respond to the taunts of his playmates that he was "only 'n adopted boy." The adopted child, fortified by the rhetoric of the chosen-child story, would flash back, "Your mother *had to take* you; but mine *chose* me!" Experts argued that the chosen-child theme allowed children to think of the difference of adoption in a positive way. But significantly, the story also provided adoptive parents with a positive way to narrate and understand *their* experience. The language of the story, like that in the first-person narratives discussed earlier, reflects the values of modern parenthood. Adoptive parents did not "just have babies"; they consciously, actively planned their families.[20]

At the same time that some adoptive mothers were using the concept of choice to move the understanding of motherhood toward a definition based on a conscious desire to mother and the reality of day-to-day care, the faith in the infallibility of maternal instinct was being challenged—at least in the scientific community. Although advice books for mothers had existed before, reformers began to argue during the Progressive Era that instinct needed to be supplemented with education to ensure the healthy development of children. By the 1920s, a full-fledged campaign had been developed to educate parents and replace mothers' "common sense" with scientific knowledge. "Mothercraft classes" and "mother training courses" appeared everywhere. Throughout the 1920s, 1930s, and 1940s, experts bombarded mothers with literature on every aspect of childhood, from physiology to psychology. Although many child welfare experts questioned the reliability (and in a few cases, even the existence) of maternal instinct, some went so far as to suggest that unchecked intuition could actually harm a child. As numerous scholars have pointed out, this advice made mothers both insecure and dependent on expert, mostly male, guidance. Yet, from the perspective of some adoptive mothers, if women needed to be educated to motherhood, physical birth no longer gave biological mothers an automatic edge.[21]

In 1929, for example, an adoptive mother used the growing emphasis on maternal education to show readers of the *Woman's Journal* the similarities between adoptive and birth mothers:

Once people believed in the existence of "a mother's instinct" and supposed it to be an infallible guide to the proper care of a baby. We know better now. The young mothers among my friends use the months of their pregnancy for a rather intensive study of baby culture. . . . I read as much during those seven months [when she was on an adoption agency's waiting list] as my friends have, and I flatter myself was no more flurried by the first bath than they were.[22]

Some women used the principle of scientific motherhood not only to minimize the differences but also to celebrate adoption in its own right. In 1922, Honore Willsie, an adoptive mother and editor of a successful women's magazine, claimed that the unique circumstances of adoption made her a better mother. As she told the readers of Century Magazine, "I am undoubtedly stricter with my children than any own mother I know, because I see my children more clearly than own mothers do." She continued, "I saw these children physically as their physician saw them, mentally and spiritually as their psychiatrist saw them. . . . And herein lay my vast advantage over own mothers. I saw my children as they were. And because my responsibility was voluntarily taken, I dare not allow my growing love for them to becloud my vision." On first glance, Willsie's appraisal of her children sounds rather clinical and cold. On closer examination, however, it simply embraces the modern ideals of science and choice and uses them to cast adoptive families' difference from blood families in a positive light. Here, finally, was a climate in which an adoptive mother could challenge the widespread belief that her motherhood was inferior and base that assertion on something "objective."[23]

Child welfare expert Jessie Taft also used the new focus on maternal education to champion and legitimate adoption. "Physical birth, flesh and blood connection," she argued in 1926, "have ceased to be the important factors in our newer vision of the parent's job. . . . Loving a child because he is flesh of your flesh is not all important but how effective and intelligent your love is in equipping him for life. Love, ignorant and blind, may hamper his development and ruin his happiness." She continued, "Thus parenthood has been taken out of its conventional setting and lies open to anyone who conceives of it as a job worthy to be done." In case readers had failed to grasp the implications of this new understanding of parenthood, she reiterated her point. "But, you say, surely you do not imply that taking a dependent child from an agency will guarantee the experience of a real parent. My answer is yes." If "real" parenthood was a "job" with the unsentimental aim of creating a stable, secure, and useful adult, then the differences of adoption did not matter. And, according to Taft, adoptive parents' "voluntary and conscious" decision to parent and the "analysis and thought" that went into that determination could even be an advantage.[24]

Although adoption was still seen as second best by most Americans, adoption advocates could represent it more positively in the context of the new family ideal, with its emphasis on planning and educated parenthood. Within the framework of the modern family, the differences between adoptive and biological families could be minimized and, paradoxically, acknowledged or, as we saw with Willsie and Taft, even embraced. Since the late-nineteenth-century debates over the declining native-born birthrate, Americans had made a distinction between women who actively chose to be mothers and those who passively accepted (or even consciously avoided) motherhood. The distinction further solidified in the discussion of family life in the early twentieth century, which established an ideal of thoughtfully and consciously planned families. The growing acceptance of choice as a fundamental principle in family formation helped to normalize adoption, and many adoptive mothers used this to legitimate their motherhood. One mother recounted how she had used the chosen-child story to tell her child of her adoption: "There are two kinds of mothers; one is a mother because she has to be, and the other is a mother because she wants to be. . . . I am your mother because I wanted to be."[25]

In this environment, a popular 1939 guide to adoption could acknowledge difference and quickly dismiss its significance. "Many people now believe that what has been uncritically termed 'maternal instinct,' a mysterious complex of knowledge and devotion that blossoms suddenly at the physical birth of a child, is nothing more or less than the acceptance of parental responsibility, something *learned*, and then fixed by habit."[26] In 1948, this strategy of both minimizing and emphasizing difference informed the creation of an adoption support group in Ohio. The Chosen Parents League, founded by a group of adoptive parents, sought to ease the anxieties and answer the questions of those considering adoption, as well as to help them find children. The founders also believed that they were in a unique position to speak to the issues of child welfare in their community. "We who have adopted children don't have them because 'oh, well, we're going to have a baby—we'll have to make the best of it'—we have them because we CHOOSE to. WE WANT THEM! . . . Anyone must realize that when we work for CHILD WELFARE we are SINCERE. We have no axes to grind!" Yet, while contrasting adoptive and biological parenthood, the founder of this organization also emphasized that adoptive parents were no different from any parents who loved and took joy in their children. "We do not quite agree with Frances Lockridge in her 'Adopting a Child' [a popular adoption guide published in 1948] that 'people who adopt children have a special quality of feeling and character,' but rather do we feel that since these our adopted children have made our lives so very rich, our happiness must overflow and invade the lives of others."[27] The issue of difference and how (or whether) to address it would continue to occupy adoptive mothers, but, for a moment, changes in the understanding of family life gave some adoptive mothers a way to lay claim publicly to being "real" mothers.

"Private" Public Stories: Adoptive Mothers' Labor Pains

In public representations of their experience, adoptive mothers first used the rhetoric of redemption and woman's nature and then the concepts of choice, knowledge, and care to assert that their motherhood was "real." But how did the lived experience of adoptive mothers—the way they *privately* felt about and understood their constructed maternity—compare with the public portrayal? Was the day-to-day experience of adoptive mothers similar to or different from that of mothers who had given birth? The few clues we have from personal letters of adoptive mothers do not suggest a radically distinct experience. For example, in 1885, a short time after she adopted a daughter, physician Eliza Mosher wrote to her sister that if she accomplished nothing else besides raising her child, "I shall feel as if my life has not been in vain." In 1925, Mabel Walker Willebrandt excitedly wrote to her parents about her newly adopted daughter, Dorothy, who was "the dearest, wisest little two year old I ever saw," and "*honestly*, no joking *looks* like Papa. . . . And her forehead is like Mama's!" In Maine, meanwhile, Mrs. Eldridge insisted that her newly adopted daughter was "the loveliest baby I ever looked upon and my love for her does not make me see her in that light for many people have told me the same thing." These private expressions of the joys, rewards, and dedication of motherhood do not strike the reader as noticeably unlike what we might expect to hear from any proud mother.[28]

Similarly, Caroline Bartlett Crane, an urban reformer who adopted an infant in 1914 and another the next year, expressed first a desire to be a mother and then an intense satisfaction as a mother. While away from home on a lecture tour in 1907, she wrote to her husband of the envy she felt when she encountered a young woman with a four-month-old child. "If I had that baby to nurse at my breast, I'd let [the child's mother] do the lecturing this afternoon." After adopting her first child, she kept a detailed diary, noting the smallest changes, the tiniest smile. She wrote to her husband that she felt she was now "a much better woman" and, later, that she was "happier in her [adopted daughter's] company, than with anyone else in the world except you."[29]

Here again, in this intimate correspondence between a husband and a wife, we see nothing extraordinary. Adoptive mothers have left few private expressions—letters to family and friends or diaries—to help us reconstruct their daily experience and their most private thoughts. What glimpses we have suggest more similarities with biological mothers than differences. Yet the fact remains that adoptive mothers did not come to motherhood in the usual way, and many Americans did see their motherhood as a thing apart. A large study in the early 1960s (after adoption had become relatively commonplace), for example, showed that although most North Americans said that they accepted adoption, on closer examination, a large percentage still considered adoption to be an inferior form of family. The study further reported that virtually all adoptive mothers had experienced comments or actions that marked their motherhood as different. Whether a seemingly innocuous remark from an acquaintance—"Isn't it wonderful of you to have taken this child!"—or the thoughtless statement of a neighbor—"How well you care for your child, just like a real mother"—adoptive mothers could not escape the view that biological motherhood was more authentic than theirs.[30]

The historical record is largely silent with regard to how this prevailing belief in difference affected adoptive mothers in the first half of this century. Did the widespread assumption of inferiority make women feel differently about their motherhood or their children, or were they able to ignore these views? Did the stigma surrounding adoption lead mothers to examine their feelings and attitudes toward motherhood more than if they had given birth?

The letters between the matron of a maternity home and a woman with whom she had placed an infant in the mid-1930s suggest that the unique circumstances of adoption forced mothers to be especially reflective.[31] As was standard, the maternity home required an adoptive mother to keep it apprised of the child's health until the adoption was final. Due to a misunderstanding, the adoptive mother (who also had a son by birth) believed that the matron was not convinced that the child should stay with her. In response, the adoptive mother wrote to the matron and admitted that she was uncertain about her feelings for her new daughter. "Now as to my own feelings. Honestly, I do not know. I love her, but whether it will grow into something big enough to be the right thing—I can't say. Four weeks contact has not told me this." She continued, "If you feel that going on mothering when I am not definitely, absolutely sure is unfair to either you or her, I, of course shall bring her back. It would be hard, I admit. I feel that to be mother of one that it takes a longer period of acquaintance than four weeks." The matron encouraged the woman to keep the child, and she did. A few years later, she wrote to the matron regarding an article she had read on adoption that emphasized difference. She declared that as "a woman who has achieved motherhood, by giving birth to a son, and by adopting a daughter, . . . [I] can say with a heart full of love, what's the difference."[32]

There is no way of knowing whether this woman's experience of adoptive motherhood was similar to other women's or if she had also felt an initial ambivalence toward her biological child. What does seem clear, though, is that adoptive motherhood was a very self-conscious motherhood. This self-consciousness becomes especially apparent in women's efforts to become mothers. And although adoptive mothers were mostly quiet about their everyday experience of mothering, some have left evidence to reconstruct the manner in which they became mothers. The actual process of becoming a mother, of course, was the primary as well as the initial difference: finding a child was not the same as giving birth to a child. Yet, as we shall see, the travails of adoption could be just as intense as the pains of labor.

As interest in adoption grew, and the social welfare policies of encouraging unwed mothers to care for their children and keeping biological families together continued (the latter aided by mothers' pensions, workers' compensation, and charitable aid), the aforementioned shortage of adoptable infants and young children persisted. Throughout the first half of the twentieth century, however, many Americans remained unaware that there were actually very few children available. Crises such as World War I, the influenza epidemic of 1918–1919, the depression (which swelled the numbers of children in institutions to an all-time high of 144,000 and pushed the foster care system to its limits), and World War II all pointed to an abundance of children in need of new families; many people did not realize that the majority of dependent children still had parents or other relatives who had legal claims on them. In the 1930s and 1940s, magazine articles that spoke of the need for foster parents (which some readers misunderstood to mean *permanent* adoptive parents) and erroneous reports that the United States was to receive thousands of European war orphans further contributed to the confusion. When prospective parents could not find a child—and thinking that they simply had not looked in the right place—some began in the 1920s to turn to the U.S. Children's Bureau for help.[33]

Established in 1912, the bureau investigated and reported on all aspects of child life in America, quickly becoming the nation's leading child welfare authority. Tens of thousands of women throughout the country wrote to the bureau each year for advice on maternal and infant health or read the bureau's pamphlets. The bureau, however, addressed adoption somewhat late in its history, publishing its first pamphlet on the subject in 1925. Soon, though, it would take a leadership role in the movement to convince states and the public of the need for professional standards in adoption placements and greater regulation (a topic discussed in detail in chapter 5).[34]

Between 1914 and 1920, the bureau received no more than a handful of letters requesting children, but as more popular magazines and newspapers addressed the topic, the number of requests began to rise, especially because articles in the 1920s and 1930s often mentioned the bureau or quoted a member of its staff. Bureau representatives also spoke on the radio about child welfare and adoption, generating more inquiries. In addition, in the late 1930s and early 1940s, prospective parents' frustration appears to have grown, and hundreds wrote to President Franklin Roosevelt or his wife, Eleanor, for help in locating children. The presidential staff passed these letters on to the bureau for a response; by 1942, the number of letters was so great that the bureau created a special filing category. These documents vividly show that adoption interested a full spectrum of Americans, from the wealthy and prominent to those with quite modest incomes. Inquiries also came from all regions of the country.[35]

The majority of these letters were short, a simple request for information, such as one from a woman who, in 1935, wrote, "We want very much to adopt a baby but don't know just how to go about it." Others provided a bit more information. In 1932, after a fruitless search, a Massachusetts woman wrote that she had "always heard that there are plenty of homeless children but it seems almost impossible to locate one at present." But many went beyond a mere request for assistance and related their desire for a child and the reason they wanted to adopt. Women wrote the vast majority of letters. Although it is impossible to know whether these letters represent the attitudes of most adoptive parents or those interested in adoption, they provide a window into at least some women's feelings about adoption, motherhood, and family.[36]

The letters, sometimes many pages in length, can be heartbreaking, detailing a succession of miscarriages, a child's tragic death, or just intense, seemingly unbearable longing. Yet, as real as these stories are—as sincere the desire, excruciating the sorrow, or singular the story—we need to remember that these are not really "personal" letters. Although retelling private stories, often in the most intimate detail, each woman wrote with a distinct purpose in mind: to convince the recipient to help her get a child. How does one prove to a stranger that one is worthy of being a mother?

Faced with this task, many women chose to recount their own experiences, apparently hoping that their accounts of pain and persistence would generate sympathy and compel action on the part of the reader. That so many letters were filled with such feelings and told with such disarming candor suggests that these women believed that emotional openness and palpable longing were qualities likely to be rewarded with a child. This, of course, does not imply that these women's stories were untrue or their emotions insincere. Rather, it suggests how the institution of motherhood (that is, the way the dominant culture expected "real" mothers to feel and behave) and the individual experience of mothering are inextricably intertwined. Did these women's understanding of cultural norms of motherhood—the belief in maternal self-sacrifice and undying love—influence the way they represented their lives? Even if these norms set boundaries on women's expression, at the same time, the letters allowed women to put forth their own understanding of motherhood. And, as one might expect, their definition challenged a number of popular beliefs.[37]

Historians have shown that at points over the last century, some members of the medical profession have blamed women for their inability to bear children. In the late nineteenth century, for example, doctors warned that too much education could lead to sterility. If, on occasion, doctors cited female behavior as the problem—what one scholar terms women's "failure of volition"—then it is possible to read many women's letters to the Children's Bureau as attempts to establish their "triumph of instinct." In requests that told of why they could not have children (and often recounted heroic efforts to bear or locate one), these women declared that their childlessness was not volitional, a result of "acts done or left undone."[38] Rather, these women asserted their worthiness to be mothers by showing their perseverance, determination, and willingness to endure tremendous pain and disappointment in their quest for a child. Far from a failure of will, these women demonstrated an undeniable conviction to become mothers—despite the fact that in many cases their bodies had failed. Just as a failed body was not the same as a failed or unwilling mother, a successful pregnancy was not a sign of a "real" mother. These letters show "maternal instinct" severed from the physical body and unconscious and grounded in the conscious desire for and diligent pursuit of motherhood.[39]

Although many women simply noted rather matter-of-factly that they could not bear children, other letters recounted the problems of a woman's body in more detail. Private stories were told to outsiders, encouraging sympathy and proving sincerity, but also highlighting the public nature of female fertility and female bodies. Despite the fact that by the 1930s fertility specialists knew that the man was responsible for a couple's inability to conceive in approximately half the cases, the medical establishment focused its treatments on women through the 1950s. In part, physicians targeted women because they were the ones who sought help in most cases. Their attention to women, however, also reflected efforts by physicians *and* wives to protect male egos that might be damaged by a diagnosis of a low sperm count. As one doctor noted, "Unfortunately, the average patient closely relates his ability to reproduce with his ability to perform coitus. As a corollary to this, most men feel that any question of their ability to reproduce casts reflections upon their virility." Women, then, often underwent painful diagnostic treatments voluntarily and unnecessarily.[40]

Although some women went to great lengths to safeguard their husbands' sense of manhood, ironically, in letters to the bureau, many women seemed quite willing to acknowledge the limitations of their own bodies. For these women, the capacity for physical maternity did not signify "womanhood"; a desire to mother did. In 1942, a wife in Los Angeles wrote to Eleanor Roosevelt that she could not "have any children because my uterus is deformed, we have tried every way to get a child, but the homes here have more people than children, then it takes around 2 years." Perhaps tellingly, this woman chose to place her infertility in the same sentence as her inability to adopt a child. In other words, the problem was not her failed body but her failure to find a child to mother. "I just don't know how I can go on much longer without a child," she continued, "I love children dearly." Her appeal concluded with a poignant plea: "Please oh Please can't you help me get a baby I grieve every time I see a baby, my heart aches to have one." Here, the desire to be a mother mattered far more than how she became one; her "instinct" was to mother, and as such, adoptive and physical maternity were the same.[41]

As this last story indicates, women felt immense pain and longing in their search for a child. Turning to a stranger for help in this most private of affairs proved frustrating as well. Women poured their hearts out in an effort to convince people they did not know that they deserved a child. Yet at least some women sensed the impossibility, even the absurdity, of proving their worth through words. A six-page letter to Eleanor Roosevelt, for example, began with the "hope" that she would be able to "read it & understand it & me also" and noted that it was "so hard to start off with what I want to say." Another woman, in the middle of her four-page request, pleaded with the First Lady not to "be borred with this letter. . . . If you only knew how bad we want a baby I am sure you would understand." Similarly, a woman from Washington commented midway through her plea to the president, "Perhaps I'm trying too desperly to show you our hearts, But I'm stating the facts as truthfully as I can, so that in case you can help us in any way, you will feel sure you are justified."[42]

In 1923, a thirty-eight-year-old woman from Ohio squeezed a note into the margins of the first page of her eleven-page inquiry to the bureau, apparently worried that it would not be taken seriously: "*Please read this thru to the end. This is a real letter by an earnest woman not gush.*" Her letter is painfully honest, detailing her "obsession" with finding a child. Her only child had been delivered by cesarian section, and her doctor had warned her not to risk another pregnancy. However, she still "yearn[ed]" for another baby, a "longing" her physician said "will make me ill if I do not obtain posession of another child to raise with the child of my union." Her sole wish was "to Mother"; "Find me [a child]," she promised the bureau, "and I will do that one thing, *well.*" Here is a document rich with feeling that uses the language of emotion to show the depth and sincerity of her plea. Yet, as her preface acknowledged, this passion could be interpreted as so much sentimental "gush." In a culture that expected women to be emotional and mothers to be devoted, this was the only vocabulary women could use both to describe their feelings and to justify their request for help. This is not to say that this woman's emotions were not real. Rather, it suggests that the institution of motherhood limited, and even delineated, the means of expressing maternal desire.[43]

On occasion, women also related their domestic talents as a sign that they were qualified to be mothers and should be mothers. In a postscript, one woman noted that she was "regular a nurse as far as taking care of babies [is] concerned, I have made two different sets of cloths for babies I thought I was going to have myself. But did not have and so I gave most of my cloths away to young mothers with their first babies. I think I deserve a child myself." A woman from Indiana, who had pursued infertility treatment and adoption for five years with no success, wrote to Eleanor Roosevelt. Although drawing a distinction between the "important" First Lady and her "humble and misfortunate" self, she nevertheless felt a connection to her. "I am sure, even if your children are all grown now, that you haven't forgotten how much they ment, . . . I guess we women are all alike some

how, the rich and poor." Her letter continued with a narrative of preparation, signifying that, except for the lack of a child, she was already a mother.
Cooking was "really fun," and her homemade bread was so good that her
"husband refusses the bakers." A backyard big enough to play, "five dozen
diapers," and a "beautiful finished baby bed" completed the family portrait.
Scholars have noted that adoptive parents often use a variety of domestic
"rituals" symbolically to claim a child as their own and to integrate him or
her into their family. Here we see a similar process used in the pursuit of a
child. The accumulation of the material items of child rearing and the mas-
tery of household skills serve as a way for prospective mothers to stake a
claim to motherhood.[44]

In addition to establishing their domestic competency and ability to care
for a child, some women used the concept of conscious choice to make their
case. A woman whose baby had died and who apparently could have no more
asked the bureau for assistance "at once" in locating an infant. Although her
"heart had been crushed since the loss of [her] child," it is possible to read
her "anxious, very anxious" request as more than a frenzied attempt to replace her dead baby. As she noted, "I feel that our lives should be filled with
something of a worth while nature and being a mother is the most natural
and the best really the best calling there is." Motherhood was her chosen (as
well as "natural") life's work, an honorable vocation whether she mothered
her own biological child or another.[45]

The expression of conviction led a number of women to contrast their
active quest with the behavior of mothers who seemed not to value their
children. "Some mothers do away with their children and more want to or
try to," a dispirited woman from Idaho argued. "Wouldn't our home be an
improvement over many such situations?" A wife in St. Louis whose repeated visits to her local child welfare institution had proved futile wrote,
"There are thousands of married & unmarried women that have babies
throw them in ash pits or garbage cans because they don't want them. People like myself would give any thing to have one to love can't even get close
to having one." Here we see choice and devotion, not blood, serving as the
primary signifier of motherhood. These examples are significant in adoptive
mothers' recasting of maternal instinct. In distinguishing their longing from
the irresponsibility of some birth mothers, these women seemed to deny the
existence of a maternal essence in all women. Although virtually all the letters imply that "real" women "naturally" want children, they also make
clear that the ability to have a child "naturally" does not necessarily make
a woman a "real" mother.[46]

The principles of choice and care as markers of true motherhood also surface in letters that relate stories of contested custody. In 1935, the bureau received a note from a Minnesota woman asking for advice on how to adopt a young boy who had been with her since he was two days old. The birth parents were married but already had four children and could not provide for another. The birth mother had approached this woman about taking her child and was willing to sign the adoption papers. The birth father, however, had continually stalled. Now, after a little over four years, the would-be adoptive mother could stand the indecision no more. "A feeling of dread hangs over us," she wrote, pleading for suggestions on how to proceed legally. "Surely the baby is ours *now*," she asserted, "we did not take him by force or coercion, yet he would be taken from us if the parents were to ask for him." The bureau, noting that both parents' consent would be required unless they could prove abandonment, offered little assistance.[47]

Correspondence from adoptive mothers among the papers of a Maine maternity home also make the argument that care given and a conscious decision to parent count as much as (if not more than) biology in determining parenthood. In 1928, the home placed a three-year-old girl with a family who wished to adopt her. The birth mother had been unable to care for her daughter and had failed to make payments for her child's board or to keep in close contact with the maternity home. Apparently, the home's matron made this placement because she believed that the birth mother would be willing to sign adoption papers and that the child should be placed in a permanent home before she grew any older.

The birth mother, however, was unwilling to sign and hoped that one day she would be able to provide for her child. The adoptive mother, frightened that she would lose the child, wrote to the home's matron. Her biological child had died, and she could not stand the thought of losing this child, too. "I do feel sorry for her [the child's] mother to have to suffer," she noted. "But I don't believe God is pleased when we neglect our own children. . . . Little do you realize how much we love her. I have got so attached to her that I would lay down my life for her if need be. And I don't believe her own mother would do that for her." In the late 1920s, it would not have been easy for an unwed mother to provide for her child, and it is unclear whether the adoptive mother considered this fact. What seems more clear, though, is her belief that "real" parents are those who are willing and able to care for their children, whatever the cost; parenthood should be intentional, and parents prepared.[48]

"Just the Average American Couple"

Women shared the most intimate details of their private lives in order to convince others to help them find children to adopt. But some hopeful adopters feared that this would not be enough. Discouraged after months and sometimes years of searching, and (wrongly) convinced that hundreds of orphans languished in institutions, many came to the (inaccurate) conclusion that wealth, not a genuine desire to mother, determined who received a child. The majority of these people, it is important to note, accepted that parents needed to be financially stable. What they did not accept was the idea that wealthy or well-to-do homes were better than hardworking or simple ones. For women of modest means, the difficult task of proving their worthiness as mothers contained the added burden of establishing that their love and devoted care were as valuable as material goods. In letters to the Roosevelts, these prospective mothers articulated a version of the ideal American family in which values such as personal commitment, self-reliance, and patriotism stood for more than material prosperity.

As historian Lizabeth Cohen has shown, during the depression, working-class Americans looked to the federal government for help for the first time. Rather than seeing the government as an impersonal bureaucracy, though, people saw President Roosevelt, the man, as the state. Thousands of individuals turned to the president, who was "at once God and their intimate friend," for help. The letters to the Roosevelts recounted in this chapter (not all of which were from members of the working class)[49] reflect this sense of personal connection and faith that the First Family would not let the correspondent down. A desperate woman from Indiana wrote to FDR that she "praide to the lord and I have done everything I know or anyone told me to do. I don't know anything to help me now if you don't." Letters to Mrs. Roosevelt referred to her as "our last hope" and expressed confidence that she would "understand and help." A few writers justified their requests by mentioning that they supported the war effort by working in a war industry, waving good-bye to a beloved soldier, or purchasing war bonds.[50]

Even before the war, however, people wrote to the Roosevelts for help in locating children. Indeed, numerous signs, including the letters to the bureau and the Roosevelts and the magazine articles discussed earlier, suggest that *interest* in adoption increased during the Great Depression. As historian Margaret Marsh has shown, despite the fact that the 1930s represent the high point of *voluntary* childlessness among married couples in the United

States, there was still strong pro-natalist sentiment. For those who could afford a child but were unable to have one of their own, adoption was the most likely answer. It is important to note that very few requests in the 1930s specifically frame adoption as a humanitarian act in a time of crisis; instead, in letters that mention the troubled economic times, most writers represent adoption as beneficial to adopter and child alike. With the end of the depression and the subsequent economic boom of wartime, which allowed people the financial security to think about a family, the number of applications to child-placing agencies increased—as did the shortage of children and the would-be adopters' frustration.[51]

When turned away from an orphanage in which children clearly resided, many did not believe the child welfare worker's assertion that there were no children available. Searching for an explanation, many determined that money—either an inadequate income or an inability to make a large donation to the institution—was the reason. Some private agencies, dependent on contributions, no doubt considered an applicant's wealth. Public agencies staffed by trained social welfare professionals, however, did not base their decisions on an applicant's income. Although they considered prospective parents' short- and long-term financial stability, this was not the determining factor in placements. In their effort to "match" children and homes, professionals made placements in families from a wide variety of socioeconomic backgrounds.

Nevertheless, people were angry. "Does one have to have a million dollars," a wife in Yonkers wrote to Mrs. Roosevelt, "is it not enough my husband has steady work, we are Honest Law Abiding Natural Citizens." A woman in Alabama worried that her family's income would disqualify her from consideration when officials began to look for a home for a child who had been abandoned in her town. "You see my husband and I dont have any money," she pleaded to the First Lady, "we are just average American citizens living a simple life. At one time we owned a house but sold it to go where the Government wanted us too for this war work. We have no savings to amount to anything because we are putting all our savings into War Bonds as most of the small people in this country are." Her appeal continued, "what can we offer except our love and devotion against the others with all there money and homes. I pray now that God will help me to have faith that America is still a place where those things are not the most important things on earth and that He would know that we will offer all we have and do our best if they will only give us a chance." These writers clearly felt that money mattered and felt just as strongly that it should not. They were not the only correspondents to assert vigorously that other factors should be considered first in determining their worth as parents.[52]

In 1939, an adoptive mother from Bellevue, Washington, marshaled a proven track record of care and evidence of fiscal responsibility in her efforts to persuade the president to help her locate another child. She and her husband, unable to have children of their own, had adopted a baby girl who had "infected eyes and rickets" in 1933. With "constant care and love," as well as expensive medical treatment, the little girl's health was now restored. The couple considered this child a "blessing" and wanted a second child, since they felt "we can care for and support one more child easly, even though we are of the common working class." All the child-placing agencies they had approached, however, had a shortage of children, and at least one had questioned the financial stability of the couple. The family lived in a two-room house on a small farm, and most agencies preferred that a child be placed in a home where the children had their own room. Although an official had told the anxious mother that building another bedroom might help her chances, she had declined. As she told FDR, "as bad as I hate to admit it I don't seem to be able to bid high enough. And I can't in all fair ness to my present family afford to buy a baby." She continued, "We sincerely thought if we could give one more baby a home, a mother and fathers devoted care it would be enough. You can tell by the conditions under whitch we took our little girl, that we don't want to pick or choose, we don't care if the child isn't pretty. . . . We just want another baby to raise, to complete our home happiness." While acknowledging that "we never will be wealthy perhaps," this wife maintained that she deserved a child every bit as much as a rich family. Her letter showed sincere desire, personal responsibility, and competent care. These were the values that other prospective mothers put forth and that were in line with contemporary understandings of ideal parenthood. Therefore, unless money really did matter most, there was no reason not to help her.[53]

The boundaries of competent care, maternal affection, and thoughtful choice were drawn further by the childless St. Louis woman, mentioned earlier, who deplored mothers who abandoned their babies to ash heaps. According to her definition, true mothers "wanted" their children and were able to care for them. However, she was quick to point out that material prosperity was not the same as competent care. As she told Mrs. Roosevelt, she knew "of a case where a child was placed in a home the people was very wealthy— that didn't matter to the child because the poor little child carried bruised marks on her from being whipped." She, by contrast, could give a child "all the care, love, & attention any real mother would give their child and even more care than some are given." In addition, she felt "as tho my husband is making enough money to support another person." As these last stories suggest, a woman's request reflected her unique situation; for mothers on the economic margins of society, this meant including a definition of family that minimized the advantages of material riches.[54]

In 1917, the *Living Age*, a weekly periodical published in Boston, reprinted a British article on adoption in England. The anonymous author urged people to set aside their fears that adoption was "flying in the face of Providence." The "deep-rooted notion" that if "Almighty God had intended that a particular woman should be a mother, He would have seen to it; and if, in disregard of His purpose, she adopts a child, He will see that she regrets it," was, in the author's view, a "piece of superstition." Nevertheless, the author believed that "it must be admitted that . . . no adopted relation is likely to be as good as a natural one. A stepmother is not a mother even when she is a very good stepmother." Stepmother? Like Cinderella's *evil* stepmother? In an article ostensibly written to promote adoption, this comparison strikes the reader as somewhat self-defeating. Yet it exposes just how tenacious was the belief that giving birth created a singular and inimitable sympathy between mother and child. In this view, consideration and choice (after all, a stepmother knowingly and presumably willingly chose to marry a man with children) counted for little.[55]

Although adoption in America was far more accepted than it was in England at this point, it still seems safe to assume that many Americans would have agreed that anything but a blood tie to a child was "second best." Even so, it is also true that attitudes about the family were in the process of changing—and in ways that would make it easier for adoptive mothers to represent their motherhood as the real thing. With the growing focus on planned families and thoughtful parenthood, adoptive mothers could claim adoption's difference as a positive good. In 1947, for example, one woman confidently asserted to the readers of *Woman's Day* that when she saw her adopted son for the first time, "the feeling in [her] heart was identical" to what she had felt after giving birth. This mother also "knew" that her "chosen son" belonged to her "far more than I ever belonged to my own parents, whom I amazed and chagrined by my advent which disarranged, but only temporarily, their plans for divorce." If biological children were sometimes unwanted, "adopted children," by contrast, were "among the very few who can be absolutely sure that their parents definitely desired and planned long for their coming. My son David can be numbered among these happy few—the luckiest children in the world, the children who truly belong."[56]

Yet to speak of a positive change in Americans' perception of adoption is not to suggest that the stigma completely disappeared. Even child welfare expert Jessie Taft, who passionately maintained that adoption offered a "real" experience of parenthood, later softened her position. In 1929, she stated that adoption could not "take the place of the actual bearing and rearing of an own child," although it was the "nearest substitute" and offered "an opportunity for a rich experience."[57]

And if adoptive mothers' conscious choice and preparedness nicely fit within the ideology of the modern family, the difference of adoption—the fact that many of these women, for whatever reason, could not give birth to the children they craved—was a red flag in another aspect of modern life: psychology. Beginning very slowly in the 1930s, the application of psychoanalytic principles in adoption placements highlighted adoption's distinctions and focused attention—and sometimes doubt—on the emotional health of infertile applicants. In addition, the new understanding of family life that helped legitimate adoptive mothers' identity included changes that made it impossible for some women to continue to become mothers through adoption.

4 | "Mother-Women" or "Man-Haters"?
The Rise and Fall of Single Adoptive Mothers

In 1940, Carol Prentice wrote a how-to guide on adoption that contained a chapter entitled "Spinsters as Parents." This chapter, as well as the one preceding it, "The Case for a Father," strongly argued against allowing single women to adopt. "First-hand knowledge" bolstered her claim. Around 1900, when she was five, her dying mother had made arrangements for her care. She was adopted by a "real old maid," who despised and feared men, and her companion, the head of a girls' school who "was nearer the modern spinster type." Prentice maintained that an adopted child was "often the sole outlet the spinster has ever had, and she is apt to lavish all the force of her frustrated emotions on one small person who cannot carry such heavy freight." Cases in which two single women lived together were not much better. In these situations, "even where there is no trace of homosexuality the child in the menage forms part of a triangle. Jealousy is probably too strong a word for the subtle interplay of emotions that the child feels, consciously or unconsciously. . . . And there is a surfeit of femininity." In addition, Prentice knew from her "own experience that a child can long passionately for a father." The clear answer, in her opinion, was to place children in "normal" homes.[1]

Prentice was not alone in her view. By 1940, many people no longer considered single women appropriate adoptive parents. The new family ideal of planned-for children and educated parenthood, while moving married adoptive mothers closer to the norm, pushed single women from the ranks of adoptive mothers. This represented a significant change, and one that casts light on the shifting understanding of both motherhood and adoption. In the late nineteenth century and early years of the twentieth century, many believed that single women made ideal adoptive mothers. A large part of society still regarded adoptable children with a mixture of pity and suspicion; allowing a single woman to adopt was not yet seen as denying a childless couple their "right" to parenthood and a child its right to a "normal" family, as it soon would be. More important, motherhood during this period was romanticized and glorified as woman's natural calling, and all "normal" women were expected to possess maternal sensibilities.

Beginning around 1920, however, many began to argue that single women should not be allowed to adopt. Interest in adoption appears to have been on the increase by this time, with greater numbers of childless, married couples scrambling for the limited number of available children.[2] Of greater significance in explaining the change of attitude toward single women, however, was the recasting of woman's identity to focus on her role as wife and sexual partner. Motherhood was still a primary aspect of a woman's role, but now it was understood as part of the experience of the sexually satisfied, emotionally fulfilled wife. If married women were sexual, unmarried women were suspect; at best, single women were not "normal," and at worst, they were sexually "deviant." In either case, they challenged the prevailing social order. Child welfare experts argued that single women should be allowed to adopt only older or "unadoptable" children, if at all. For example, an article written in 1945, which ironically called for social workers to be more flexible when approving adoptive applicants, noted that "unmarried people" were "obviously disqualified," along with the "mentally ill" and "alcoholics." Single women still adopted after 1920; however, there was no longer popular support for their motherhood. And by the 1950s, it appears that virtually no single women adopted.[3]

Single Adoptive Mothers: A Profile

As one would expect, single women were always a small minority of adoptive mothers, given that, during this time, approximately nine out of ten white women married at some point in their lives.[4] Nevertheless, in the late nineteenth and early twentieth centuries, single adoptive mothers were visible and, evidence suggests, largely accepted. A number of articles on adoption before 1920 raised the question of the appropriateness of their motherhood, and virtually all answered in the affirmative. Physicians and others doing private adoption placement who were interviewed for these stories agreed that it was natural for unmarried women to find an outlet for their maternal longings through adoption. Journalists mentioned that homeless children were "regularly in demand" by childless women or that "not infrequently" single women asked to adopt.[5]

These advocates for single women were not anarchists urging the destruction or modification of the nuclear family. They can be described best as forward-looking traditionalists who strongly believed in the existence of a maternal instinct in all women and believed just as strongly that this instinct should find—needed to find—a productive outlet. Often, the single adoptive mothers portrayed in fiction and profiled in magazines were ordinary women who had missed out on marriage and motherhood through the misfortunes of fate, not through a blatant disregard of traditional gender roles. In the Progressive Era, one social commentator argued that leftover women and leftover children made a perfect match, urging single women, "like the wife in a childless marriage," to adopt to "enrich her life and partly satisfy her motherly feeling."[6]

Although it is impossible to know how many single women adopted, it is possible to make some broad generalizations about the type of unmarried woman who adopted.[7] Included in my definition of single women are widows, divorced women, never-married women living alone, and women living or romantically partnered with other women. Before a woman could adopt, she needed to know that she could financially support herself and the child. Consequently, single adoptive mothers were either women of independent means or professional women whose skills provided them with an adequate wage to care for a family on their own. Despite the profession's notoriously low pay, some librarians adopted in the first two decades of the twentieth century. Female physicians, social reformers, and teachers also took children; these were, of course, the professions that women most often entered, but women in these three occupations might have had an easier time adopting because their work put them in contact with dependent children, unwed mothers, and deserted wives. In 1929, for example, Miriam Van Waters, a leading figure in women's prison reform and superintendent of the Massachusetts Reformatory for Women, adopted a young girl she had encountered through her work for the juvenile court.[8]

Although many women found children through their work, single women came to motherhood in a variety of ways. Some approached orphanages and foundling homes, although this avenue, at least by the 1920s, seems to have led mostly to disappointment. In 1914, at the age of forty, Gertrude Battles Lane, editor of the *Woman's Home Companion*, adopted a French war orphan. Others became mothers after taking the child of a relative or friend. When in her early fifties, writer and educator Edith Hamilton adopted the five-year-old nephew of her partner, Doris Reid, who was in her thirties. Throughout the 1920s, the three spent every summer in Maine, enjoying the sea; later, when the young man came home from college with some friends, the couple fretted over whether they should serve them "cocktails and highballs." They decided against it.[9]

Generally, unmarried women adopted when they were in their late thirties, forties, or fifties. (During the period under consideration, all adoptive parents averaged ten or more years older than biological parents; that is, adoptive parents were at least in their thirties when they adopted.) They adopted children of varying ages, from cuddly newborns to rough-and-tumble ten-year-olds. One commentator speculated that unmarried adoptive mothers were "women who would probably describe themselves as having been too busy to marry, who, on reaching middle age, discover quite unexpectedly that life is intolerable without a child." Maybe. But for women who were not independently wealthy or supported by husbands, those years also provided the time to establish themselves in well-paying careers and create support networks to help meet the demands of unmarried motherhood, without which adoptive motherhood would have been impossible.[10]

Magazine articles reported that single women often raised their adopted children with the help of female friends, but most stories and fiction focused on the single woman raising her child alone. For a woman to raise a child alone, she would have to be either independently wealthy or employed at an occupation in which she earned enough to support herself, her child, and a nurse to care for the child. Consequently, it appears that women often raised their adopted children with female partners or within a community of women. Such domestic arrangements, often referred to as "Boston marriages," in which two career women shared a home and their lives, were common in the early twentieth century. Around 1915, for example, the progressive educator Elisabeth Irwin legally adopted at least one child whom she raised with her lifelong companion, the biographer Katherine Anthony, in their Greenwich Village home. Irwin and Anthony were part of a vital community of women involved in education, reform, and the arts and that included at least a few other unmarried adoptive mothers. Irwin and Anthony likely knew Harriet Johnson, a health reformer who adopted a baby girl in 1916 to raise with her partner, Harriet Forbes, a nurse who worked in New York settlement houses. In the 1930s, an unmarried colleague of Irwin's at the Little Red School also adopted a young son.[11]

Single women adopted for a variety of reasons. Many unmarried women worked in professions that put them in contact with needy children, and it is possible, even likely, that some women adopted for altruistic reasons. Yet, it is important to remember that helping a child and loving a child are not mutually exclusive. Miriam Van Waters, for example, spent part of her professional life assisting children and was active in the lives of her nieces and nephews. Still, as she pointed out, it was not the same as being a mother. Van

Waters wanted a child "every day and every night under [her] own roof."
Van Waters loved Sarah, the seven-year-old she "saved" in 1929, with
"intense feeling," because Sarah *belonged* to her.[12] Other unmarried women
also expressed an interest in adoption motivated by a desire to experience
motherhood. In 1941, a thirty-three-year-old, college-educated woman from
Kansas wrote to the Children's Bureau asking for information on institutions that would place a child with a single woman. She was unemployed
but had an independent source of income and had helped raise two nephews;
her letter expressed nothing but longing for a child.[13]

It is also possible that some single women, whose professional lives centered on child welfare issues, took children, in part, because of the knowledge
they would gain from raising a child. Dr. Frances Ilg, a child-development
expert who coauthored the popular syndicated newspaper column "Parents
Ask" in the 1950s, adopted a child in the 1930s while studying in Sweden for
a year. She later said of her daughter, "My perceptions were greatly sharp-
ened by living with a child from day to day and growing up with her. She
became an intimate part of the work and of the books."[14] Similarly, in 1929,
a fifty-year-old Texas librarian contemplated giving up her eighteen-year
career to adopt three little girls. She considered this dramatic life change
because her "maternal instinct" was "strong" and because she had "always
been interested in the study of environment versus heredity." Here, a single
woman's interest in adoption seems to reflect personal as well as intellectual
motives; for some educated, professional women, motherhood and career
were closely intertwined.[15]

The preponderance of evidence shows that adopted children were treated
as children, not as domestic help. Elizabeth and Emily Blackwell, the United
States' first two female physicians, each informally adopted a young girl in
the midnineteenth century. Although these children lived with the women
for many years, according to the Blackwells' biographer, they were never
treated as family but always as domestic help. We must consider that some
single women did take children in predominantly for their labor, especially
in the nineteenth century, when adoption laws were new and indenture still
existed. Evidence suggests, however, that the case of Dr. Cordelia Greene,
another nineteenth-century physician who ran the Castile Sanitarium in
upstate New York, was more representative of the attitudes of the majority
of single adoptive mothers. Greene adopted six children, all of whom called
her "mother." She walked one of her daughters down the aisle at her wed-
ding, placing the young woman's hand in that of her bridegroom, and
delighted in her grandchildren.[16]

Although there seems to have been a good deal of support for single adoptive mothers, at least before 1920, they were not completely immune to criticism or gossip. A positive article in the *Medical Woman's Journal* in 1929 noted that "single women frequently adopt babies, and this is especially true of women doctors and nurses." Why this was so, the author could not definitely say. Instead, she wondered whether "their service to humanity stimulates this desire to exercise the maternal role, or whether it is simply an inherited inborn and indomitable passion that must be reckoned with, or both." Whatever the reason, "unmarried women who adopt babies do it in the face of exciting suspicion of their own moral conduct." In other words, on first glance, there was nothing to distinguish a single adoptive mother from an unwed mother. It is impossible to know how often adoption cast doubt on an unmarried woman's character, but it seems likely that this would depend on the unique circumstances of each case. Although a stranger would not know how a single woman came to be a mother, a woman's close friends surely knew. Even so, her adoption of a child could be a point of speculation and a potential source of disapproval.[17]

Adelaide Hasse, head of the Economics Division of the New York Public Library in the 1910s and remembered for her work in developing a classification system for government documents, adopted a young boy around 1911 and another a few years later. Hasse, who was in her early forties when she adopted, lived with the children in Greenwich Village. Outspoken about library issues, she attracted attention; in 1915, the *New York Evening Mail* featured her in a story headlined, "Being adopted mother to red-headed boy her relief from her highbrow job. Though she's chief of dept. of Economics in daytime Miss Hasse is more interested in kiddie's shoe and stocking problems." Although most of the article focused on Hasse's professional accomplishments, it also noted that she recommended adoption to "all business women who have been too busy hitting the bulls-eye of success to marry and have sonnies of their own." The newspaper took a lighthearted approach to her single motherhood, but according to Hasse's biographer, the proper and conservative men who ran the library and sat on its board were not likely to be amused. Already annoyed by her assertiveness with regard to library policies, Hasse's adoptions might have contributed to their negative assessment of her. It is also possible that some believed that the first child was actually her biological son, the product of an affair with her previous boss. Hasse's behavior—she liked to shock people by introducing herself as Miss Hasse and son, without revealing that he was adopted—probably did not help the situation.[18]

If, on occasion, some people wondered whether a single woman's adopted child was really her own, their suspicions were not always unfounded. In 1917, Frieda Miller, then a research assistant at Bryn Mawr College and later director of the Women's Bureau in the U.S. Department of Labor, met Pauline Newman, an organizer for the Women's Trade Union League, and the two embarked on what would be a lifelong partnership. In the first few years of their relationship, Miller apparently had difficulty committing exclusively to a woman and had a secret affair with a married man. Miller became pregnant in 1922, and she and Newman decided to raise the child together. Eager to protect Miller's reputation, the two women traveled to Europe, where Miller gave birth. When they returned to the United States with the child, they told everyone that Miller had adopted an orphan girl. The two women publicly stuck by this story their entire lives and raised Elizabeth as their adopted daughter in Greenwich Village. Elizabeth was seventeen before she learned that Miller was her biological mother.[19]

"Virgin Mothers": Representations of Single Mothers

The single adoptive mother also appeared as the subject of a number of works of popular fiction. As many literary critics have noted, popular fiction aims for a large audience. To be successful, it must reflect the prevailing beliefs and values of the society.[20] Literature shows us what life scripts are imaginable at a given moment in time; the number of unmarried adoptive mothers that appeared in turn-of-the-century fiction and the popularity of the works and their authors suggest that the concept of single women adopting was largely acceptable or, at the very least, conceivable.

In Mary Wilkins Freeman's "A Gatherer of Simples," published in 1887, Aurelia, a simple, independent loner, finds her hidden emotions awakened after adopting Myrtie, a young orphan. When the child's grandmother comes to take her away, Aurelia states, "I can't help thinking that Providence ought to provide for women. I wish Myrtie was *mine*." When the grandmother dies before claiming the child, we are left to believe that Providence does indeed provide for women by making sure that even single women can find an outlet for their deep maternal needs.[21]

The popular author Margaret Deland wrote of unmarried adoptive mothers on more than one occasion. In her 1898 story "The Child's Mother," Dr. Lavendar, the purveyor of truth, justice, and wisdom in many of Deland's stories, decides after much contemplation that a young girl belongs to

Rachel, the single woman who raised her after her birth mother abandoned her. When the birth mother returns, married and somewhat respectable, Dr. Lavendar refuses to tell her the location of her child. He has decided that Rachel is the mother of the child's spirit, a claim that takes precedence over the biological mother, who is "only the mother of her body." Deland takes pains to show readers that Rachel is deserving of the child and is simply expressing what Deland believes is a normal woman's desire to mother. Rachel had lost her chance for physical motherhood because she was too maternal, giving up her opportunity for marriage to take care of her mother, who had regressed to a childlike state after suffering a breakdown.[22]

Deland's runaway best-seller *The Awakening of Helena Ritchie*, published in 1906, also dealt with an unmarried adoptive mother.[23] The beautiful, wealthy young widow Helena moves to a small town where she knows no one and keeps to herself. When Dr. Lavendar needs to find a home for David, a seven-year-old orphan, he approaches the lonely Helena. After much persuasion, she agrees. Helena, however, is not really a widow. Thirteen years before, her reprobate husband killed their only child, and she left him. Expecting that he would soon drink himself to death, she began an affair with Lloyd, who promised to marry her when her husband died. Helena's husband, however, does not die, and so Lloyd, whose interest is waning, now poses as her brother. As the story unfolds, Helena is forced to choose between her love for David and her passion for Lloyd. When Helena's husband finally dies and she presses Lloyd to make good on his promise of marriage, he agrees, but only on the condition that she give up David. She refuses.

It is at this point in the novel, as Helena must confess her adulterous sin and earn the right to keep David, that Deland puts forth her views on motherhood. For Deland, motherhood is powerful. Helena's love for David can "save" her, can offer a path to moral redemption. The belief in the power of motherhood to redeem was not uncommon in 1906; indeed, it was a concept that guided social reformers' mandate that unwed mothers keep their children. Reformers believed that once a woman's maternal instinct was aroused, her love for her child would keep her on the straight and narrow path. For many years, in fact, Deland herself provided temporary lodging in her home for unwed mothers and their infants until they could find a domestic situation.[24] What is fascinating about this novel, however, is that Deland's presentation of redemptive motherhood does not depend on a blood tie; motherhood derives its power from caring for a child, not carrying a child to term.

For Deland, the identity of "mother" must be earned through behavior that Deland sees as "motherly." Helena's moral lapse has disqualified her for motherhood, but she can make herself worthy through hard work and self-sacrifice for the child. It is a conscious action that comes at some cost to the woman that makes a woman a mother. In the case of Helena Ritchie, choosing to stay with David and abandon her chance of a life with Lloyd was not enough of a sacrifice. As Dr. Lavendar points out, she chose David because she wanted him more; it was a choice made with her happiness, not David's, in mind. Only when Helena realizes that her selfishness makes her unfit for motherhood and decides to move away and return David to Dr. Lavendar is a true sacrifice made. Like the biblical tale of the mother who, in abandoning her claim for the good of the child, proves to Solomon that she is the true mother, Helena's decision to leave David proves her worth as a mother in Dr. Lavendar's eyes. The story ends with Dr. Lavendar returning David to Helena and the stagecoach pulling away to lead them to their new life together.[25]

The adoptive mothers that Freeman and Deland portray inhabit a world in which decisions about child custody are made by members of the community, not the legal system or child welfare professionals. They are self-sufficient women who are part of a community. Although single women in the nineteenth century might have come to their motherhood in similar ways, in the twentieth century, it appears that unmarried adoptive mothers were more likely to be professionals.[26] Grace Duffie Boylan's *The Supplanter*, published in 1913, tells the story of Janet Allen, a thirty-year-old nurse who becomes an adoptive mother. This novel was included in the list of "New Feminist Books" sold by the Women's Political Union. It also contained the urging that "any unmarried woman who finds time hanging heavily on her hands should take a house and bring up a baby."[27]

In *The Supplanter*, Janet recounts her path to motherhood. Head of surgical nurses at a large California hospital, she assists a physician friend at a wealthy woman's difficult delivery. The birth leaves the mother in a catatonic state. Janet agrees to care for the child until the mother's health returns, in large part because at the moment of the boy's birth, she felt a "flash" of connection with his soul. When the mother's health does not immediately return, Janet chooses to continue caring for Teddy rather than returning to her job as a nurse. Janet forces herself to remember that she is not the boy's mother, but only a caregiver. She insists that Teddy refer to her by her nickname and conscientiously reminds him of his mother.

When Teddy is four, it appears that the mother might soon be able to care for him, and Janet realizes that she feels as though she is his mother.

The mother, however, suffers a relapse, and Janet resumes her care of Teddy. Janet's friends question her decision. They believe that her devotion to Teddy has precluded her from marrying and having children of her own. She responds that Teddy "is worth more than careers and conjugalities. . . . I [have] learned that physical motherhood is not the only maternity." Soon after, the doctor confides to Janet that he believes that all the birth mother's maternal feelings died when Teddy was born. Janet rejoices. She interprets this as an "annunciation" that she is truly Teddy's mother. A "primal ecstasy" sweeps through her. She whispers to the doctor, *"He is my child, even as I have been his mother from that first deep glance. He came to me a willing son of my spirit."*[28]

Although Janet is the child's spiritual mother, she has no legal right to the child, a status that gives her no real position in society. Janet and Teddy's father have engaged in the slightest of flirtations and bonded over their concern for the child. The stage seems to be set for a formulaic romantic conclusion: Teddy's comatose mother will die, Janet and the father will be married, and the "real" family will at last be united. But, in a dramatic plot twist, the birth mother sets the house on fire, Janet rescues her, the birth mother regains her senses, and Janet forces Teddy to return to his parents, despite his desire to stay with her. Janet is devastated and struggles to build a new life without Teddy.

Soon, however, Teddy returns to Janet, his "real" mother. Ties of care, not blood, create the true mother–child bond. As the boy's father explains, "one might think that this mother [the birth mother] and child, so curiously separated, would fly to each other's arms in perfect love and sympathy. But as a matter of fact they do no such thing—they are still strangers." Teddy's birth mother adopts a baby girl and lets Teddy, who made "her head ache," return to Janet. At last, Teddy calls Janet "mother," making her "perfect in [her] womanhood."[29]

Magazine articles told similar, but true, stories of single women who reached their fullest potential in adoptive motherhood. Miss Mary Hildreth, profiled in *Harper's Bazaar* in 1912, was the adoptive mother of ten children, whom she raised on a farm in New Hampshire. She adopted her first child in the late 1880s after a friend, "to whom she was deeply attached" and with whom she had spent much of her time, married and had a child. Miss Hildreth fell in love with her friend's new baby and decided that she "could not endure to be without a possession so wonderful and desirable." She adopted a baby of the same age, and the two women—one married, one not—spent the next few years comparing infant accomplishments. It was her deep conviction (and one the author acknowledged would be disputed by most biological mothers) that "she could not love the children more if they were her own." Although Miss Hildreth's desire for children did not challenge any gender norms, in other ways, she was a gender renegade. She was an ardent suffragist, argued that men should be taught the essentials of domestic housekeeping, and confidently stated that she had no regrets that she had not married or given birth.[30]

Positive representations of unmarried adoptive motherhood that appeared before 1920, whether fictional or real, rested on two fundamental assumptions: first, that these women were celibate, and second, that their decision to adopt signaled their steadfast belief in traditional gender roles. In a culture that idealized maternity but denied women's sexuality, single adoptive mothers in some ways could be understood as the truest of "true women." As historian Linda Gordon has argued, "the female analog to the male sex drive was the maternal instinct. . . . The desire for maternity was presumably the only selfish reason that women submitted, literally, to sexual intercourse."[31] As "virgin mothers"—a term that Janet in *The Supplanter* uses to describe herself—unmarried adoptive mothers have not had their purity and innocence spoiled by the physical realities of sex and pregnancy.

A woman's sexuality—or lack thereof—was of paramount importance in determining her suitability for motherhood; indeed, their differing sexual subjectivity was what made unmarried adoptive mothers acceptable and unwed mothers lamentable. Of the examples discussed earlier, *The Supplanter* most clearly addresses the question of sexuality. Janet describes her spiritual acceptance of her role as Teddy's mother as the moment of annunciation, a direct reference to the Virgin Mary. When her friends continually urge her to marry to experience the "supreme passion," she responds that her role as Teddy's mother fills all her needs; Janet is a "mother-woman," and as such, she has no desire for marriage, no longing for sexual pleasure. Nonetheless, in case some readers may have questioned her attitude toward men, the author takes pains to show that Janet is heterosexual, filling the story with a number of male suitors whom Janet considers but rejects. *The Supplanter's* ending also hints that Janet will ultimately marry an old friend who has ardently pursued her. The marriage, however, will not be a grand passion but a pleasant companionship to ease the hours after Teddy has grown up and left Janet to begin a family of his own. In cases in which the unmarried adoptive mother is clearly not a virgin, such as Deland's *The Awakening of Helena Ritchie*, sexuality is what a woman sacrificed to become an adoptive mother.[32]

These stories argue for a definition of motherhood centered on a spiritual, not a physical, connection with a child. They also share a Victorian understanding of a woman's role. As discussed in the last chapter, by the mid-nineteenth century, motherhood had been elevated to "cult" status, and the mother–child bond surpassed in intensity and importance even that between husband and wife. Womanhood became virtually synonymous with motherhood. As one early-twentieth-century author stated, single women might "cease to regret the husband [they] might have had, but never the children who might have been [theirs]." Positive public representations of unmarried adoptive mothers show motherhood, not marriage or a career, as the path to a woman's true fulfillment. Even *The Supplanter*, with its feminist endorsement, shows a woman giving up a career for the joys of motherhood.[33]

As long as the culture understood single adoptive mothers as "mother-women," they were acceptable, because they posed no challenge to traditional gender roles; in fact, they seemed to celebrate them. Many scholars have noted that by the late nineteenth century, the belief that all women possessed a maternal instinct and had a duty to spread their moral influence into the larger society had provided single women with the ideology to move into the public sphere. Single women took over areas such as teaching, nursing, and child welfare work, for which their "womanliness" seemed especially well-suited. But although society accepted that women were uniquely fit for these occupations, by the early twentieth century, some feared that too many of the best and brightest were opting for careers and forgoing marriage and motherhood. Within this context, unmarried adoptive mothers proved reassuring: these women might have bypassed marriage, but they still understood, even embraced, the importance of woman's role as mother. Unmarried adoptive mothers possessed a strong maternal instinct; they were women who had not shirked their natural duty. One popular women's magazine noted in 1913 that "more and more often does one hear the unmarried woman confess the hungry longing for motherhood" and interpreted this confession as "A New Sign of National Health."[34]

The maternal model of womanhood provided single women with a clear rationale for adopting that allowed the public to understand and accept their unmarried motherhood. Within the context of this ideology, even those women who were consciously creating families without men were not seen as directly challenging the social order. For example, in her interview with the writer from *Harper's Bazaar* in 1912, Miss Hildreth clearly stated that she never felt it was necessary or desirable to "have a man about the house." The author assured readers that Miss Hildreth was not a "man-hater," but she also noted that Miss Hildreth believed that a "man is a domestic feature easily dispensed with, and that a father's influence is by no means necessary in the training of children."[35] In 1912, readers might have found Miss Hildreth a bit eccentric, but they would have appreciated her motherly emotions. Soon, however, the public's perception of Miss Hildreth and women like her would drastically change.

"Parthenogenetic Fantasies" and "Manless Menages"

In the 1920s, an array of voices, which included social workers, sociologists, psychologists, members of the legal profession, and married adoptive parents, began to inveigh against allowing single women to adopt. Victorian constructions of sexuality, marriage, and parenthood had been replaced by a more modern sensibility. By the 1920s, children had become a "priceless commodity," fathers had become vital to a child's healthy psychological development, and women had become sexual beings. An assortment of social scientists and other professionals defined the best "family" as one in which husband and wife enjoyed emotional intimacy and sexual pleasure and nurtured a few children, to the personal fulfillment of all involved. If marriage partners were now equal, there was no reason for women, even feminists, not to marry. And with the new Freudian emphasis on women's sexual needs, women who did not marry were looked at suspiciously.

The "spinster" had no place in the modern family, and her possible deviation from the new sexual norm unsuited her to head a family of her own. As historian Nancy Cott observed, "Nineteenth-century ideology of women's moral influence and glorious maternity, by veiling female eroticism, had made same-sex intimacies innocent." In the context of modern sexual norms, "romantic friendships" and "Boston marriages" were no longer "ennobling"; they were "abnormal." It was the presumed celibacy of single women that had suited them for adoptive motherhood. Now, however, the specter had been raised that at least some of these women were not celibate at all. And, in the cultural ranking of sexual sins, lesbians occupied a rung even lower than that of unwed mothers, whose sexuality was at least directed at the "right" object.[36]

In the span of a few short decades, social attitudes had changed enough that what had once been understood as innocent was now seen as sinister. In 1912, a reporter for a popular magazine had nothing but praise for Miss Hildreth's story; viewed through the erotic lens of the 1920s, it is unlikely that the reporter would have viewed her so positively. Now readers might have wondered about the relationship with the friend to whom she was "deeply attached." Maybe Miss Hildreth was a "man-hater" after all. For those who had seen unmarried adoptive mothers as champions of traditional gender roles, the new interrogation of the motives and normalcy of single women called this interpretation into question. Maybe single adoptive mothers were not upholding tradition; maybe they were direct challenges to the normative family.

As early as 1916, the Children's Aid Society in New York had stopped placing children with single women. In 1920, an article in *American Magazine*, which praised single adoptive mothers, challenged those who were against placing children with single women. The article was written by an adoptee who had been raised by a single woman who was "the most wonderful mother in the world." The writer's mother, a New England schoolteacher in her late forties, had adopted her when she was just eight months old. The adoptee went on to lament current child-placing policies that insisted on placing children in "normal" homes with a mother and father; child-placing experts, she believed, would have found her mother "too old, too poor," and "not at all desirable" and would have deprived her of a "very happy childhood." By the 1930s, even women physicians were having a difficult time adopting. Dr. Evelyn Holt encountered a hostile legal process but ultimately was able to adopt a child. Dr. Harriet Hardy, however, was unable to get through New York State's red tape to adopt a young boy she had encountered while working at a foundling hospital.[37]

Even wealth could not guarantee a woman a child. In 1940, a maternity home in Maine, which occasionally placed infants for adoption, received a request from a fifty-year-old "spinster." The home had a policy against placing children with single women, but this particular woman posed a special case. She was "exceedingly cultured and public spirited" and so wealthy that the home's board realized that her "resources and ability to educate and develop a child would be almost unlimited." The home consulted with the state's welfare board, which showed the woman an older child. But her heart was set on an infant, and the woman returned to the maternity home, only to be refused.[38]

It appears that by the 1920s, adoption was becoming more popular among married childless couples and that virtually all healthy, adoptable young children could find homes in such families. Given that demand far exceeded supply, many felt that it was only natural that childless couples should be given first choice. Yet a close examination of the reservations expressed by those set against allowing single women to adopt shows more than just concern for the well-being of the child. These critiques of single adoptive mothers are as much about cultural fears surrounding lesbianism, the maintenance of distinct male-female gender roles, and the stability of the traditional family as they are about the best interests of children. They also reflect the growing influence of psychology, not only in adoption but also in the definition of appropriate adult emotional adjustment and the determination of child-development practices. And finally, they vividly highlight the cultural reinterpretation of mother love as a selfish, smothering affection that endangered a child's healthy development and justified experts' control over child rearing.

Adventuring in Adoption, published in 1939, was one of the first books specifically designed to answer the questions of prospective adoptive parents. Although the authors were not definitively against single motherhood, their assessment was filled with enough caveats that any single woman contemplating adoption would be given pause. In addition to the financial pressures of single parenthood, the unmarried adoptive mother had to contend with what the authors vaguely defined as the "intricate emotional problems arising from her single estate." In addition to her child-rearing responsibilities, a single woman would need to "maintain for herself an extra-familial life, interesting and stimulating enough to keep her from projecting herself upon the child and crushing his independence, or losing her perspective and exaggerating his importance." To make up for the lack of male influence, the unmarried adoptive mother needed to possess "a generous share of the so-called masculine qualities." However, the authors were quick to add that by masculine women they did not mean the "non-feminine, swaggering type that affects masculinity." And they were quite clear that two women adopting a child together was "no solution" to providing a child with two parents.[39]

As the preceding paragraph suggests, single adoptive mothers fell victim not only to the culture's fear of gender nonconformity and lesbianism but also to the growing emphasis on the importance of fathers in inculcating appropriate gender roles. Beginning in the 1920s, family experts began to focus especially on the role of fathers in their discussions of the crisis in family life. A boy needed a father's influence to show "how he must behave to be a man," whereas a girl needed her father's companionship to ensure that she would "pick out the right kind of man for her husband." Children adopted by single women and raised solely by women would, as the esteemed family sociologist Ernest Groves noted in 1927, receive "an over-supply of the mother-element." With the spotlight on the family as the primary site of gender-role socialization, even clearly heterosexual women such as widows or divorced women found themselves out of favor as prospective adoptive parents.[40]

Members of the burgeoning child welfare establishment—even some single social workers who were adoptive mothers—were among the most vocal opponents of single adoptive motherhood. During the 1920s, social welfare professionals began to work to gain control over adoption placements and policy as part of their child welfare agenda. Although the judiciary retained the ultimate authority to approve or deny an adoption petition, child welfare workers had cultural authority; the media contacted them, not judges, when looking for the latest information on adoption for a story. And more and more institutions that placed children looked at these professionals as the experts.

In February 1930, the *Saturday Evening Post* published a long article on adoption that painted an unattractive picture of single adoptive mothers. Adoptive parents were not interviewed for the article, but child welfare professionals were, and they clearly stated their opposition to adoption by single women. When the author asked the "expert" about adoption for a single woman or childless widow with "strong maternal instincts," she shook her head. Why, she asked, deprive a child of two parents when the demand for children exceeds the supply? And, as she told the author, social workers "are not trying to fill the psychic or emotional needs of the unmarried women; that's their problem, not ours."[41]

The anonymous expert acknowledged that there were many single women who had an abundance of both the financial and the emotional means to provide for a child, but she saw that as "the hitch! We don't want a foster parent who will put all her emotional life into that one relationship; it's abnormal, and the strong emotional impact is very bad for the child. . . . It is likely to produce a neurasthenic, hothouse child." In fact, she would as soon place a child with a single man, since "they are less likely to obtain a possessive, imperious stranglehold on the emotions of the child and warp its life to their needs." The behavioral psychologists who held sway in the 1920s scrutinized the behavior of all mothers to make sure that they did not drown their children in excess affection. Psychologists urged those mothers who emoted a little too much to redirect their affections toward their husbands and adult sexuality. But without a man around on whom to dote, the experts believed that single adoptive mothers would necessarily suffocate their children. Maternal instinct, which had once been seen as natural in all women, which was popularly thought to be womankind's best and defining quality, was now constructed by a small group of "experts" as likely to be excessive, even neurotic, in women who were not married.[42]

Jessie Taft, a child welfare expert who wrote a number of articles on adoption, was opposed to single women adopting. She was also the unmarried adoptive mother of two. Taft adopted in the early 1920s and raised the children with her life partner, Virginia Robinson, in a home they purchased in Flourtown, Pennsylvania. At least once in her professional career, Taft had to acknowledge this contradiction.[43]

In 1936, the journal *Independent Woman* printed an article entitled "Would You 'Bootleg' a Baby?" which informed its single, professional readers that although they had succeeded in a man's world, they would not succeed in obtaining a child from any credible child-placing agency. The article also noted that some single professional women who had adopted children, such as the progressive educator Elisabeth Irwin, were challenging the views held by experts such as Taft. Irwin and others believed that single adoptive mothers were more likely to be educated on children's issues than most mothers. They disputed the idea that they would emotionally smother their children. Enlarging the concept of a selfish, excessive maternal love to include both parents, these women argued that childless adoptive couples were more likely to overindulge their children because "they have been starved for children to love—and the emotional exploitation of a child by two persons can be just twice as bad as by one." Taft responded that she believed a child needed a mother and a father—a "normal" home—but also admitted that her adoption experience had been successful for both her and her children.[44]

This was not the only time child welfare professionals found themselves tiptoeing around the issue of single adoptive motherhood, lest they step on the feet of colleagues and possibly even friends. In 1938, the U.S. Children's Bureau was involved with the League of Nations in writing a report that would establish child-placement principles. Part of the draft, written by the director of the Canadian Welfare Council, addressed the adoption of children by "bachelors or spinsters." It read:

> Some organizations are fairly definitely opposed to the placing of a child with an unmarried person, whether spinster or bachelor. This is based in part upon the need of two parents, but more particularly upon experience which has shown that the relationship developed is nearly always highly abnormal. While the relationship may not be homosexual, yet the mere presence of a child in such a home often indicates an adult in need of compensation to assist in overcoming

poor adjustment to life. The child is not treated as an individual searching for wholesome interest, good friends and natural independence, but is considered unconsciously as a satisfaction for a craving which should have been met in a more normal manner.

This assessment was seen as so potentially inflammatory that it prompted a cable from bureau chief Katharine Lenroot to the Canadian author. "SERI-OUSLY OBJECT . . . STOP URGE CHANGING NEARLY ALWAYS TO FREQUENTLY . . . OMITTING REMAINDER OF PARAGRAPH STOP WOULD HAVE SERIOUS REPERCUS-SIONS IN UNITED STATES AS IT STANDS STOP . . . WIRE IMMEDIATELY IF YOU APPROVE THIS SUGGESTION."[45]

In the next weeks, bureau staff drafted a new statement that consciously downplayed any mention of homosexuality. Staff member Elsa Castendyck, in her cover letter to the original author, noted that she agreed with Lenroot's criticism, but "not so much because of the several prominent unmarried persons who have adopted children but because, as now written, the emphasis is upon the effect rather than the cause of the difficulties usually encountered in such cases." She continued, "I wonder if we do not want to throw into greater prominence the abnormal situation in the home which may or may not result in homosexuality rather than the latter possibility." And, finally, she suggested the following substitute:

Some organizations have opposed the placing of a child with an unmarried person, whether bachelor or spinster. This is based primarily upon the lack of two parents and the resulting abnormal home situation. Deprived of the outlets which a satisfactory marriage provides the foster parent, whether bachelor or spinster, may unconsciously warp or thwart the child development by bestowing upon and accepting from him the full measure of affectional regard usually shared by the other parent. Child placing agencies have recognized this as a possible obstacle to the growth of normal interests and independence of the child and seek to guard against over-indulgence and selfish love on the part of the foster parent.[46]

Adoption, these letters suggest, was an issue that had the potential to divide women who worked in social reform. With so many prominent single adoptive mothers in the welfare field, social workers who opposed the practice found themselves criticizing the private decisions of women who in many ways were just like themselves. These women, similar in their educational achievement, professional dedication, and, often, devotion to improving the situation of mothers and children, nevertheless could differ when it came to defining an acceptable family. That the question was tied to sexuality and the taint of homosexuality further complicated the issue.

As numerous historians have noted, although many women reformers in the late nineteenth and early twentieth centuries spent their lives in committed and romantic relationships with other women, they rarely *publicly* identified themselves as homosexuals. Lesbianism implied "mannishness," "perversion," or psychological pathology and was associated primarily with working-class or African American women—not educated, professional, middle-class, white women like themselves. Miriam Van Waters, for example, never "consciously claimed" a lesbian identity, despite a forty-year relationship with Geraldine Thompson; nor, to my knowledge, did any of the other adoptive mothers I identified who were partnered with women. What we do know, though, is that, given the stigma surrounding homosexuality, associating single adoptive motherhood with lesbianism could destroy careers.[47]

One of the last popular magazine articles to portray single adoptive motherhood positively in the period under consideration appeared in the *Ladies' Home Journal* in 1937. The article is especially striking, in that it had been well over a decade since such a glowing endorsement of single motherhood had appeared. Yet, when we examine the story closely, it is easy to understand why the magazine printed it. The story, written anonymously, recounts a divorced woman's recent adoption. Although the author lives a modern life—professional, well traveled, divorced—she is also extremely traditional, believing that her life will not be complete without the experience of motherhood. The author had wanted children desperately while married, even seeking medical treatment to increase her chances of conceiving. But before she conceived, her husband asked her for a divorce. The author waited a few years before she adopted, determined not to use an innocent child to ease the pain of her failed marriage. After a time, she approached a private adoption agency, convinced the director that she would make a fine mother, and quickly received a child.

This woman, heterosexual and open to marriage if the chance presented itself (or at least portraying herself as such), did not reject marriage or men. Rather, she was adopting to make the best of a bad situation and to realize her dream of becoming a mother. Her adoptive motherhood was not a direct challenge to the institution of marriage but an alternative for a woman who found her access to the usual path to motherhood blocked. Adoption served as the means to reach her "destiny" as a woman. As many scholars have noted, women's magazines reiterate traditional gender roles. When the magazine accepted this first-person account, it no doubt felt that the woman was an ideal hybrid of the modern yet traditional woman. However, at least one reader, a married adoptive mother, challenged the article and fired off a letter to the magazine. The magazine's editors responded that they had reread the article and agreed that it was not an accurate representation of reputable adoption practice.[48]

In the 1940s, still more experts spoke out against single women, this time using Freudian theories. Adoption expert Florence Clothier argued that a child needed two parents to attain "psychosexual maturity." "Normal Oedipus development," Clothier believed, "cannot occur in an environment in which one parent figure is lacking." A boy needed a father with whom to identify in order to "strengthen his masculinity" and a mother "to awaken and call up his love impulses and tenderness." Girls, meanwhile, needed a "happy" relationship with a father to ensure that their adult relationships with men were "not overshadowed by fear and aggression." In *The Psychology of Women*, published in 1945, Helene Deutsch further delineated the pathology of single adoptive mothers who fell into three distinct camps. The first group consisted of "bachelor girls" whose motivation was "rooted in the parthenogenetic fantasy 'I do not need a man for that.' " Other women, the "aging spinster" and "motherly aunt" types, were liable to smother their "unexpected gift of fate" with excessive emotion. And finally, she despaired of those "female couples" who adopted and often overly intellectualized their relationship with the child. According to Deutsch, the outsider viewing this family was often left with the "slightly comical impression that their manless menage lacks a feminine member."[49]

In the end, single women lost their chance to experience motherhood through adoption. They were excluded for a number of reasons. The newly sexualized society marked them as deviant. The increased emphasis on the importance of a father figure to ensure appropriate gender-role socialization defined woman-headed households as inferior and lacking. The mounting distrust in women's natural competence as mothers and increasing disdain for women's maternal emotions fell especially hard on those who, without visible romantic interests, did not quite measure up to the new psychological standards of healthy adjustment. And the growing authority of social workers in adoption, whose primary professional objective was to maintain the stability of the traditional family, effectively closed off their access to children.

Most important, society found something quite frightening and foreboding about women who created happy and whole families without men. As this study argues throughout, adoption serves as a site on which the culture plays out its fears about the stability of the family and, more broadly, its anxieties about the ever-changing, unknowable future. To accept single women as adoptive mothers would be to accept, even to invite, a change in one of the fundamental, bedrock institutions of society—the family.

The evidence suggests that single adoptive mothers were not as uncommon as we have previously thought; in the first few decades of the twentieth century, although there would not have been an unmarried adoptive mother on every block (with the possible exception of Greenwich Village), an unmarried adoptive mother would not have been a complete surprise. Yet it is possible that single adoptive mothers received so much attention because they were such oddities and because their presence struck at the heart of some profound cultural beliefs and fears. At the turn of the century, when maternal sensibilities still served as *the* marker of womanhood, it would be inconsistent with the prevailing gender ideology to deny single women the opportunity to adopt. However, once the indicator of womanhood shifted to mother *and* wife, single adoptive motherhood no longer made sense. Now it was unnatural, deviant, and a possible threat to social order and stability.

Mabel Walker Willebrandt, an assistant attorney general in the Harding administration who is most often remembered for her work on Prohibition, was another single woman whose life and decision to adopt posed an alternative, even a challenge, to the nuclear family and traditional gender roles. Willebrandt divorced in 1924. Feeling that her life was incomplete without a child, she began to search for one to adopt. She visited orphanages and alerted her friends to be on the look-out. In August 1925, she found two-year-old Dorothy through a woman she had helped when she had been a police court defender in Los Angeles. Willebrandt had the loving support and approval of her parents; her mother assured Mabel that she would be "such a fine Mother" and that she would "rejoice" in Dorothy "as a grandmother." Willebrandt raised Dorothy with the help of her two female housemates, Louise Stanley and Annabel Matthews, and her parents, who visited often.[50]

Although she worried about the cost of raising a child, Willebrandt expressed no concerns about her ability to raise and nurture a child by herself. She immediately immersed herself in child-rearing manuals and developed her own philosophy, which she detailed in an article in *Good Housekeeping*. Like any single working parent now or in the past, Willebrandt almost immediately began to worry about and feel guilty over the amount of time she had for Dorothy.[51]

Nonetheless, she decided not to remarry when the opportunity presented itself a few years later. Willebrandt cared deeply for the man, who could have helped shoulder her financial burdens, but she worried that he did not understand her commitment to her career. Although monetary concerns continually plagued her, she knew that she wanted to make money herself, "especially since there's no such thing as getting it out of a clear sky with no donor attached!" Like many of the first women professionals, Willebrandt could not find a way to meet the demands of marriage and a career. But although she found it difficult to meet the challenge of motherhood, she did not find it completely impossible to blend Dorothy and her work. Although marriage and a career were out of the question, motherhood and a career were not.[52]

Willebrandt had found a way, with the help of her friends and parents, to fulfill her desire to mother, but she still felt an emptiness in her life. As she wrote to her parents in 1926, "Only sometimes a sigh that you are too far away and Dorothy too young to have joy in my triumphs—we all want to feel our success for somebody. There's the love of doing it and keeping standards high but I long for something more. You see I *am* in my life and profession a *man*. I want a wife and family reaping vicarious pride in my success and being noticed for it." Willebrandt felt like a man and, through adoption, had created a family without a man. In short, although she might have wanted a man, she certainly did not need one. For a society bent on keeping traditional gender roles and male hegemony, Willebrandt and other women like her posed a threat to the institution of marriage, the structure of the nuclear family, and the dominance of men. Many Americans had long been worried, especially during the race-suicide panic, that native-born, married women were rejecting motherhood. Here, however, was something even more frightening: women rejecting not only marriage but men, and embracing motherhood and careers.[53]

In the spring of 1946, Ann Barley, a single adoptive mother, made headlines nationwide. The thirty-six-year-old former War Department employee had inherited a nice sum of money and, after hearing a Dutch official talk about the sad plight of European war orphans, determined to adopt one. Since the government had suspended travel to Europe for all but those traveling in the national interest, Barley pretended to be a foreign correspondent. Getting to Europe proved to be the easy part. Only after six months of dead-end leads, endless red tape, and wretched living conditions did she finally locate a baby boy in France. While they waited for transport back to the States, Barley and her new son stayed in a Paris hotel supposedly open only to American businessmen. There, they met a number of newspapermen. Smelling a good story, a journalist for the *Herald Tribune* wired a piece back to New York as the mother and child boarded a plane for Washington. By the time they arrived, other reporters had picked up the scent and welcomed the plane with a burst of flashbulbs. Joyful stories of Barley's successful quest appeared in newspapers from coast to coast the next day. In 1948, Barley published a book-length account of her journey, *Patrick Calls Me Mother*, to positive reviews.[54]

By 1946, child welfare experts had been openly critical of single motherhood for two decades. What, then, are we to make of the press's enthusiastic response to Barley's tale? Moreover, what does her determination tell us about single women's maternal desire? Barley's story implies that some single women continued to dream of having a family, despite their inability to locate children through reputable agencies. Meanwhile, the press's reaction suggests that many Americans still believed that some single women's maternal drive could be natural, not neurotic, and, in exceptional circumstances, worthy of fulfillment.

The press's initial zeal is easy to understand: Barley's search was great copy. Her adventure gave a human-interest twist to reports on the shortages and troubles of postwar Europe. And although the circumstances surrounding her adoption were unusual, it also seems fair to assume that her single status was an important part of the interest. At the very least, her unmarried state provided an opportunity for clever puns; *Time*, for example, recounted her "international labor pains." In 1948, her story was still newsworthy; at least twelve major magazines and newspapers reviewed her book.[55]

Patrick Calls Me Mother begins by unequivocally establishing Barley's heterosexuality. "One evening . . . I was having a final, tense talk with a man I had thought I might marry. We had waited for each other through the war. Now he was back and time and distance had subtly changed his feeling. He thought that we had made a mistake. There was nothing much I could do but agree." In the taxi home, she contemplates her future. "Perhaps I would not marry at all, now." Determined to move on with her life, she tells the taxi driver to change course and drop her at a friend's house. There she encounters the Dutch official. When she humbly expresses interest in adopting an orphan—"If there are Dutch children who need mothers . . . perhaps I'd do"—he is encouraging. When she tells him she is single, his enthusiasm does not wane. Apparently, "the psychological nuances that an American social worker might have thought of, such considerations as whether a child with one parent might feel shortchanged, did not seem to strike any echo in his practical mind. He felt that the question of first importance was whether I had money enough to educate a child."[56]

To Barley, this "seemed an unrivaled opportunity. If Dutch children needed help, then I need have no qualms about offering a home without a father. Just a home with three square meals a day would be better than nothing." Before the war, Barley had lived in New York and earned enough to support a small family. She had then thought of adopting a child, but the war and falling in love had brought an end to the idea. Now, the thought returned. A week of serious contemplation furthered her conviction. By the end of the week, she had decided both that she "had a right to establish a life for myself" and "that such a chance as this might never come around again."[57]

The rest of Barley's book (almost 90 percent of the text) details her dogged search for a child throughout war-ravaged France and Holland. Page after page describes the terrible situation of children and the difficulties facing those who are trying to help them. One little girl dies before Barley can adopt her. Two Dutch children, sickly and distant after the experience of war, tug at her emotions even as they fill her with revulsion. She endures hunger, illness, and loneliness in her quest, thereby showing both the sincerity and the depth of her maternal desire. When she finally locates Patrick, it is a well-deserved triumph.

This narrative structure is important in understanding reviewers' favorable reception. By establishing her sexuality and acknowledging the concerns of social workers, Barley effectively removes the most obvious objections to her adoption. She does not claim that a father is unnecessary or that her situation is ideal. But, as her story goes, she is not keeping a child from a "normal" family, she is rescuing a victim. Barley also takes pains to show that hers is a thoughtful, rational decision, one she has considered for some time, not an impetuous attempt to find an outlet for her emotional needs. Within this setting, the potentially controversial aspects of Barley's story are easy to miss. Her provocative assertion that she has a "right" to a family remains buried between the telling of her personal heartbreak and the children's heartbreaking stories.

It also is easy to overlook Barley's critique of professional adoption practice in the United States. After the initial news stories, she received dozens of letters from people who had tried to adopt children but had failed. Social workers, these letters suggested, were insensitive, their standards too high. The largest number of letters came from single women. A woman from Michigan told Barley that child welfare workers had given her a solid rating until they discovered that she was "an old maid." A St. Louis businesswoman had saved five thousand dollars to adopt a child but had been turned down because she was single. She offered Barley the money if she would serve as her "personal stork." After reading these letters, Barley determined that adoption in the United States "was becoming over-institutionalized—a great, bewildering, complicated rat race."[58]

None of the reviews, however, focused on the acceptability of single women as adoptive applicants or on the state of adoption in the United States. Instead, reviewers highlighted the story itself and its telling. The *Saturday Review of Literature*, for example, noted that the story was "told with such debonair gaiety and amused good nature that it is obvious young Patrick will grow up in an enviable home." This, however, was not the primary reason the reviewer recommended the book. Instead, she proclaimed that the "moving and poignant" descriptions of war orphans were "hard to put out of the mind." Similarly, the *Herald Tribune* stated that the book was "not merely a gay account of the rescue of one child. It is also a tragic story of the misery of Europe's children." And finally, the *New York Times* review focused exclusively on the "grand adventure" and described it as "happy reading." With single adoptive motherhood embedded in heterosexuality (the book ends with Barley's assertion that she and Patrick are "a family," but a paragraph later she hints that romance awaits with a man she met in Paris) and humanitarianism, reviewers apparently felt free to ignore the challenge to the traditional family or, possibly, even failed to read the story as such.[59]

If some journalists were sympathetic to single women's desire to adopt in some circumstances, social workers were not. By the 1950s, child welfare professionals were united in their opposition to single women. In 1941, the Child Welfare League of America's *Standards for Children's Organizations Providing Foster Family Care* excluded single women and recommended that widows be accepted only in "unusual situations"; by 1958, in the league's first *Standards* focused exclusively on adoption, even this small exception had been eliminated. A 1954 survey of 270 agencies that placed children for adoption conducted by the Child Welfare League of America showed that single women—including widowed, divorced, or never married—were considered ineligible to adopt in all but four agencies. There is no evidence to suggest that these four agencies actually placed children with single women, and it is likely that single women were simply not specifically excluded. In the mid-1950s, California's Department of Social Welfare declared unequivocally in its *Manual of Adoption Policies and Procedures* that applications would not be accepted from any single person, whether never married, widowed, or divorced.[60]

Limiting adoption to married couples (and thereby minimizing the differences between adoptive and biological families) possibly helped lessen the stigma of adoption, if only by making the differences less publicly visible. Yet, once adoption was restricted to those who could pass the "just-like" test, an unprecedented opportunity to expand the cultural definition of what constitutes a "normal" family vanished. For one brief moment in history, the culture's belief in all women's maternal instinct and the relative unpopularity of adoption overlapped and allowed unmarried, theoretically celibate women to become mothers with little, if any, public disapproval.

Adoption was not necessarily the perfect solution for women who wanted children and had the financial means to care for them but, for whatever reason, were not in a position to give birth. Yet when single women were allowed to adopt, they at least had the ability to meet their desires and to create families of their choosing. Often the families they created were similar in structure to the traditional family, with the exception that they were headed by two deeply committed women, rather than a husband and wife. Sometimes, however, they were unique structures, filled with more than two adults or with adults of varying generations. These families had fluid boundaries, as contrasted with the often isolated nuclear family. Gender roles were blurred as children saw women serve as "mother" and "father," as caretaker and breadwinner. With the exclusion of single women from the ranks of acceptable adoptive parents, adoption lost what had been the potential to radically expand the culture's definition of family.

5 | "The Best" or "Good Enough"?
Child-Placing Professionals, Adoptive Parents, and Definitions of Family, 1920–1950

In 1935, an article on adoption in *Parents' Magazine* began with the following story. "A well-known child psychologist was recently asked, 'Is it safe to adopt children?' His reply was, 'It depends on why you adopt them.' In response to the puzzled look of the inquirer, he added, 'I wasn't thinking of you, I was thinking of the child.'" The person asking the question had good reason to be puzzled. Americans' understanding of adoption and adoptive parenthood had changed dramatically in the eighty-five years since Massachusetts passed the first adoption law. Then, an interest in adoption had been understood as a sign of an individual's generosity of spirit largely benefiting the child. Now, in the new psychological age, an urge to adopt signaled either a natural instinct or a neurotic desire, a benefit or a detriment to the child. Change and puzzlement— these two themes pervade the history of adoption in this period as child welfare professionals struggled to take control of adoption and many adoptive parents resisted the experts' efforts to create and define their families.[1]

The 1920s mark the beginning of changes that, by 1950, had significantly altered the practice of adoption. Adoption lost its association with the rescue of dependent children and began to be thought of as distinct from temporary foster care. In the 1920s and 1930s, adoption achieved a new level of public acceptance and even became a fad in some social circles of Hollywood stars and political power brokers. By 1940, one commentator noted that interest in adoption had "spread over this country with the indiscriminate enthusiasm of a contagion." As more and more people turned to adoption, the shortage of infants and young children worsened. By the mid-1930s, one state-authorized child-placing agency noted that applications outpaced available children by eight to one. In the same years, the U.S. Children's Bureau routinely began to "warn" those who wrote requesting information on adoption that "the number of families who wish to adopt children far exceeds the number of children available."[2]

But for many applicants, the shortage defied common sense. Hadn't the depression disrupted American families? What about those children? Mistakenly equating families in distress with children available for adoption, many applicants blamed social workers' "red tape" for their inability to find children. The red tape to which some would-be parents objected referred to the new placement policies social workers began to develop in the 1920s. Since the requests so far exceeded the supply, social workers sought to find not just a home for a child but the "best" possible home. The best did not necessarily mean the wealthiest home. Rather, child welfare professionals tried to "match" children and parents so that, in the words of one social worker, "no one will ever say to a[n adoptive] mother or father, 'This cannot be your natural child.' "[3] To this end, professionals used the latest developments in a variety of scientific disciplines to ensure that children and parents were physically, intellectually, and temperamentally suited to each other. In addition, social workers vigorously screened prospective parents to ensure that they were able to care for a child financially *and* had psychologically sound motives for adoption. Social workers attempted to create adoptive families that not only mirrored biological ones but also reflected an idealized version of them.

Not everyone, however, wanted a "perfect" family. Although social workers increased their ability to oversee adoptions in this period, they failed to achieve complete cultural authority. By the mid-1940s, social workers placed children in only about half of all adoptions by nonrelatives.[4] In privately arranged or nonprofessional agency adoptions, adoptive parents worked out the creation of their new families in personal ways that spoke to their understanding of family life and offered them a level of control and privacy over this most intimate of experiences. Social workers' involvement in adoption and the ever-increasing shortage of adoptable children focused attention on the questions of what motivations deserved the reward of parenthood, what relationships counted as "real" family, and what emotions represented genuine parental feelings. These questions were, of course, not easy to answer. They were also questions of the utmost importance as many individuals increasingly looked to the private family for personal fulfillment.[5]

Adoption "Experts": Social Work and the Struggle for Authority

The first two decades of the twentieth century witnessed efforts by social workers to establish their occupation as a profession distinct from the sentimental philanthropy of volunteers. The principle underlying social work held that those dispensing aid should be guided not by social class, the rich helping the poor, but by science, the expert assisting the uninformed. A six-week summer training course for charity workers held in New York in 1898 marked the beginning of social work education; by 1920, seventeen schools of social work existed. The establishment of professional associations and the development of theories, methods, and investigatory techniques further promoted the transition from moral duty to skilled service.[6]

Social workers, however, came to adoption slowly. The idea of adoption conflicted with their efforts toward family preservation and their belief in the primacy of the blood tie. Social workers thought that unwed mothers should keep their infants, a philosophy that continued unchallenged within the profession through the 1930s. In addition, beginning in the 1910s, social workers, influenced by the findings of the new intelligence tests, felt that a definite link existed between illegitimacy and inherited feeblemindedness— a link that they believed made most illegitimate children unadoptable. Consequently, social workers focused their efforts on issues other than adoption.[7]

Meanwhile, in the 1910s, individuals, generally well-to-do women, began to establish private adoption agencies. Imbued with a philanthropic spirit, they strongly disagreed with social workers, especially regarding the disposition of illegitimate infants. They believed that these children were adoptable and that an unwed mother and her child did not make a real family. In New York in 1911, for example, Alice Chapin, wife of a prominent physician, began to care for the foundlings brought to her husband's hospital. After restoring the infants to health in the nursery she constructed on the third floor of their home, Chapin placed them in the many homes that had heard about her work and requested children. In 1919, she established the Alice Chapin Adoption Nursery to meet the growing demand for children.[8]

In Chicago, Florence Walrath found herself in the adoption business after locating an infant for her sister, whose firstborn child had died shortly after birth. Soon word of Walrath's success spread, and friends and acquaintances began to approach her to find infants for them. Walrath officially opened the Cradle, Chicago's first formal adoption agency, in 1923. The Cradle quickly achieved a national reputation as such Hollywood stars as George Burns and Gracie Allen flew to Chicago to claim their own bundles of joy. In addition, individuals such as the *Houston Post*'s humor columnist Judd Mortimer Lewis became unofficial "baby bureaus," to much public acclaim. These private adoption agencies and individuals like Lewis accepted babies for adoption and approved adoptive parents based largely on intuition. Lewis, for example, placed a child in a family only after he had "patiently, personally investigated" and determined that the home "rang true." Lewis and the others firmly believed that caring individuals working independently did a better job placing children than professional home-finding societies.[9]

RELIGION AND SOCIAL SERVICE

A HUMORIST'S "BABY BUREAU"

MOST PEOPLE who make a business of writing or talking about human-welfare problems condemn unorganized charity, and perhaps they are right as regards a majority of cases, but there are some notable exceptions to the rule. One of these is the work of Judd Mortimer Lewis, staff poet of the Houston *Post*, who is helping to lessen the need of orphan asylums. Mr. Lewis writes a column of verse and jokes every day, but he finds time to place many homeless babies in babyless homes. Experience has convinced him that persons working independently can do much more satisfactory work than home-finding societies such as are operating in many of the States. He says that he has placed less than two-score babies since he started his "baby bureau" six years ago, but that "every home in which I have placed a little one has been thoroughly, patiently, personally investigated; I know that every home in which I place a baby is all right." Mr. Lewis says the daily newspaper is the best medium on earth for a clearing-house between the orphan asylums and foundling homes and the babyless homes. The newspaper man has no trouble in finding out from local institutions what babies there are for adoption. He can write descriptions of the babies which will reach thousands of readers, and after a while he will be depended upon — become a sort of institution himself. Being a poet, Mr. Lewis, if we are to take his word for it, has very little money to spend, but, fortunately, his work does not require much capital. Kind-hearted women of Houston frequently render personal assistance to the "bureau." Mr. Lewis's work has already been mentioned in these pages, but that was before any detailed account of it was ever written in quotable form. If you have any doubts about its being a real human-interest story, read this from Mr. Lewis's pen:

"What is needed more than anything in the work is people. People give a dollar or two dollars or a thousand or a million dollars to charity, then go their ways with their nose in the air and a 'holier than thou' look that would be the funniest thing ever put into this column if I could only corral it. They think they have played thunder. And they probably have. I read of a case in Chicago recently of a widowed mother who was in need of help and applied to organized charity. The record of the case shows that she received $300 in driblets, and FIVE THOUSAND DOLLARS were spent investigating her case! Our charity is not organized; it is the most unorganized thing you ever saw. There are no salaries; and there is no hesitation. When a baby is flung homeless on life's troubled sea we get to it! Nobody calls a secretary, who calls another secretary, who calls another secretary, who calls another secretary, and so on until some one is finally found to visit the case, and ten chances to one the baby

has died and been buried, or has grown up and raised a beard by the time the investigator has arrived. This business is not in need of money or of salaried officials. What it wants is you, it needs you to put some of your own self into the business. Put yourself into it!

"A lady who gives much of her time to this work visited two foundlings with me the other day, and owl-eyed, monkey-faced little humans they were. They were not properly assimilating their food. The boy had a well-shaped head and good features, but he was gaunt from starvation, and wrinkled until he looked a thousand years old. The lady with me exclaimed: 'Oh, Thotmes III!' And he actually looked like a mummy of Thotmes or Rameses. I tell you in a time like this is when a feller needs a friend. If I had the wealth necessary I would build a model baby home. Every foundling should have the attention of a physician and a trained nurse and be loved and fattened for a month or two before prospective parents were permitted to see it. I have never yet seen a foundling home which bathed, changed, fed, and cared for every baby all the time as it should be cared for. They evidently do the very best they can, but their best does not seem to me to be quite good enough. Perhaps I'm too particular. If you give money to a charity your money may do the charity some good, but the charity won't do you a bit of good. And real charity must benefit him who gives as well as him who receives. Come on in, fellows, the charity is fine!"

The demand for babies always exceeds the supply. Only a few days ago Mr. Lewis said he had orders for four babies. He recently wrote to an orphans' home in Cincinnati for two little girls, and expects to get them. He has placed babies in homes as far away as Florida and Georgia, but the greater part of his work is confined to Houston and Texas. In another issue of The Post Mr. Lewis tells more about his experiences:

"The people who procure a baby through my efforts must 'ring true' as regards morality, kindliness, and cleanliness. If they have a child of their own, their references must be exceptionally fine; for they are unusual people indeed who can give an adopted baby a square deal under such circumstances. They need not be wealthy; there is as much, sometimes more, love in the home of the laborer as in the home of the millionaire. That a child is illegitimate almost never cuts any figure with the people who are looking for a baby to adopt. Just so the child is a normal, healthy child a home can easily be found for it.

"The demand is almost altogether for girl babies; for light-haired, blue-eyed girl babies generally, and as more girls than boys are offered for adoption, supply and demand seem to fit perfectly. I can always find a home for a boy baby. I have placed four boys very happily.

"Some people worry themselves unnecessarily about heredity. If the child inherits a healthy body I believe it is all they should ask. It is my theory that environment amounts to a great

JUDD MORTIMER LEWIS.

A newspaper poet who makes jokes for a living and places "homeless babies in babyless homes" for an avocation.

A number of popular magazines, including the *Literary Digest* in July 1913, profiled *Houston Post* humorist Judd Mortimer Lewis, who served as a "one-man baby bureau" whose services were "free from red tape." (Library of Congress)

The shortage of adoptable children made headlines in Philadelphia in 1929.
(Library of Congress)

Although a few private agencies existed in the 1910s in addition to the social agencies that sometimes placed children, such as the Children's Aid Society, many parents adopted their children through personal networks. In these adoptions, birth parents or biological relatives directly placed a child with parents, or a physician or an attorney served as an intermediary between those desiring a child and those wanting to surrender one. Social agencies were not involved. Although it is impossible to determine the number of privately arranged adoptions, evidence suggests that they accounted for half, if not more, of all stranger adoptions. Throughout the 1910s, adoption gradually gained popular acceptance, largely without the oversight or advice of the social welfare profession.

As a result, social workers had an uphill battle in the 1920s when they began to look at child placing and tried to bring adoption under their professional jurisdiction. They had to both assert their unique qualifications to be in charge and convince the public that the current practices were dangerous to the child, the adoptive parent, the biological parent, *and* society at large.[10]

Changing popular opinion and behavior was a daunting task. Legislative efforts focused on establishing laws that required an investigation into the circumstances surrounding the placement by a child welfare professional or the state welfare department and a six-month trial period of residence in the prospective home before any adoption could be finalized. In 1917, Minnesota passed the first such law, and by the end of 1941, thirty-four states required an investigation before the court issued an adoption decree.[11] These legislative victories were impressive. As legal analyst Brian Gill has shown, judges usually followed the recommendations of investigators. Judges disregarded an investigator's determination that an adoptive home was unsuitable only when the child was clearly attached to the applicant and his or her safety or health was not in danger. Gill further notes that in placements made by public agencies, social workers had almost complete authority; the court was in no way involved with an agency's initial decision to reject or approve an applicant and virtually always granted an adoption that a public agency recommended. Still, despite social workers' increased involvement, even in states that required an investigation, judges had the ultimate power to deny or approve a petition.[12]

The U.S. Children's Bureau also aided efforts to increase the authority of social workers in both the legal and the public realms. Aware that "popular interest in adoption has been consistently furthered by popular articles on the subject," the bureau worked with authors and editors on stories. It sent letters of praise to magazines that published articles championing social work standards and notes expressing its "disturbance" to those that did not. To the hundreds, mostly women, who wrote requesting information on how to adopt and where to find a child, the bureau responded with the names of reputable agencies and an exhortation about the importance of professional standards. "No doubt you realize," began the typical response, "the importance of making application for a child only to an agency that maintains high standards of work." As the number of letters to the bureau dramatically increased in the 1930s, its professional and authoritative responses influenced the adoption decisions of countless Americans.[13]

Social workers in the field also contributed to efforts to convince the public of the benefits of professional placements. In 1924, at the National Conference of Social Work, A. H. Stoneman of Michigan's Children's Aid Society urged his colleagues to begin a public-relations campaign to promote placement policies with a "scientific basis." Stoneman lamented the emotional appeals that appeared in popular magazines and moved readers to adopt a homeless child "no matter how bad his family history." Stoneman called for children's agencies to send out "an equally strong emotional appeal" in favor of scientific placement procedures. Stoneman's preferred method for arousing the right kind of emotions was to publicize adoption horror stories, the "unhappy developments" of independent placements to counter the many "happy" stories, which he believed were nothing more than "the lucky outcome of a reckless adoption."[14]

Even before Stoneman's call for scare tactics, a few social workers involved in adoption had begun the arduous process of formulating guidelines. In 1921, Sophie van Senden Theis, superintendent of child placing for the New York State Charities Aid Association, published the first comprehensive manual for social workers. The standards she advocated, and which social workers would expand upon and refine over the next three decades, included a thorough investigation of prospective adopters (including an examination not only into the material and religious conditions of their lives but also into their "intimate traits of personality") and a complete physical and mental examination of the child. Conducting a thorough examination meant that a child would not be placed until it was at least six months old. In addition, workers were to compile a detailed history of the child's background, "gathering every scrap of significant information about his family, including his grandparents, aunts, and uncles." A questionable heredity could permanently mark a child as "unadoptable." Some agencies, for example, refused to place a child (or delayed placement) if its mother scored too low on her intelligence test. "Queer" or "bizarre behavior" in a child's immediate family could also unsuit it for adoption; for instance, a survey in the 1930s of mental hygienists involved with adoption showed that almost half believed that a child with homosexuals or transvestites as close relations should not be placed.[15]

Social workers also had difficulty establishing that their training and experience made them uniquely qualified to oversee adoption placement, as laywomen asserted that a finely tuned "maternal instinct" was qualification enough. As social work struggled to claim its place as a legitimate profession, an unavoidable tension developed between social workers and the volunteers who had previously controlled the care of the poor and dependent classes. Historians have documented this conflict both in the field of social work writ large and in specialized areas such as the treatment of unwed mothers. The professionalization of adoption followed much the same path, with a few notable differences. In adoption placement, the idea that a volunteer could make decisions as sound as those of a professional proved especially tenacious. As early as 1910, a volunteer who placed children in western Pennsylvania argued at the annual meeting of the National Conference of Charities and Correction that mothers made the best placements: "Surely mothers with their sympathetic hearts and innate intuition, can get at the facts in the various cases better than all the men in the universe, and we feel the service has been done for the love of humanity, not in the perfunctory way of paid workers along similar lines." In response, Henry Thurston, one of Chicago's leading child welfare experts, acknowledged that "nature and experience" qualified mothers. He also believed, however, that unmarried men and women were just as sympathetic and, importantly, more efficient.[16]

The controversy continued throughout the 1920s and 1930s. Social workers argued that child placing was a "most exacting" science that required "careful preparation and study." Meanwhile, volunteers such as Eleanor Gallagher of Chicago's Cradle vocally asserted otherwise. In 1936, Gallagher published *The Adopted Child*, one of the first popular books on adoption. Gallagher stated that fifteen years of experience had convinced her that volunteers could have as much "insight and understanding . . . as those with a degree from a school of social work." Social workers, Gallagher believed, had sacrificed sympathy for "understanding the problem"; in their "lust for power" and search for "the truth," social workers had ceased to be a client's "friend." Social workers responded that it was "regrettable that the first book written on adoption is so unsatisfactory."[17]

Although child welfare leaders called for social workers to develop systematic theories of child placing and to apply the developing methods of casework to adoption, it appears that rank-and-file social workers did not run to embrace adoption as their area of expertise. There were a number of reasons for this reluctance. As historian Daniel Walkowitz notes, social workers' status and authority came from the power they held over their poor, needy clients, who looked to them for advice and help. Although prospective adopters had to gain the caseworker's approval, they did not require the social worker's aid in the traditional sense. In fact, although they needed something from the caseworker—a child—they also gave something to the caseworker that she needed: a good home for a dependent child. This dynamic, as one social worker observed, "contradict[ed] the customary need of the caseworker to be the giver."[18]

The social reality of class further complicated the relationship between caseworkers and prospective adopters. Adoption "clients" were not poor and uneducated but were often "people whom she might find socially attractive and interesting." Consequently, a caseworker might "over-identify" with the client or show an unfortunate "tendency to take much that he says at face value." Adoption, then, tested the caseworker's skills. One guide warned home finders that "the better educated person is also better read and better informed; presumably his discussion of children and their needs is colored by what he knows to be approved current thinking. Although this could also happen with a less educated person, the probability is that his discussion of attitudes in relation to children would be less intellectualized and more revealing of his own personality problem." Caseworkers were trained to dig beneath the surface to unearth a client's true self. This task proved difficult to achieve with "the better educated person," who "quite automatically" expressed attitudes likely to be approved; an adoptive parent's "superior education" could "act to conceal personality deficiencies."[19]

Child placing, or, as one social worker described it, "playing God," could also be emotionally difficult for the caseworker. Professional articles urged caseworkers to examine their attitudes toward their own parents, lest their dissatisfactions with that relationship "send [them] on a will o' the wisp hunt for perfect adoptive parents." Unlike other areas of social work in which the caseworker helped a client, in placement work, caseworkers judged applicants. Although a caseworker could take pleasure in an adoption placement that turned out well, if a placement failed, the responsibility, fairly or not, rested with the caseworker. Although controlling adoption placements and policy gave the social work profession as a whole more status and power, for the individual caseworker, adoption work could be especially difficult and only moderately rewarding.[20]

As social workers developed adoption policy and refined the practice in the 1920s, 1930s, and 1940s, they claimed expertise in three areas of special concern to prospective adopters. First, social workers spoke to adopters' fear of a child's heredity. Social workers promised to evaluate a child's heritage thoroughly by extensive interviewing and testing. Second, and directly related to the first, social workers maintained that through the extensive evaluation of a child and his or her biological parents, they could "match" a child to the adoptive parents. Social workers asserted that they could find a child "who might have been born to you." Children would "fit" their adoptive homes in physical characteristics, intellectual capacities, temperament, and religious and ethnic affiliation. The policy of matching assumed that this affinity would lead to easier assimilation. And finally, responding to the adoptive parents' fear of biological parents changing their minds, social workers maintained that their procedures ensured that the child was really free to be adopted and that the biological parents would stick to their decision.[21]

Matching: The Politics of Culture and Class

At first glance, matching makes sense. It is easy to accept on face value the assertion that a physical, even temperamental or intellectual, likeness between a child and its adoptive parents facilitates the child's acceptance into the new family. Social workers believed that as a "child grows up and approaches maturity, it will be easier for him and for the adoptive parents if his appearance and constitutional type are not too foreign to that of the family of which he is a part." Even the Cradle, the private adoption agency in Chicago that disagreed with social workers on virtually every aspect of policy, agreed that the principles behind physical matching were sound. The Cradle took pains to match ethnicity, body type, and hair and eye coloring, which it could do because of the large number of children it placed and its even larger pool of prospective parents from which to choose. On closer examination, however, the policy of matching reflected deeper cultural beliefs about the social functions of families and the real basis of family ties.[22]

In 1957, Joseph Reid, executive director of the Child Welfare League of America, stated that matching came about as social workers scrambled to "sell" adoption to a skeptical public. In these accounts, a shortage of adoptive parents led social workers to promise that they could provide perfect children who would match the adoptive family. But the evidence clearly suggests that since at least the early years of the twentieth century, there was never a shortage of adoptive parents for infants and very young children. Consequently, we must look for other explanations for the development of matching. One obvious reason is that social workers' ability to match a child to his or her adoptive parents was a service that a doctor or lawyer placing one child at a time could not easily provide. In the struggle for control over adoption placement, *scientific* matching was a strong selling point for professional social workers.[23]

It was a selling point that many adoptive parents would find hard to resist, since they could anticipate repeated comments from those eager to point out the difference between their families and ones based in biology. The matching of physical characteristics provided one way to minimize the difference by making adoption invisible to outsiders. In this regard, matching seems both productive and considerate. Yet erasing difference also suggests that Americans believed not only that families should look alike but also that a similar physiognomy assisted in the creation and maintenance of a familial bond. Winifred Cobbledick, an adoption worker in California, articulated this position in a study of matching in the 1940s. "Natural parents derive a normal satisfaction from the similarity of their children to themselves," Cobbledick argued. "It is understandable that adopting parents experience this need as well, and the physical and mental traits of an adopted child which seem like those their own child might have shown are a tie which helps to bind them together more closely." However, the concern with masking difference reinforced physical difference as an important marker of "otherness" and reflected social workers' belief that adoptive families should be modeled as closely as possible on biological families.[24]

Social workers tried not only to match physical characteristics (including ethnicity, race, coloring, and body type) but also to ensure that a child intellectually "fit" its adoptive parents; in simple terms, intellectually promising children would be placed with educated families, and children who showed less potential would find homes with adoptive parents who had less education. In 1921, Sophie van Senden Theis, in the first placement guide for social workers, noted the importance of placing a child in a family where it had "the capacity for satisfying his parents' hopes." Relationships "between a family with ambitions for educating their child and a child dull at school, between a family with high standards of refinement and a child who develops a coarse-grained temperament" were "full of pitfalls." Efforts to determine a child's potential led social workers to require relinquishing parents to provide detailed medical and social histories. This policy complicated social workers' relationship with unwed mothers, because they felt that such mothers never told the complete truth about a child's father. Social workers used this information about the biological parents' health, IQ and educational attainment, and personality traits to gauge a child's "adoptability" in general and "mental prospects" in particular. In addition to gathering information on a child's biological background, agencies increasingly required that an infant undergo a battery of developmental and achievement tests before placement.[25]

The emphasis on a child's intelligence reflected the hereditarian views of the 1910s and 1920s, which argued that intelligence was heritable *and* immutable. Hereditarians such as Lewis Terman, who developed the Stanford-Binet IQ test, believed that an inherited IQ marked an individual for a specific and inevitable station in life. In this worldview, class boundaries were natural, a mere reflection of the innate intelligence of the group. With regard to children, hereditarians denied that environment affected a child's development. As Terman stated in 1916, "The common opinion that the child from a cultured home does better in tests solely by reason of his superior home advantages is an entirely gratuitous assumption." Instead, Terman declared, "the children of successful and cultured parents test higher than children from wretched and ignorant homes for the simple reason that their heredity is better." In 1917, the hereditarians' concept of IQ and testing left the realm of theory and entered into America's popular imagination with the testing of 1.75 million World War I soldier recruits; the era of mass testing, as Stephen Jay Gould notes, had begun.[26]

In the mid-1920s, Arnold Gesell, director of Yale University's Psycho-Clinic and a well-respected psychologist, first argued that intelligence tests could be used successfully on even very young children to determine their potential intellectual abilities. Although acknowledging that it was "impossible to cast a horoscope," Gesell maintained that it was "unnecessary to proceed blindly in the dark." To this end, he argued in the Child Welfare League's *Bulletin* that all infants should be examined thoroughly before adoption.[27] Gesell's views quickly appeared in the professional literature of social workers and became a staple topic for those writing on adoption. Not all social workers, however, were convinced of the predictive value of intelligence testing on infants. Many argued that the results should be used as only one of many "tools" in determining the type of family in which a child should be placed. Nevertheless, no one disputed Gesell's larger point that every possible effort should be made to ensure that children were not "overplaced" ("dull" children placed in educated families) or "underplaced" ("bright" children placed in homes with little opportunity for intellectual or cultural growth). As one social worker noted, "a misplaced child, either over-placed or underplaced, often becomes the center of a tragedy."[28]

Social workers involved in adoption placement never went as far as the hereditarians in their belief in the power of heredity; they had long argued that environment played an important role in a child's development. Nonetheless, none argued that heredity could be ignored. It is important, then, to consider the influence of this scientific thought on the policy of intellectual matching. The focus on matching that began in the post–World War I era corresponded with a period in which hereditarian ideas abounded. Although social workers maintained that matching IQ was important for the happiness of both the adopted child and the adoptive parents, the policy also functioned as a form of social control by ensuring (as much as possible according to the scientific thought of the day) that a family's social class standing would be maintained through the subsequent generations.

Social workers attempted to form adoptive families in such a way as to replicate the prevailing social class structure. A 1936 editorial in the Child Welfare League's *Bulletin* argued that adoptive families "should be safeguarded against receiving with high hopes a child who in the long years ahead will prove to be a disappointment to them."[29] Two years later, the league made this opinion, and the principle of intellectual matching, part of its "minimum safeguards" for adoptive parents: "The child should have the intelligence and the physical and mental background necessary to meet the reasonable expectation of the adopting parents"—a guarantee that many birth parents might like for their children, and a safeguard based on the principle of social class hierarchy.[30] In the 1940s, one popular adoption guide, written in consultation with a leader in child placing, noted that a child with an IQ of 100 (children who score 100 are considered to be of normal intelligence) would not be placed with a college professor and his wife, because "such a child, however chubby and delightful—however blue of eye and blond of hair—might prove a disappointment as he grew older and be unable to profit fully by the education facilities placed at his disposal."[31] According to these views, parental love, at least in adoptive families, was not unconditional but dependent on a child's achievements.

It would be unfair to present social workers as the lone advocates of matching. After all, even the Cradle sought to match the physical characteristics of adoptive parents and children. The difference between social workers and others who engaged in matching can be understood best in terms of degree and kind. Private adoption agencies or individuals placing children "independently" often considered a child's background when placing a child, making sure that children and families broadly matched in socio-economic characteristics. In many independent adoptions, matching took place almost as a matter of course; if a physician placed the child of an un-married patient with a patient who was longing for a child, it is likely that the two parties shared similar social backgrounds.[32]

The placement practices of the Cradle serve as one example of the match-ing that took place in agencies staffed by nonprofessionals. The Cradle usually placed children when they were around forty days old, too young for most achievement tests. And only on occasion did the Cradle have a birth mother take an IQ test. In addition, for the most part, it took the birth mother's word regarding the educational level, employment, and physical characteristics of the birth father, using "intuition" to determine the truthfulness of her re-sponses. The agency then used the relatively small amount of information it had gathered to try to generally match intellectual capacity. Many of the unmarried mothers who used the Cradle, for instance, were well-to-do or col-lege students drawn to its promise of anonymity and secrecy. Using this knowledge, the Cradle placed children with couples of a similar background in a method of matching that simply lacked scientific pretense.[33]

Yet even if the underlying value system was the same, there were some important differences between the practices of social workers and those of individuals or nonprofessional agencies. Only social work professionals—as specially trained child welfare experts—had the expertise to proclaim that the principle was sound and for the larger social good. And as journalists and authors increasingly asked social workers for their opinions on adoption, they had an outlet to influence public opinion. Professionals' assertion that they used the latest in scientific technique also served to imbue matching with the prestige and legitimacy of science. Finally, only social workers made intellec-tual matching a fundamental tenet of their adoption placement policy.

The intended effect of matching might seem paradoxical in a nation with egalitarian principles and rags-to-riches myths, especially given that these tra-ditions are sometimes cited to explain why adoption first gained popularity in the United States as opposed to Europe. However, at least one commentator, a woman who was an adoptive mother and involved in establishing profes-sional adoption standards in her community, believed that it "is not a denial but an affirmation of our democratic principles." Overplacement and under-placement, she felt, were "wasteful," and matching was simply "an acceptance of the fact of mental and temperamental limitations and differences." While the "absence of caste in the social life of America" allowed for the easy accep-tance of adoption, the practice of matching did "not strain the point beyond human ability." One can see the conservative implications of matching when compared with the idealism of early leaders of the French Revolution, who briefly envisioned adoption as a way to create a new class-free society by having noble families adopt the children of peasants, and vice versa.[34]

Social workers' commitment to matching intellectual expectancy or achievement capacity set the stage for a battle between social workers and adoptive parents over the meaning and purpose of "family." Some social workers refused to believe adopters who claimed not to care about a child's IQ and who simply wanted a healthy child to love, especially if they were educated or professional. One social worker believed that professional applicants were not "unreasonable or neurotic in requesting a child whose intelligence is in the superior group and whose background does not read like a story of William Faulkner's." In fact, this social worker would be concerned if they did not request such a child. She went on to warn her colleagues, "Even if they assure [you] as they occasionally do that they would be quite contented with a potential truck driver, the chances of happiness of the latter in such a family would be very slight." Refusal to take adoptive parents at their word not only created a potentially antagonistic relationship but also ensured that social workers' understanding of the ideal "family" prevailed in professional placements.[35]

As the preceding paragraph implies, intellectual matching was not a policy wholeheartedly embraced by all prospective adoptive parents. Evidence drawn from letters to the U.S. Children's Bureau and even the professional literature of social workers suggests that although the majority of those interested in adoption worried about heredity, matching—especially intellectual matching—was much less of a concern. In 1922, a childless couple from North Carolina inquired about finding a child whose parents "would never seek it out" and who was from "good, honest parents for we yet believe in heredity." But even for this couple, uncomplicated custody trumped genetics: "We have often said we wished some one would leave an infant on our poarch at night with no clue as to whoes it was." In the early 1940s, one woman wrote to Eleanor Roosevelt asking for help in locating a child. She and her husband were "both blonde. I have blue eyes and he has brown. So a little tow head or red head could fit in real well." Yet even for this woman, to whom appearance apparently mattered, finding a child mattered more. Her letter continued, "But that part really doesn't matter. We just want a precious bundle to love & cherish & bring up to love God and its country."[36]

For a few people, even a child's mental and physical condition was of little concern. Frustrated by her inability to find a child through a reputable agency, and in response to a popular magazine article that warned of the dangers of privately arranged adoptions, a woman wrote to the Children's Bureau that, "as for the question of taking a risk on the health of a Black Market Baby what insures us that a child of our own would be normal?" And in 1945, one of the first professional voices to call for a rethinking of "adoptability" standards reminded her colleagues that "many [adoptive applicants] . . . are undemanding in specifying the kind of child they want. A familiar statement made by dozens of applicants is: 'We want just a normal healthy baby; his background isn't important to us; almost any descent is all right with us.' "[37]

Some adoptive parents, however, were concerned about a child's potential. Letters to the U.S. Children's Bureau and to a number of child-placing agencies provide examples of prospective parents who expressed fear about a child's heredity and IQ and appealed to the social work "expert" for verification of a child's promise. An examination of these letters suggests that prospective adopters who were members of the professional class were the most apprehensive. In 1929, for example, a woman from Connecticut whose husband worked in education wrote to the Children's Bureau requesting information on child-placing agencies. She and her husband were "both college graduates, in the early forties, Protestant and Anglo-Saxon and have a comfortable home," and she specifically requested information on organizations that believed "in testing a child's mental capacity" and had information on the child's parentage.[38]

Similarly, in 1934, a childless woman who had heard a Children's Bureau representative discuss adoption on a radio show wrote for information on finding a child. Although her husband's income was "not large," he was an attorney, and the couple lived "comfortably" in a neighborhood filled with "young professional people." Able to provide a child with "the things that are essential to a happy and useful life," including education and "culture," they "naturally" wanted a child "capable of assimilating these things." In addition, they did "not want a child who would compare unfavorably" with the "superior children" of their friends and neighbors. It is possible that these people, because of their educational background, were more aware of the latest scientific theories and so more concerned about a child's heredity. It is also likely that, as a result of their professional training, they placed more faith in the competency of experts and tests; a study of adoptions in Baltimore from 1938 to 1952, for example, showed that more professional families used licensed child-placing agencies than any other socioeconomic group. For professionals or anyone wary of a child's heredity, social workers' background checks, tests and examinations, and efforts to match the child to the home no doubt went far to alleviate worry and provide the confidence and security to adopt.[39]

In addition, men's voices, heard only occasionally in the records of adoption, appear with regard to issues of heredity and IQ. These men, most often well educated and professional, expressed concerns that seemed to be based on equal parts of masculine pride and professional fear. A physician in Maine who adopted a six-week-old daughter in the 1930s from a private maternity home staffed by untrained benevolent women expressed considerable concern about the child's heredity.[40] Before placement, the maternity home's matron had assured the couple that the child's background on the mother's side was "particularly desirable" but clearly stated that little was known about the child's paternity. After the couple had the child, the doctor began to press for information about the child's father. Although he acknowledged that it would cause the matron "a lot of trouble and annoyance," the doctor urged her "to have several chats with the mother and see if more cannot be extracted from her about [the father]."

The very next day, after speaking with a well-respected colleague, the doctor wrote to the matron again. This time, he encouraged her to try to convince the birth mother to divulge the name and whereabouts of the biological father. Once this information was known, the doctor intended to have a detective conduct an investigation "in a quiet fashion" into the man and his immediate relatives. This method, the doctor believed, would prove more reliable than taking the birth mother's word about the father's background.

The matron responded immediately. Although she was "deeply in sympathy" with the physician's desire to know more of the child's paternity, she expressed reservations about interrogating the birth mother too intently. She also wondered, using the professional language of the experts, how "scientific" it was to allow the child to stay with the family, given their reservations, especially since a family from Ohio was quite willing to take the child with no questions asked. The physician was in a bind. His wife had grown attached to the child and was unwilling to give her up. Nonetheless, he wanted and needed the security of knowing that the child's paternal background was satisfactory. He confessed to the matron that they would keep the child even if no information could be found. But he continued to urge her to question the birth mother, arguing that if the child's paternal history included insanity or feeblemindedness, no one should adopt the child. This, he assured her, should not be construed as criticism of her policies, but simply as scientific fact. The matron, apparently not wanting to disrupt the placement, spoke with the birth mother. It appears that rather than providing the adoptive parents with the name of the biological father, the matron conducted an investigation on her own. A few months later, she sent the doctor a two-page letter detailing the father's educational and occupational history and the occupational and medical history of his parents. There is no record of the physician's response to this information, but he and his wife did legally adopt the child after the mandatory waiting period.[41]

In the late 1940s, similar concerns about heredity beset another physician. This Philadelphian, who had a low sperm count, wondered how he could love a child "not my own." He also worried that one of the biological parents might be "retarded" and asked his wife, who had no qualms about adopting, "How can someone in my profession assume such a risk?" After a few years, he put aside his fears. The couple adopted a young girl whose unmarried mother was "of normal intelligence" and worked as a secretary. The child's biological father was an enlisted man in the navy. Most important for the doctor, the eight-month-old had tested above average and so was "appropriately placed with professional parents."[42]

Physicians were not the only professionals to worry about a child's background. In 1935, one man, apparently unaware that women headed and staffed the bureau, wrote to the "Gentlemen" of the Children's Bureau, requesting information on agencies "that keep a careful record of the children's health and that of their parents." This letter, typed, short, and to the point, continued, "I am in the engineering profession and employed by the government, and will require intelligent children as we plan to give them a college education."[43]

These stories suggest that husbands approached adoption much more cautiously, much more "rationally," than did their wives. Men's letters to the U.S. Children's Bureau requesting information about adoption also raise the possibility that men and women experienced the adoption process differently. Many women expressed their desire for children in a language of longing and with an emotional candor that implied their ability, worthiness, and readiness to be nurturing mothers. These emotions, however, are notably absent from the correspondence of men. These letters are straightforward, professional, and impersonal, often utilizing the language of the market. "Wife and I are well and married 14 years," one man wrote. "No children. But like to adopt one as we own our beautiful home. No debts. And we are Christian people, attend our church Regular. And our credit rating is 100% recorded." If an outpouring of intimacies regarding their infertility, loneliness, or desire for children often characterized women's letters, a résumé of accomplishments and possessions distinguished those by men. Breadwinning, as historian Robert Griswold has shown, was at the heart of fatherhood, and men's letters reflect this primary concern with economic competency; given that social workers investigated prospective fathers' earning potential, the men's concerns were not misplaced.[44]

A series of letters from 1921 in the Children's Bureau's records allows us to compare a husband's and a wife's representation of their interest in adoption. Concerned about heredity, Mr. Jones wrote to the American Social Hygiene Association (ASHA) for "advice as to the best method of selecting" a child. As Mr. Jones noted, he and his wife were able to provide a child with "the widest opportunities in its future life and growth" and so were interested in learning "of any characteristics discernible or subject to analysis, etc., which could give to us a proper and conscionable clue to the fortunate child we expect to select for adoption in to our home." His letter concluded, "We would be greatly pleased to receive any pamphlets or otherwise, you might condescend to forward—information, of course, laying great stress upon hereditary traits and their detection. We will forward any monies you might have to ask for compensating your labors. We expect to hear from you and let us thank you very much for any interest you decide to display toward our desires." Unfamiliar with adoption, the ASHA forwarded this letter to the Children's Bureau and asked for assistance. The Children's Bureau told the ASHA to have Mr. Jones contact it.

Mrs. Jones—not Mr. Jones—wrote to the Children's Bureau. Like her husband, she emphasized that they "want to be certain that the child is perfectly healthy both mentally and physically." She also stressed that they could care for a child financially, noting that Mr. Jones was an architect. Yet the similarities end there. Mrs. Jones told, in intimate detail, why they wished to adopt a child. "We are both very fond of children. I have been operated on and tried every way to have children of my own but with no success. . . . We are . . . two young people anxiously waiting to love and cherish [a child]." Her letter also concluded in a different manner, expressing her "hope" that they would hear soon from the Children's Bureau.

The tone of Mrs. Jones's letter suggests that she felt more helpless, more dependent on others, in fulfilling her dream for a child and less entitled to a response from the government or a professional organization than did her husband. In addition, Mrs. Jones appears to feel the need to justify her desire for a child, whereas her husband seems to believe that his ability to provide for a child is justification enough. And while Mr. Jones emphasizes how "fortunate" a child would be to have him for a father, Mrs. Jones, in her description of her reproductive failure and anxiousness to locate a child, suggests that she will gain as much as the child. Her letter, in its details of surgery and search for a cure, hints at vulnerability; his, with its promise of "opportunities" and expectation of a response, only confidence. These differences are telling. No doubt it was easier, given traditional gender roles, for Mrs. Jones to appear in need of help. Possibly her need was greater than his. Mr. Jones, regardless of whether they found a child, had a career and a sense of masculine competency. Mrs. Jones, however, given the gender expectations and limitations of the time, might have felt that she had failed as a woman without a child to mother.[45]

A Normal Home for a Normal Child

As social workers looked to develop a philosophy regarding adoption placement, they began to interrogate an applicant's "motives" for adopting. Social workers' focus on motives reflected the growing influence of psychoanalytic theory in the field of social work, which first began in the years after World War I. Psychiatric social work in the 1920s and 1930s remained largely in the realm of theory, especially outside the social work centers of the East Coast; by the 1940s, it had filtered down to the level of casework practice. In 1927, Charlotte Towle of the Children's Aid Society of Pennsylvania introduced the psychiatric perspective into the literature on adoption placement. According to Towle, the very nature of adoption signaled emotional maladjustment. Adopted children had experienced trauma and deprivation that made them insecure and emotionally unstable; meanwhile, the infertility or inadequacies of the adoptive parents suggested emotional problems of their own. As social workers slowly began to accept psychoanalytic principles in the 1930s, the basic premise on which placements had been made changed. Psychiatry focused on the interior self, rather than the exterior environment. No longer would caseworkers accept a home as suitable for adoption simply because it was "unblemished by dirt and distinguished by correct deportment." Now adoptive parents had to prove that they were psychologically fit. Undoubtedly, a careful examination of prospective parents' motives and emotional health increased the likelihood that a child would be safely and happily placed. However, social workers' critical evaluation of some motivations also led to a narrowing of the types of families created through adoption.[46]

In 1921, Sophie van Senden Theis's placement guide had urged social workers to go beyond a rote gathering of facts to a "keen, close, and unprejudiced observation" of an applicant. It was, she argued, "more important to know of a woman that she is easy going and indecisive than that she is a careless housekeeper. A child may grow up to be a satisfactory citizen in an untidy household," she continued, "but he has a poor chance of it if his foster mother changes her mind about what he must or must not do every day or so." Theis wanted adoption agents to unearth an applicant's "character," but she also expected them to take applicants largely at their word when they described their reasons for wanting to adopt. This trust would soon be broken.[47]

Psychological theory held that a caseworker needed to "really know why" a couple—especially the wife—wanted a child in order to ensure their fitness for parenthood. Underneath the applicant's stated motivation lay the true reason, which a skilled and "insightful" caseworker could ferret out; as one social worker noted, it is "important to know their expressed motive . . . and to understand their real motive." Dorothy Hutchinson's 1943 placement guide *In Quest of Foster Parents*, which soon become a classic in the field, emphasized these psychoanalytic principles. Hutchinson, a professor at Columbia University's School of Social Work and a child-placement agency supervisor, acknowledged that "the wish for a child is a healthy, normal, and universal desire of every woman." But, she cautioned, the desire also might be "neurotic and destructive." For every applicant who wanted to experience the "normal, genuine satisfactions of motherhood," there existed one who would adopt to "perpetuate [her own] early neurotic relationships . . . or . . . to realize their immoderate specifications for love." What had once been a "natural desire" was now a motive to be analyzed.[48]

Social workers scrutinized certain "motives" under a very bright light. Adoption stories recounted in earlier chapters include cases in which the death of a loved child moved a family to adopt—a reason that many people accepted as both normal and healthy. Psychiatric social workers disagreed. Grief and sorrow were "emotional problems" that made placement questionable. Social workers were concerned that families would adopt to replace the dead child and would demand that the adopted child be an identical replicate. Although a legitimate concern, it also put the "experts" in the position of control. They would decide whether the family had come to terms with their loss or whether their desire to adopt represented "an attempt to interrupt the mourning violently—a mistake that is usually followed by bad consequences." A professional social worker, not a family, would define the appropriate expression and determine the appropriate length of grieving. The subjectiveness of these decisions can be seen in a 1946 social work article that urged extreme caution in these situations. The author, after describing in detail the circumstances of the death of a couple's baby, concluded that this woman was ready to adopt because she "was able to talk about her difficult confinement and the loss of her baby, with some emotion to be sure, but one felt that it was by no means running away with her." Too many or too few tears could indefinitely postpone an applicant's approval.[49]

Couples over the age of forty, even if childless, also found their motives interrogated and their suitability harshly judged. Historically, adoptive parents averaged about ten years older than biological parents; adoptive parents were commonly in their thirties, forties, or even fifties when they took a child. Many were childless couples who came to adoption only after abandoning their hopes for biological children. For others, adoption signaled a second cycle of parenthood, a continuation of the joy and satisfaction they had experienced with their biological children. Beginning in the 1930s, social workers began to focus on placing children in the homes of younger couples, those in which there would be a "natural" age difference between parent and child. As with the policy of matching physical characteristics, a "natural" age difference served to make adoption invisible and the family appear "normal."

A social worker had real concerns to address when considering older applicants. Would their health enable them to care for a rambunctious youngster or raise the child to maturity? Yet for some social workers, physical health seemed less of a concern than the mental health of someone over forty. Older couples lived a "routine" and "well-ordered life" and possibly had a "rigid personality." Or, their longing for a child finally quenched, older couples might "cling" to a child and "limit its capacity for development by an oversolicitous, overprotective attitude." Social workers, however, did encourage this group to adopt older, less "adoptable" children. Individuals over forty who wrote to the U.S. Children's Bureau in the 1940s, for example, were repeatedly urged to consider older children. Although the bureau acknowledged to one woman "the enjoyment you probably would get from a baby," it urged that "now it might be wise for you to give some consideration to the possibility of taking an older child who would be nearer the age of an 'own' child you might have had." This policy helped social workers find good homes for hard-to-place children while still holding to their policy that there should be a "natural" age difference between parent and child.

By the 1950s, over-forty applicants were at such a disadvantage for adopting infants from a professional child welfare agency that popular books on adoption devoted a special chapter to their plight.[50]

Requests from those who already had one or more biological children also presented a problem for social workers. Parents often approached agencies about adopting a child as a companion for an only child. Social workers considered this a sound motive (after all, ideal families had more than one child), but they also had to determine that this was the real reason. A couple might desire another chance at parenting because they had failed their biological child or for some other unhealthy reason. Social workers also had to make sure that the parents would be able to love the children equally. And, given social workers' belief in the sanctity of blood ties, this was difficult to establish.[51]

Adoptive families, social workers determined, should parallel the "natural" family as closely as possible. In this regard, social workers viewed a childless couple's motive for adoption—the "normal" desire of a young couple for a family—as the most legitimate. As a result, by 1945, infertility became virtually the only readily acceptable reason for adopting a child. But by limiting adoption to infertile couples and perpetuating the belief that through adoption these couples could finally become "families," social workers further enthroned the nuclear, biological family as the ideal. This focus also meant that adoption was seen only in terms of its relation to the "normal" family of a husband and wife of childbearing age whose sexual union had produced one or more offspring, a comparison that necessarily made adoption seem second best and artificial.

Throughout the 1920s, 1930s, and 1940s, the demand for children greatly exceeded the supply of adoptable infants. And, without a doubt, social workers felt immense pressure to meet the desires of desperate, young childless couples. Given this, we could look at social workers' policy of placing children with young infertile couples and excluding older couples or those with "questionable motives" as simply a reasonable response to the shortage of children. Age, in particular, was used by some agencies as an "arbitrary" but seemingly "natural" way to eliminate applicants.[52] Nonetheless, their decision that the adoptive relationship should mirror that of biological parents and children worked to further constrict the culture's family norm. Excluding older couples and rarely placing a child with a family that had a biological child served to exalt the symbol of "blood" as the marker of true family and to privilege the nuclear family as the "best" family. Wholeheartedly and unreservedly accepting the principle that those with biological children should be allowed to adopt, for example, extends the bounds of family beyond ties of blood to include ties of care and affection. Likewise, accepting the legitimacy of an older couple's desire to adopt moves the joy of "family" beyond a mere instinct to reproduce and challenges a traditional understanding of the life cycle.

Social workers' vigorous efforts to separate good motives from bad denied the fact that in our culture a family's functions extend beyond nurturing children. According to one social worker, childless couples should be motivated "entirely by their wish to be parents, to share their love and to enjoy all the experiences of parenthood." This was the only legitimate motive for adoption. Anything else was a "selfish personal need" and so was unacceptable. Included in the category of selfish needs were reasons such as wanting "a son to carry on your business, or a child to 'perpetuate [your] name' and inherit your worldly possessions," or even wanting "support in old age." Yet these were the very concerns that had in large part prompted the creation of adoption laws in this country. They were also themes that pervaded the history of adoption not only in the United States but also in cultures worldwide. Social workers invalidated these motives in the name of concern for the child. In doing so, they presented a false picture of "the family" as a "natural" unit devoid of any cultural or temporal particularity or social function beyond providing for a child's biological need for care. This family portrait obscured the fact that in American society families historically have served as units that hold and transmit property, an important link in the maintenance of our class system.[53]

By the 1940s, social workers had decided that only a "genuine, wholehearted longing to have children" qualified a couple for adoptive parenthood. This determination romanticized the parent–child dynamic and hid the fact that most relationships between children and parents were ultimately not one-sided but entailed mutual obligation and assistance. A family's internal functioning went beyond natural urges to meet any number of concrete and common needs. Women seeking children before 1920 sometimes mentioned "for company" as their reason for requesting a child. These parent–child relationships appear to have been no different in commitment, outcome, or affection from those in which childlessness was given as the motivation (and in fact, some of those who gave this reason were childless and had chosen to represent the outcome of their childlessness, loneliness, as their motivation). Yet, by the 1940s, most social workers judged this motive, too, as selfish and insufficient. As Hutchinson noted, "children are not essentially companions for adults. True, they bring satisfaction, but not in the sense of providing a leisure time activity." In a real sense, however, a child was a companion. With women relegated to the private home and largely isolated from other adults, a child provided both company and a vocation.[54]

Neurosis and Infertility: Ensuring the Purity of Motives

Although social workers believed that infertile couples should receive priority and that their motive was the most pure, these applicants were not spared an examination under the psychiatric microscope. Beginning in the 1930s, the medical establishment published articles claiming that previously childless couples often conceived after adopting a child (this myth persisted well into the 1960s, despite numerous studies that showed no link between adoption and subsequent conception). These articles, which also received coverage in the popular press, maintained that psychological factors were responsible for a woman's infertility in up to 75 percent of all cases. A woman's inability to conceive could be caused by any number of psychic conflicts, from a deep-seated antagonism toward a husband to an "unconscious rejection of motherhood." According to the Freudian psychoanalyst Helene Deutsch (whose work was sometimes cited in professional articles), the "miracle" of pregnancy after adoption was based "upon the discharge of fear, of guilt feelings, and of the neurotic belief 'I cannot be a mother.'" Deutsch's analysis continued, "Maternal love for the adopted child" acted as a "healing agent," and the adopted child became "a heavenly messenger, an angel of peace . . . help[ing] a woman to motherhood."[55]

Deutsch might have believed that the supposed adoption cure was a miracle, but for social workers involved in child placing, an adoptive mother's possible neurosis was a potential calamity. Social workers wanted adoptive homes in which husband and wife, according to the marital ideals of the time, enjoyed a healthy sex life, supported their partner's dreams, and accepted their socially prescribed gender roles. A strong marriage, many home finders agreed, provided the most solid basis for a successful adoption, so they looked for couples who had a "mutually satisfying marriage." If, however, as a team of doctors concluded in a study published in 1941, sterile women "displayed unusual self centeredness in social and personal relations, clearly seen in a sexual frigidity, with abnormal reactions to coitus," they were obviously not ideal adoptive mothers.[56]

Hutchinson, in her guide on child placing, warned caseworkers about applicants for whom doctors had failed to identify a physical cause of infertility. In these cases, Hutchinson noted, "there is possibly a neurotic basis for childlessness." Hutchinson echoed the physicians and the psychiatrists as she informed her readers that a woman "may unwittingly feel that she has no right to [children] or feel too guilty to allow herself this very common privilege. She may fear birth itself, or she may be unable to give honor to the husband." Of more concern for those who placed children was Hutchinson's statement that such a woman also might be someone "whose love needs and requirements were so deprived and thwarted in childhood that she must continue to be mothered herself rather than to give mothering to someone else."[57]

If a woman could express a profound desire for a child yet conceal a "dread of childbirth . . . even a deep-down, unconscious dislike of children," a social worker had a difficult task indeed. As a result, social workers in the 1940s increasingly required a full medical examination of both husband and wife to determine whether there was an organic cause for their infertility. In cases in which no physical reason could be found, some social workers suggested "consultation with a psychoanalytically trained psychiatrist." Others believed that preference should be given to couples whose sterility could be "definitely established." One social worker took a couple's refusal to seek medical treatment for their infertility as a sign "of a deeply ambivalent attitude toward having a child, . . . in effect almost an unconscious wish to have the agency recognize the part of them that does not want a child and so perhaps refuse their application." A woman's infertility might be a sign that she rejected her feminine role. Given that proper gender-role socialization remained one of a family's primary functions, social workers also looked for evidence that a woman accepted her womanliness. The agent in one case noted that a prospective adoptive mother "sounds feminine and as though she enjoyed being so, considering her collection of recipes, her cooking, her interest in children, and her pleasure in family life."[58]

Infertile women were not the only women in this period to have their "maternal instincts" and their femininity called into question; the experience of adoptive mothers and unwed mothers was surprisingly similar during this time. As historians Rickie Solinger and Regina Kunzel have shown, beginning in the early 1940s, psychiatric social workers redefined white unwed mothers as neurotic and therefore unfit as parents. According to Kunzel, although social workers agreed that illegitimacy was a symptom of neurosis, they failed to reach consensus on the deeper pathology that prompted a woman to engage in premarital sex. Illegitimacy might represent anything from a woman's "self-punishment for forbidden sex fantasies" to an unhealthy dependence on her mother or a sexual attraction to her father; regardless, the experts maintained that illegitimacy had little to do with sex and much to do with psychological sickness. Social workers encouraged these "sick" unwed mothers to give their children up for adoption; in cases in which an unwed mother wished to keep her child, the encouragement could turn into coercion. These women's illegitimate infants quickly found adoptive homes among the many infertile couples clamoring for children.[59]

In the 1940s, therefore, some adoptive mothers became mothers through a process that denied unwed mothers the right to mother. Given this practice, the relationship between the "unfit" birth mother and the "fit" adoptive mother appears on its face antagonistic, oppositional, and exploitative (this relationship has become openly antagonistic in recent years, as adoptable infants have grown more scarce and distinctions between "fit" and "unfit" mothers more sharply drawn). But unwed and adoptive mothers also shared an identity as mothers outside the culture's ideal. Many, if not most, Americans considered their motherhood as less legitimate, less true, than the motherhood of a woman who had given birth or a woman who had conceived within marriage. This outsider status opened them up to expert scrutiny and evaluation. Ultimately, each required the unacknowledged assistance of the other to return to the path of ideal womanhood. Childless married women became mothers by adopting illegitimate children, unwed mothers gained a second chance at marriage and legitimate childbirth, and both forever carried the secret shame that they were not quite ideal women.[60]

Adoptive Parents Resist: "Good Enough" Parenthood

The families created through adoption with social workers using the previously described theories and practices (which, admittedly, existed more in theory than in practice) were "scientifically perfect." Caseworkers used the latest developments in the fields of psychology and psychiatry, medicine, and child welfare to ensure that children were physically and mentally sound, adoptive parents emotionally and materially stable, and the two, when united, perfect "matches" to create a "normal" as well as ideal family whole. Yet professionally assembled, scientifically perfect families were not the norm. Social welfare policies, by limiting both the number of adoptable children (by encouraging unwed mothers to keep their children and rigorously screening the children) and the number of acceptable adoptive parents, forced many to look outside professional agencies to privately arranged or even black-market adoptions.[61]

Rejected applicants, if they were determined to find children, had no choice but to turn to an agency that did not follow social work practice or to an individual such as a physician, attorney, or even birth mother. In addition to the applicants who could not use reputable agencies, many others chose not to use the services of the experts. Some, for example, were unwilling to endure the wait that accompanied application to a professional agency (the time between application and placement was usually well over a year, and often much longer) and looked elsewhere. Independently arranged adoptions also appealed to parents who, according to one commentator, objected to "the necessity of proving periodically to case workers that grandfather was not a horse thief and that only grapejuice is served in the house." Still others determined not to use professional agencies for ideological reasons. Social workers not only failed to gain control over adoption placement in terms of absolute numbers, they also failed to achieve cultural authority over the meaning and practice of adoption. As a 1941 article in the *Bulletin* of the Child Welfare League noted, there was a "wide gap between the case work and community points of view on the whole subject of adoption."[62]

The private nature of the family was one area in which opinions diverged. Social workers maintained that "adoption is not and should not be a private matter." Their extensive investigations into the backgrounds of both the children and the adoptive parents, their mandate that adoptions not be finalized until after a supervised probationary period of at least six months, and their use of the case record, filled with information and permanently stored at the agency, all underscored the public nature of professional adoptions. Some prospective adopters, however, disagreed that the creation of a family should be a public affair. These individuals continued to focus on the family as personal, the home as a private space. They did not want adoption to alter this understanding of family and so sought to keep outside intervention to a minimum.

In 1939, for example, a couple from Massachusetts approached a social welfare agency and, according to the social worker, "were very cooperative and understanding about the need for intake study; they were frank in discussing their family problems, and gave a list of five references." But although this couple understood the need for an investigation into their background, they "were loath to have the information given kept on file."

Discussing their private lives with an individual social worker was one thing; having a permanent record, "the story of their private affairs . . . in print," another. Although this couple preferred to use a social worker, they also maintained "that if their story must become a matter of record they would seek a child through other channels." In fact, they contended that the reason people turned to family doctors or private agencies was because of social workers' insistence on a *permanent* record. Social workers believed in the primacy of blood ties and kept such detailed records in case a child or birth parent someday returned and asked for information. Private agencies like the Cradle or individuals who occasionally placed a child, in stark contrast to the policies of professional social workers, did not keep detailed records. Their only goal was to find a new home for a child that would replace its biological family; to them, assembling and storing a detailed record of that process seemed superfluous to their aim of placing the child successfully.[63]

Setting aside questions of an adoptee's right to information about his or her biological family or the possibility that this couple's distress reflected their intention to hide the fact of their child's adoption, it is also possible to read this resistance as an assertion of their right to privacy. The social worker's notation that the couple objected because "they felt that in later years it might be embarrassing to their child if some friend working in the [agency] might come across their record" is ambiguous: were these people merely concerned about "secrecy," or did they have a legitimate concern that the extremely personal information regarding their income, marital relationship, and sterility or the circumstances of their child's birth and relinquishment was too intimate to risk disclosure to an outsider? This particular social worker believed that it was a valid question and wrote to the Children's Bureau for its opinion. The bureau's response was one of surprise; the staff member stated that this problem had "never occurred to [her] before" and noted that it "seems to me that it strikes at our whole philosophy of case records." No further advice was given. Yet this story shows how professional practices and some adoptive parents' preference for privacy conflicted.[64]

Independently arranged adoptions or those through private agencies in which an individual—not an expert who existed only "for the purpose of giving or withholding a child"—made an "intuitive" decision about an applicant's worthiness to become a parent also seemed more personal. As one physician noted, many prospective adopters "distrusted the professional approach because they thought it did not have the 'heart' and 'warmth' that goes with the personal approach." Anthropologist Judith Modell notes a similar perspective in her work on contemporary independent adoptions. Participants state that independent adoptions seem more "natural" and allow adoptive families to maintain their own understanding of kinship.[65]

In addition, private agencies purposefully intruded little into the private realm of the family. For example, Eleanor Gallagher, who worked at the Cradle in the 1920s and 1930s, repeatedly emphasized the importance of familial privacy in her book on adoption and believed that social workers' supervision exceeded what was necessary to ensure a child's safety. Gallagher believed that "from the moment the baby is taken into the [adoptive] home, one has no more right to enter that home, inspect, supervise, or criticize, than one has to enter the home of any other neighbor or relative. None of us wishes an outsider to inspect, supervise, give instructions, or even advice." For Gallagher, privacy was as much a matter of principle as of personal convenience. Although social workers could "scientifically" assure a family a child who "fit," for many adoptive parents, privacy, control, and autonomy were worth the potential risks of independent adoptions.[66]

A custody case in Nebraska in 1946 further highlights some of the differences between social workers' understanding of adoption and family and that of many Americans. The question in the case was whether a childless couple, John and Rose Yunick, fifty and fifty-four years of age, respectively, should be allowed to adopt the three Van Horn children, ages four, three, and two.[67] Mr. and Mrs. Van Horn (the children's court-appointed attorney later described them as "young, irresponsible and of poor character") had paid the Yunicks to board the children for six months in early 1945. A few months after the children had been returned to their parents, the Van Horns again asked the Yunicks to care for their children because they "made them nervous." At that point, Mrs. Yunick told Mrs. Van Horn "that she did not want to take the children again unless she could adopt them because it was too hard on her to have the children leave her." The Van Horns agreed and signed the adoption papers.

When the Yunicks petitioned the court to finalize the adoption, however, the judge denied their request. He determined that they had not met the state's requirement of a six-month trial period, since a number of months had elapsed since they had initially cared for the children. The judge appointed a guardian, Edson Smith, for the children, ordered the Yunicks to undergo physical examinations, and continued the adoption hearing for six months.

After investigating the Yunicks and consulting with child-placing professionals, Smith determined that it would be in the "best interests" of these "healthy, attractive, blonde, blue-eyed youngsters" whose IQ tests showed them to be "of average or higher than average intelligence" to be found "more satisfactory" adoptive parents. At the hearing, Smith alleged that the Yunicks were "not proper and suitable persons to adopt" for a number of reasons. For one, Smith believed that "their ages so greatly exceed the normal age of parents of children of the ages of the three children [that] it is highly improbable that they would be able to properly rear, counsel, and discipline such children with the necessary sympathy and firmness, especially when the children will be going through the critical adolescent period."

The health of the Yunicks was also an issue. Both had tested positive for syphilis, although the physician testified that the disease in its present stage was "not communicable" and that "there were 26 different ways in which the disease could be innocently contracted." In addition, Smith asserted that the Yunicks' financial condition was questionable, as they still had a large mortgage on their farm and other bills. And finally, he pointed out that the children were Methodist and Mr. Yunick Catholic. Smith's position was reinforced by the testimony of the executive secretary of the Child Welfare Association, an "expert" who argued that even though the children had been well cared for and were clearly attached to the Yunicks, it would be in their "best interest" to place them in another home. The Yunicks also took the stand to plead their case. The judge, however, agreed with Smith, and the Yunicks' adoption petition was denied.

The Yunicks, however, appealed the court's decision. And, improbably, the case was decided not by the judge of the juvenile court but by a jury. Smith had had an easy time convincing the judge to deny the Yunicks' petition, but he would find the jury less open to his arguments. The jury consisted of eleven women, three African American and eight white, and one African American man—probably not the typical jury of 1947. Testimony at the jury trial covered much the same terrain as the first hearing. They learned that Mrs. Yunick had a sixth-grade education and had been divorced. They heard about the Yunicks' health problems and debts and Mr. Yunick's lukewarm Catholicism. They listened to not one but three child welfare experts state that it would not be in the children's best interest to stay with the Yunicks. The experts, and Smith in his closing argument, noted that all reputable child-placing agencies would exclude the Yunicks because of their age, lack of financial security, questionable health, and lackluster religious commitment. Finally, Smith assured the jury that there were "large numbers of childless couples of appropriate age, health, financial security and religion" who would eagerly adopt this healthy, attractive, and intelligent trio. He concluded by noting that it was not unlikely that when the children were in their teens, they would be supporting the Yunicks, rather than the Yunicks supporting them.

But as Smith himself acknowledged in a letter to Dorothy Swisshelm, chief of Nebraska's Child Welfare Department, the "jury appears not to have been too greatly impressed with my arguments." Indeed, it took the jury only forty minutes to decide in favor of the Yunicks. The jury was not alone in its failure to be persuaded; the local newspaper also sided with the Yunicks throughout the case, repeatedly presenting Smith and the experts as cold, impersonal bureaucrats. Smith had a strong case—the Yunicks were clearly not the best possible parents by any objective standards—so why did the jury and the press embrace them? For the jury and the press, parents apparently did not need to be "the best": love and commitment were good enough. Child-placing professionals believed that it was their responsibility to place children with the best possible families, and since the number of applicants so far surpassed the number of available children, they had a surplus of families from which to choose. In the eyes of the social welfare professionals in Nebraska, the Yunicks were not "the best" family. "The trial by jury it seems to me," noted Swisshelm, "did away entirely with the intent of the adoption law, which is to decide whether 'such adoption is for the *best interests*' of the child." She continued, "Whether or not the Yunicks are unsuitable is only one phase of the problem. If the jury did not consider whether this is the best possible placement for *these particular children*, then the interests of the children are not being protected at all."[68]

Unlike the experts, the jury believed that the Yunicks were the best parents for the children. The evidence it found compelling consisted of the testimony of four respectable witnesses who believed that the Yunicks would be "fit and proper" parents and an exhortation on famous elder fathers with infants. The jury members heard this testimony. They also saw the Yunicks and the children together in court; as even Smith later admitted, it was "apparent that the Yunicks have been giving the children good food and clothing, and the children appear to be fond of her." Smith had argued that the Yunicks "undoubtedly have much love and affection for the children, but that is only a side issue in this case." The jurors disagreed. Apparently, for them, age, religion, and wealth were the side issues. What mattered was the Yunicks' commitment to the children (as evidenced by their willingness to fight for custody) and the reality of their existing relationship; by the time of the trial, the children had spent over a year and a half of their young lives with the couple. These concrete facts mattered more to the jury than the experts' abstract notion of "the best" and made the Yunicks, as one juror reportedly told Mrs. Yunick after the trial, "so deserving" to be the children's parents. The jury showed respect for the relationship between the Yunicks and the children. It also is possible that the decision reflected a belief that the children's biological parents—and not the state—had the right to make decisions about their children's care.

The public side of the Yunicks' story ended in late February 1947 when the local newspaper carried a brief story describing the celebration of the youngest child's birthday. Although the article was small, its message was larger. Homemade "frosted cakes" delighted the three children, but the child's present was but a trinket: the Yunicks had spent over a thousand dollars on the trial, and their young son received a present only because it "was payday." The jury's quick decision against the experts, the newspaper's obvious disgust with the trial and its expense, and the social welfare establishment's assertion that the whole affair was "a disgrace to the State" indicate just how far apart were the public's and social workers' views on adoption—and on "the family."[69]

Many prospective adopters scoffed at what they believed to be the overly high standards of social workers, especially with regard to the issue of heredity and a child's "adoptability." An article in the *Ladies' Home Journal*, for example, complained that the standards set for a child's adoptability were so high that if applied to the general public, "most of us should never have been born." This author knew of a case in which an overzealous social worker had compiled "a dossier on the baby as long as that of an international spy." The child had been declared unfit for adoption because of "insanity in the family," yet the crazy relative "turned out to be an uncle who was in an asylum as the result of being shell-shocked in the war!"[70]

And although social workers' IQ tests and thorough background checks reassured many prospective adopters, many others wanted a newborn and did not want to wait until a child had received the social workers' stamp of approval. Social workers, in fact, knew that their policy of observing a child for a number of months before placement discouraged adopters from seeking their assistance, but they paternalistically justified the delay in the name of protecting "oversanguine" adoptive parents. Thousands of illegitimate children were adopted each year without any "expert" evaluation and despite the popular belief that these children had an increased risk of feeblemindedness. These individuals put their trust in the word of whoever placed the child and their faith in the power of love and a good home. With regard to social workers' evaluation of applicants, many frustrated would-be parents of modest means actively challenged what they (inaccurately) believed to be social workers' determination that the best families were the wealthiest. Instead, they put forth a definition of the ideal that centered around commitment to family, personal responsibility, and hard work rather than riches; their definition of "best" was measured in values, not valuables.[71]

Experts scrutinizing applicants' psychological motivations also came under attack. Social workers during the 1920s, 1930s, and 1940s became increasingly familiar with psychoanalytic principles and methods. Yet it was not until after World War II that these concepts—repression, the Oedipus complex, and unconscious drives—filtered into the awareness of the average American. Many prospective adopters simply did not possess a psychological awareness that would have predisposed them to probe their "inner lives"—or their motivation to adopt. In 1944, one frustrated applicant fired off a three-page letter to the director of the Children's Bureau asking if she "knew how hard they make it for ordinary people to get a child?" She, like countless others, felt that money was an issue and believed that her family's inability to give the child a college education had landed her at the bottom of the waiting list. She also criticized the social worker's assertion that "it may not please our own son to have a strange child to come live with me." Social workers worried that parents would favor their biological child or that such applicants thought they had not "done well" with their biological child and wanted "another chance." These considerations appear not to have occurred to this woman. Instead, she was "mad" and "disgusted" that "it doesn't matter [to the social worker] that we love children and are young enough to still want them."[72]

Similarly, a Chicagoan in 1936 wrote to President Roosevelt urging him to encourage children's homes to "soften" their qualifications so more people could adopt. This man, like many others, believed that institutions kept qualifications "unnecessarily" high because housing dependent children was "a very profitable sort of racket for those in the 'know'!" Adoption, he believed, would "create happiness and a better desire to live for something worth living for besides ones selfish self, for everyone of normal intelligence *loves* children." For these would-be parents, there was no hidden "deeper need," just what they believed to be a natural desire. They spoke in the language of a "normal" love for children, not motives, and were puzzled when social workers did not immediately accept this as motivation enough. Furthermore, social workers' focus on motives marked adoptive parenthood as different from biological parenthood. As Eleanor Gallagher pointedly noted in her adoption guide, which criticized social workers' emphasis on uncovering hidden issues when interviewing applicants, "If a child had been born to them, I doubt very much if they would have discussed their motives for bringing the child into the world."[73]

In 1907, the *Delineator*'s "Child-Rescue Campaign" began the task of pairing up "the child that needs a home and the home that needs a child"—what seemed to be a simple and natural act of bringing together two halves to make a whole. By 1927, psychiatric social workers understood adoption as "the problem of selecting a home to fit the child and a child to fit the home," a process of such "intricate coordinations" that it required "the discriminative technique of science blended with the creative spirit of art." Something this "complicated," they believed, should not "be entrusted to sheer impulse or to unassisted common sense."[74]

Social workers had only partial success in their efforts to control adoption placements, restrict privately arranged adoptions, and make professional evaluation a mandatory part of the legal adoption process. Although by 1941 most states required an investigation by the state department of social welfare or an authorized representative prior to the finalization of all (including independent) adoption petitions, independently arranged adoptions continued in large number throughout the 1940s.[75] Professionals also failed to persuade much of the public that their way was the best way. In 1948, an editorial in the Child Welfare League's *Bulletin* noted that many people still did not recognize the value of "suiting the child to the home and the home to the child."[76] If anything, this was an understatement. The next year, a newspaper in Berkeley, California, condemned matching as a practice that kept "thousands and thousands of little ones . . . out of fine homes while bureaucracy hems and haws and primps and preens over a parentless child trying to match eyes, mental characteristics, even types of blood."[77]

As the demand for children continued in the immediate postwar years, social workers found themselves and their policies increasingly under attack. The postwar family mandate meant that even more couples craved a baby—and were willing to do anything to get one. Unregulated agency and privately arranged adoptions continued, as did a small black market where baby brokers sold infants for a hefty profit. If professionals wanted a say in adoption policy, they would have to address their bad press and become a bit more flexible. They did. The Child Welfare League held national conferences in 1948 and 1951, which led to some important changes in professional policy. Meanwhile, the number of adoptions grew by leaps and bounds. In 1937, child welfare officials estimated that approximately 17,000 adoptions occurred annually, of which at least half were nonrelative adoptions. In addition, applications from prospective adoptive parents were on the rise. By 1944, the Children's Bureau estimated that the number of adoptions had more than doubled; the number would double again over the next decade and continue to climb throughout the 1950s and 1960s.[78]

Although the shortage of children continued in this period, the increase in the actual number of adoptions can be explained by an increased availability of children as illegitimacy rates exploded and more and more unmarried mothers relinquished their children. As the number of adoptions rose, social workers ultimately gained more control. More pregnant, unmarried women turned to professionals as social workers abandoned their long-held belief that these women should keep their children. Also, as the number of adoptions dramatically escalated, more states passed regulations; by the late 1960s, less than a third of all adoptions of unrelated children were independently arranged.[79]

An important change in the postwar period came when professionals began to expand their definition of "adoptability." Social workers become more flexible in their placement of illegitimate children and eased their standards, no longer placing only "blue-ribbon" children. Finally, agencies would take applicants' word that they did not need a scientifically perfect baby. As the Child Welfare League's director noted in 1957, social workers have "come to see what the general public probably saw before they did—that having children naturally or through adoption involves risk. There are no guarantees in life and there is no reason for adoption to be an exception." He continued in a vein that echoed what many adoptive parents had been proclaiming all along: "we have recognized the strength, the courage, and the fiber of families in America to accept what comes and also to be really accepting of less than perfect children. In essence, we have recognized the power of love."[80]

Social workers at long last had abandoned the belief that "adoptive parents were doing a child a favor," so "it was only fair to guarantee them as good a child as could be found." Social workers had argued that this was the attitude of the majority of adoptive parents in the prewar period; in other words, their restrictive policies had been a response, at least in large part, to the demands and expectations of adoptive parents. However, the evidence is clear that many adoptive parents just wanted a child and were willing to assume a great deal of risk. Long before the social workers, adoptive parents believed that they gained through adoption every bit as much as the child.[81]

Professionals might have moved closer to adoptive parents with regard to a child's adoptability, but overall, they did not change other aspects of their policy that had the potential to create conflict with some applicants. In the postwar period, the adoption placement philosophy that social workers had developed over the last three decades became standard, with only a few modifications. The examination of applicants' motives and the belief that "they may or may not be consciously aware of their true motives" continued unchallenged.[82] And, in the conformity-focused, nuclear family–obsessed 1950s, infertility became even more entrenched as *the* most legitimate motivation, and adherence to traditional gender roles became even more significant.[83]

However, with regard to intellectual matching, important change did occur. By 1951, one placement worker acknowledged that it was "practically a truism that performance 'on a baby test' alone is no accurate indication of the level of intellectual development of an individual in the future."[84] This inescapable fact, coupled with adopters' demands for very young infants and the theories of psychiatrist John Bowlby, who emphasized the importance of early mother-infant bonding, led the more progressive agencies to embrace early placement and abandon IQ testing by the mid-1950s. Although scientific intellectual matching fell out of favor, the principle still held; in 1954, a Child Welfare League survey showed that of 254 agencies, 253 believed that it was important to match intellectual potential. In the absence of tests, professionals relied on the maxim that "it is more likely that a child of superior [biological] parents will be superior than will a child of dull parents." The same study showed that the matching of physical characteristics, religion, and cultural background also had widespread support. As the decade wore on, agencies began to incorporate a small degree of flexibility in matching, but it would not be until the 1960s that the concept was challenged directly.[85]

Professionals' efforts to create idealized families deserve one final note. The unwillingness of some social workers to take applicants at their word says something about their fears about the American family. Adoption supposedly represented a "natural" and universal desire for parenthood and the pleasures of family life, yet social workers saw a dark side. Their unceasing quest to uncover something hidden suggests that they believed there was something to find: women, secretly frustrated with their gender role; men, privately miserable in their workaday world. Adoption also supposedly represented human goodness—altruism, generosity, love—yet social workers saw that an individual's desire for a family could bring out the worst in a person. A "conservative solid citizen," for example, tired of waiting for a child, told a social worker "that it would be almost worthwhile to pay some girl to get herself illegitimately pregnant."[86]

He was not alone in the lengths he would go to get a baby. Turned down by adoption agencies because she was married to a man of a different religion, was thirty-five years old, and had been divorced, a woman from St. Joseph, Missouri, desperately approached the reproductive specialist John Rock, who had recently succeeded in fertilizing a human egg in vitro. Having failed to find a child through adoption, she wanted "to try the fertilized egg deal." Unfortunately for her, a baby would not be born through in vitro fertilization for almost twenty-five years. Nonetheless, these stories demonstrate that despite social workers' vigorous efforts to control adoption and the creation and definition of families, some people refused to accept social workers' understanding of family and looked for other ways to find children that did not involve the "experts." Their definition of "perfect" could test the boundaries of the law, science, and tradition. In the ensuing decades, adoptive parents would push these limits even further to create families previously unimaginable.[87]

Epilogue

In New York City in 1947, the anthropologist Margaret Mead spoke to a large group of child-placing professionals, adoptive parents, and philanthropists about adoption in other societies. Adoption was found around the world, she stated, wherever infertility, the death of a child, or the birth of a child of the wrong sex had spoiled the family picture envisioned by that culture. Mead also maintained that there was no reason to think that a baby one produced oneself was better than any other child. Dismantling cultural assumptions about family, she noted that Americans generally believed that children would (or should) look, think, and act like their parents, ultimately enjoying the things they enjoyed and marrying someone like themselves. Often, though, life did not turn out that way. Highlighting the socially constructed aspect of adoption, she suggested that experts could stylize the placement procedure so that parents could get children who lived up to their cultural expectations. In other words, adoption allowed parents to create families that had been denied them by nature and were closer to what they desired than nature had permitted.[1]

At the time Mead gave this speech, many of the families created through adoption did improve on nature, in that the practice of matching ensured that families at least began with children who looked like their new parents and had the intellectual potential to think like them. Yet if matching represented a conservative approach to family—simply constructing an idealized biological family—Mead's discussion also hinted at adoption's radical potential. If nature placed limits on individuals' ability to parent or to create the family of their dreams (not only infertile couples, but also older couples and celibate single women, for example), adoption could remove those limits. Of course, by 1947, older couples and single women, who had once used adoption to form the families that nature had denied them, had lost their access to children, at least from agencies staffed by social welfare professionals.

Even with the growing restrictions on adoption placements, the concept of adoption never lost its transformative power. During the 1940s, 1950s, and 1960s, when adoption's popularity soared, the practice's radical potential was largely hidden, with a few notable exceptions. Efforts to provide homes for Japanese children orphaned by the dropping of the atomic bombs led to a number of interracial adoptions in the United States. Similarly, the end of the Korean War in 1953 saw the beginning of a movement toward intercountry adoptions, especially of Asian children, the numbers of which would dramatically increase in the ensuing decades. In these families, conspicuous racial differences *visibly* challenged the genetic ideal of family. Moreover, these adoptions represented a definition of parenthood that emphasized the rewards of care. In many cases, prospective parents turned to transnational adoption after having been rejected by local agencies; their desire was simply to parent, not to parent a child who could have been born to them.[2]

In the mid-1960s, further changes in adoption practice, such as placing African American children with white families and hard-to-place children with single parents, resulted in the creation of even more families that represented an alternative to the biological norm. International and interracial adoptions moved families beyond the bonds of physical and cultural resemblances. Adoptions by single persons and, more recently, adoptions by gays and lesbians and "open adoptions," in which the birth parents and adoptive parents know each other, have reconfigured the roles of "mother" and "father" and further problematized the connection of these identities to sexual reproduction. Of course, advances in reproductive technology also have severed the link between sex and conception. These advances have contributed to Americans' increasing focus on the significance of genetic connections in creating immutable and profound family relationships. This emphasis has served to stigmatize adoption, with many Americans approaching adoption only as a better-than-nothing alternative after the old-fashioned way and modern technology have failed. Nevertheless, by focusing on care and conscious commitment, adoption represents an important counterpoint to ideals of family that center on and romanticize blood ties.[3]

Although many of today's adoptive families might look different from most of the families described throughout this work, in many ways, their experiences are strikingly similar. Adoptive parents continually struggle to create families that reflect their beliefs about the real meaning of "family." And adoption continues to function as a site on which the culture at large works out its understanding about "family," including the issues of who should be in a family, what roles family members should play, and what functions (both public and private) the family should fulfill.

Changes in placement practices that led to new family forms were not conscious efforts to expand the definition of family, but rather responses to the reality of supply and demand. Efforts in the 1950s and 1960s to recruit

African Americans as adoptive parents had some success but still fell short of meeting the needs of black children. As the shortage of white babies continued, agencies began to place black children with white families. By the early 1970s, estimates placed the total number of transracial adoptions that had occurred since the mid-1960s at around 15,000. A few proponents praised these adoptions as promoting "color blindness" (and some adoptive parents specifically cited their commitment to an integrated society as a primary motivation), but critics maintained that they were a form of cultural genocide. In 1972, the 5,000-member National Association of Black Social Workers (NABSW) issued a statement that unequivocally condemned the practice and rejected the "fallacious and fantasied reasoning" of those who believed that it could lessen racism. In the years after the NABSW's proclamation, the number of transracial adoptions dropped as agencies enforced (and some states required) same-race placements.[4]

The debate over transracial adoptions highlights cultural questions about both the ideal form and the primary function of families in our society. The controversy over transracial placements centers on retaining cultural heritage, not maintaining specific genetic ties. Critics focus on the function of the family, arguing that even if a white family takes pains to teach the child about black culture or learns how to care for black children's hair, this extra effort "puts *normal* family activities in the form of *special* family projects to accommodate the odd member of the family." They also believe that white families cannot teach black children the coping techniques necessary to survive in a racist society. In this case, the importance of function overrides form: a major criticism of agencies that made transracial placements in the late 1960s and early 1970s was that their allegiance to the superiority of the nuclear family caused them to view the placement of a black child with a white couple as superior to the placement of that child with an unmarried African American. From the perspective of the black child, critics maintained, this view was "erroneous."[5]

The controversy over transracial adoption has heated up again in recent years, and the issues remain the same. Prompted by the overwhelming number of African American children who wait in a "limbo of parentlessness" while social workers search for black families, white foster parents and politicians have taken steps to promote transracial adoptions. A number of white foster parents who had cared for black infants that were taken away when social workers found black placements brought antidiscrimination cases to federal courts. Interestingly, some advocates of transracial adoption also focus on the function of families, although from a different perspective. Law professor and adoptive mother Elizabeth Bartholet, for example, argues that these placements do not represent cultural loss as much as community gain. Adoption "creates a family that is *connected* to another family, the birth family, and often to different cultures and to different racial, ethnic, and national groups as well." Adoption, in her view, can lead to a unique acceptance of difference and a breakdown of the barriers that often exist between the private family and the larger community.[6]

In its discussion of the socializing function of the family and in the establishment of counterpoles of culture and care, today's debate over interracial placements in many ways relates to the issues surrounding adoption in the early years of the twentieth century. Then, magazines like the *Delineator* urged white, middle-class women to adopt homeless children to ensure that they would grow up with dominant, middle-class American values, which, in many instances, meant erasing any traces of the child's ethnic or class background. In this sense, African-American social workers are right to worry about how adoption shapes a child's identity. Many of the *Delineator*'s readers, however, had little concern for this "redemptive" aspect of adoption. Instead, adoption met their desire to provide care and a child's need to receive it. If, in the case of interracial adoptions, this focus on care is expanded to include a child's need to know of and celebrate his or her heritage, it would seem that interracial adoption does not have to lead to the loss of cultural tradition.

The profiles of adoptive parents and adopted children changed in other ways in the late 1960s. Faced with an overwhelming number of so-called hard-to-place children who were older; mentally, emotionally, or physically challenged; or nonwhite, agencies began to consider single applicants for these children as an alternative to extended foster care. In a society in which more children were being raised by single parents through divorce and in which unmarried mothers were deciding to keep their children, the idea of placements with singles seemed increasingly less radical. On the other side of the equation, changes brought by the women's movement of the 1960s and 1970s allowed women to envision lives and families without husbands. It also encouraged women to see themselves as capable breadwinners. Single (and later gay and lesbian) adoptive parenthood complicated the categories of family, mother, and father.

Contemporary accounts of single adoptive parenthood that discuss its history usually place its beginnings in the mid-1960s. In the span of only a few decades, the rich history of single adoptions discussed in chapter 4 had been lost. Adoption had come to be understood solely as the placing of an infant with an infertile couple. In 1966, the Los Angeles Department of Adoptions challenged this definition by placing forty special-needs children in single-parent homes. By 1973, single adoptive parents had started a national support group to inform and assist singles who wanted to adopt. By 1990, single women and men constituted about 25 percent of all adoptions of special-needs children and about 5 percent of all other adoptions.[7]

Agencies virtually always place a child with a single parent only when a two-parent home cannot be found. Many agencies unequivocally tell singles that they reserve young, healthy children for two-parent families. In other words, although agency-sponsored single-parent adoptions give sanction to an untraditional family form, the "better-than-nothing" attitude toward single parenthood also works to underscore the ideal of the two-parent norm. Some singles have criticized this policy, complaining that agencies treat them as the "dumping ground" for special-needs children. Even after a positive home study, singles often find themselves "back burnered" unless they are willing to take a child with disabilities. Singles who do not want to parent a special-needs child often sidestep public agencies by arranging independent or international adoptions.[8]

Single applicants choose adoptive parenthood and, like earlier generations of adoptive parents, argue that their conscious and assertive decisions and their perseverance in looking for a child give them a unique claim to parenthood. When dealing with agencies, they undergo an exhaustive screening process that weeds out all but the most determined. Single men face even greater scrutiny than women. Ironically, some agencies now praise single women for the same qualities social workers condemned them for beginning in the 1920s and 1930s. As one director of an agency specializing in special-needs placements noted, "Since the single parent has fewer distractions, he or she can perhaps spend a fair amount of time analyzing and responding to a child's needs and building a relationship." What was once regarded as "smothering" is now seen as "focused nurturing."[9]

Guides for singles considering adoption can be a startling amalgam of the old and the new, exposing the tenacity of gender-role stereotypes (or at least acknowledging the effectiveness of gender-role socialization) while encouraging gender blending. As one guide to single adoption reminded its mixed readership, "You are it, both mom and dad. . . . Dads you need to be 'good enough' moms. Show affection, you are the only person your child may get a hug from. . . . Try to remember the positive things your mom did and, if possible, do them." The advice continued, "Moms you need to be 'good enough' dads. . . . Your child needs security; they need to know that someone is in charge. That you are in control and can make the necessary decisions for their life. . . . They need to see that you can persevere and not lose your clear head." If, on the one hand, these admonitions treat gender differences as natural or inevitable, on the other hand, they at least allow for the possibility of conscious change. Single adoptive parents in some ways have conflated the categories of "mother" and "father" and received legal sanction to do so. Meanwhile, some gay and lesbian couples have used adoption to challenge the legality of the dominant American belief that families should be headed by one mother and/or one father, no more and no less.[10]

The right of gays and lesbians to be adoptive or foster parents is hotly contested, and only in a few areas of the country have agencies been willing to consider their applications; some states have even passed specific statutes prohibiting lesbian and gay adoptions. Of course, lesbians and gays can arrange independent adoptions directly with the biological parents, although before the adoption can be finalized, they need to undergo a home study or other type of review, according to the laws of their state. Some have adopted through agencies simply by presenting themselves as heterosexual singles. For gays and lesbians involved in long-term relationships, the parental status of their partners is also an area of contention, since adoption statutes require that unmarried persons adopt only as single individuals. In recent years, however, gays and lesbians have won some important legal cases challenging these statutes. The controversy over same-sex, second-parent adoptions obviously centers on American society's reluctance to accept homosexuality in general and gay and lesbian families in particular. However, the fact that some courts are now allowing these adoptions also shows how adoption both reflects and creates changes in the culture's understanding of what constitutes a legitimate family.[11]

Successful second-parent adoption cases have urged the courts to interpret adoption statutes liberally and to base their decisions on the child's best interests. In this regard, material as well as emotional benefits are considered, and courts have often cited such tangible gains as health insurance coverage, inheritance rights, and Social Security benefits in their favorable decisions. In many of these cases, petitioners have called on the language of choice and preparedness that adoptive parents have long used to claim status as "real" parents.

For example, in one recent case, a nonbiological mother successfully petitioned the court to adopt her partner's daughter, whose birth the two women had jointly planned. The expert witness argued that "the fact that this parent–child constellation came into being as a result of thoughtful planning and a strong desire on the part of these women to be parents to a child . . . stands in contrast to the caretaking environments of a vast number of children who are variously abused, neglected and otherwise deprived of security and happiness." The two mothers also argued that the best interests of the child demanded "legal recognition of her identical emotional relationship to both women." These cases show that adoption is on the cutting edge in redefining kinship terms—and in a public forum. While conservatives loudly proclaim that allowing homosexual marriage would threaten the American family, gay and lesbian adoptions, and especially second-parent adoptions, are already quietly—albeit slowly and against considerable odds—changing concepts of mother, father, and family.[12]

Other changes in adoption practice have redefined the categories of mother, father, and relatives. In "open adoption,"a term first introduced in the mid-1970s, birth parents (most often the birth mother) and adoptive parents know each other, in relationships that range from an initial exchange of nonidentifying information or letters and pictures to ongoing relationships in which the birth parent continues to have contact with the adopted child throughout its life. Although arrangements such as these existed throughout the history of adoption, in the 1970s, three social scientists involved with adoption developed theoretical underpinnings for these practices in response to the critique of closed records. In the early 1970s, some adult adoptees began to challenge the secrecy that increasingly characterized adoption after World War I. Members of the adoption reform movement called for an end to the practice of closed records and worked to gain access to records for adult adoptees. The movement also called attention to the fact that some adoptees struggle to reconcile the known and unknown parts of their identities.[13]

Open adoption also reflected profound changes in American society. In the conformist 1950s, white unwed mothers faced intense disapproval, and social workers encouraged them to give up their babies; estimates suggest that more than half of all white unwed mothers placed their children for adoption between 1952 and 1972. Within a decade, however, the percentage dropped to around 3 percent. Americans' growing acceptance of premarital sex and the growing number of children raised in single-parent households through divorce created a climate in which unmarried mothers could more easily raise their children. The legalization of abortion in 1973 also appears to have reduced the number of children available for adoption. These factors contributed to a dramatic and rapid decline in the number of unrelated adoptions, from an all-time high of over 89,000 in 1970 to approximately 50,000 in 1975.[14]

Together, the shortage of white infants, the diminishing stigma of illegitimacy, and the critique of secrecy have changed the nature of the relationship between birth and adoptive parents. Some unmarried mothers refused to consider adoption because they could not envision losing contact with their children forever. One young woman summed up her attitude toward adoption as follows: "You want me to leave my baby with strangers? I wouldn't leave my child for thirty minutes with a sitter who wouldn't tell me her last name. How could I leave my child for a lifetime with someone I don't know?" For these women, open adoption was a workable option. For that option to work, of course, adoptive parents had to be willing to welcome not only a child but also its biological mother into their family. Motivated by the shortage of white infants, which by the late 1970s was extremely acute, some intrepid individuals agreed to try the new arrangement. These first open adoptions usually were arranged independently; that is, an attorney or physician, not an agency, arranged for the transfer of the child. In 1971, independent adoptions accounted for only 21 percent of the total number of unrelated adoptions. Since then, the movement toward openness has resulted in an increase in the number of independent placements, which now account for perhaps half or more of all unrelated adoptions.[15]

By its very nature, adoption has always forced would-be parents to reflect hard on the implications and responsibilities of parenting an unrelated child. The movement toward openness has only increased the pressure brought to bear on adoptive parents. Prospective adopters no longer grapple only with the question of whether they can fully love a child not born to them. Now they must immediately consider the reality of the birth parent and determine what this means about the nature of adoptive parenthood and how it relates to their understanding of family. For some, this new dimension of concern has led to an expansive understanding of family and parenthood and a lessened sense of children as parental property. As one adoptive mother wrote to her child's birth mother, "Tho he is our child now, he will never stop being your child too."[16]

Openness has also diminished one of the fears that has plagued parents throughout the history of adoption in America: that a birth parent would try to reclaim the child. Opponents of openness have maintained that contact would increase the adoptive parents' uneasiness, but evidence from an early study found that those involved in fully disclosed adoptions had less fear than those in confidential adoptions. As one adoptive mother noted, "whenever there is something that you don't know, it seems worse than if you know. . . . When you're involved in openness you see every day that [reclaiming the child] is not the thought that is on [the birth mother's] mind." Openness also can contribute to adoptive parents' feeling of entitlement to the child. In an age that witnesses anguished custody battles and romanticizes blood ties, adoptive parents often feel, as one adoptive mother admitted, "that I had kidnapped a baby!" According to some adoptive parents involved in open relationships, this feeling often disappears because they know the birth mother has picked them to parent her child.[17]

Although virtually everyone agrees that the trend is toward greater openness, many passionately believe that adoptions should remain confidential. The main concern expressed by those who oppose open adoption (and one of the initial fears for those contemplating open adoption) centers on the belief that the child will not know who its "real" parents are, and adoptive parents will feel like nothing more than "glorified baby sitters." Proponents are quick to respond that open adoption is not shared parenting, thereby drawing a clear distinction between parenthood as a physical state of being and as the culmination of always being there. Birth parents, advocates maintain, are a child's relatives, not his or her parents. To make this point, guides on open adoption consistently contain "true stories" in which a child shows that it knows who its parents "really" are—even if adults might find the concept confusing.[18]

As this concern indicates, open adoption nips at the notion of family privacy and parental autonomy, in that there is a conscious acknowledgment that an "outsider" has a legitimate interest in the adopted child. Those involved in open adoption are literally opening the family circle to include new relatives (to a greater or lesser degree, depending on the level of openness) and recognizing a family tie with genetically unrelated individuals based on a shared interest in a child. As one adoptive couple explained it in a letter to their child's birth mother, even "though we have not met you we are united in a deep bond of love with you for this beautiful child." However, a letter from another couple to the woman who had given birth to their son subtly suggests the difficulty of finding a place for this new relation. "Thank you for giving him life—thank you for entrusting that life to us. We love him truly for himself, and we love you." While admitting a tie, even an obligation, to the birth mother, the letter also clearly delineates the limits of her parenthood. Moreover, although the letter acknowledges a connection, the structure of the last sentence also works to separate and minimize that link. The affection for both is there, but the love is qualified in important ways. The child is loved "for himself," an entity complete unto himself and separate from his origins. The birth mother is loved for what she has done—giving birth and making a responsible decision in regard to his upbringing—not for her continuing role as a parent.[19]

By sanctioning the creation of families across the boundaries of race and sexuality, adoption today achieves some of the radical potential that Margaret Mead envisioned by stretching or even shattering the conventional model of the two-parent, racially homogeneous, heterosexual, and heterosocial nuclear unit. But in other ways, adoption practices continue to underscore or to reinforce the customary understanding of family and of women's traditional role as family caregiver, even as men have taken a larger role in adoption. Men's increased involvement reflects changes in Americans' attitudes toward gender roles and the growing belief that men should share in both parenting and domestic responsibilities. As a result, men have become more involved in the process of both creating the adoptive family and raising their adopted children. Nevertheless, whether it be writing autobiographies, creating search and reunion networks, or lobbying for legislation that would open adoption records, the majority of those actively talking about adoption are women.[20]

In part, women's greater involvement can be explained by the fact that despite changes in men's participation in the home, women continue to perform the bulk of a family's (and society's) domestic and emotional work. However, the association of adoption and women also seems to be furthered by Americans' tendency to rely on an easy paradigm of adoption as the exchange of one mother for another, regardless of the circumstances of a particular adoption. On the biological side of the equation, this scenario works: birth mothers are more involved than genetic fathers. (Despite the fact that two of the most famous custody disputes between biological and adoptive parents, Baby Jessica and Baby Richard, turned on the fact that the biological fathers had not agreed to sever their legal rights, biological fathers contest very few adoptions.) Yet on the adoptive families' side of things, fathers often take an active role in locating a child. Despite this, in current popular discussions of adoption, fathers tend to recede into the background. A recent episode of the television news show *48 Hours,* for example, followed the story of a ten-year-old girl as she struggled to decide whether to stay with the family who wished to adopt her or return to the mother who had abandoned her four years earlier. Although the would-be adoptive family consisted of a husband, wife, and two sons, the show framed the dilemma as a battle between mothers. In the show promos, the adoptive mother proclaimed, "I just want to be her mommy and I want to do her hair," while the birth mother asserted that "I feel like she's trying to rob my daughter from me."[21]

A similar sentiment is expressed in a poem in a popular book on open adoption, which begins, "Once there were two women / Who never knew each other / One you do not remember / The other you call mother." It is clear that birth mothers are the structuring element in open adoptions. However, virtually all the adoptive families profiled in that book were infertile *couples* in which fathers took an active role. It is a paradox that although adoption can stretch our understanding of family, it can also work to sustain traditional gender roles that fuse women's identity with family creation.[22]

Advocates of open adoption often say that it is not new; that historically, adoptions have not been secret and have involved people who knew one another, from the colonist who "adopted" the English orphan who worked for him to the unwed mother whose family placed the child with a distant relative or a childless member of the community. Although this scenario certainly contains more than a grain of truth, it is misleading. Profound cultural changes, including the privatization of the family, the idealization of motherhood, and especially the sacralization of children, have rendered the comparison as useless as likening the kitchen duties of the contemporary family to the subsistence household of the eighteenth century.

These references to the past (and, in many ways, idealization of the past), if not entirely accurate, do reflect a nostalgia for the time when neighbors knew and cared for one another in times of trouble and families consisted of large networks of relatives. Many of those on the cutting edge of open adoption now speak of their relationships in terms of the extended family; birth parents take their place alongside aunts, uncles, cousins, and grandparents. In the best open adoptions, then, a child simply has more people who love him or her. These references to the past are also more than coincidental. Changes in adoption cannot be understood solely in terms of the concerns of those involved with adoption. These changes, such as the move toward openness, reflect the concerns of Americans, such as the belief held by many that individual families are isolated and self-concerned and cannot handle alone the difficult task of rearing citizens for the modern world. Only in a culture that has begun to rethink the relationship between families and their communities, and in which former first lady Hillary Rodham Clinton argued that it takes a village to raise a child, could openness succeed.[23]

Today, Americans live in a society in which, thanks to advances in reproductive technology, there are at least ten ways to create a baby. In this context, adoption seems like a rather quaint way to form a family. Nevertheless, as adoption has become more infrequent relative to the peak numbers of the late 1960s, its innovative potential has resurfaced. Some popular commentators, though, have read this innovation as a sign of weakness rather than strength. In 1994, an article on adoption in *Newsweek* warned its readers that "adoption as an institution has never been in such turmoil." The problem with this pronouncement, however, is that it assumes that adoption has a static and largely unproblematic past. In fact, as this study has shown, the history of adoption is rich with nuance, conflict, and change. Adoption as a legal institution and courtroom process developed at a specific historical moment because it responded to the needs of that moment, and it changed as American society changed. In a culture as deeply troubled by and divided over the meaning, function, and future of the family as America has been for virtually all of the twentieth century and remains today, adoption as an institution necessarily will be contradictory and conflicted.[24]

Appendix

Children in the Custody of the Pennsylvania Children's Aid Society, 1880–1920

The society's primary aim was to find foster, not adoptive, homes for its dependent wards. To focus on adoption, only the case histories of children aged five and under were examined. (A total of 480 children entered into CAS care during the periods examined. Of these, 191 [39 percent] were aged five and under; see Table 1.) There were a number of reasons for this decision. First, child-care workers in the nineteenth century knew that younger children generally found adoptive or permanent homes. In the early 1890s, for example, Boston's overseer of the city's young dependent children noted that it was rare for an adoptable child to reach the age of three without finding a home. Second, adoptive parents routinely and often vehemently maintained that the child should not know that it was not their biological child. Given this, children old enough to have conscious or vivid memories of their birth parents would not be wanted by prospective adopters; one woman who was considering adopting a three-year-old, for example, asked a child welfare expert, "At that age would a child completely forget the past and be like my own?" On the whole, the younger the child, the more desirable it was to those interested in adoption.[1]

Finally, focusing on young children minimizes the chance that a family took a child for its labor value rather than to be raised as the family's "own" child. Contemporary critics of placing out and adoption contended that a family would adopt a child to get cheap labor and to ensure that a social worker would not come to inspect. The CAS knew of possible abuses in the placing-out system and noted that "the happiest results [in placing out] are attained in the cases of very young children. About such children the family tenderness

Table 1. Entrance Dates and Number of Cases
Examined: Children Aged Five and Under

1882–April 21, 1890	115
January 1, 1895–December 31, 1895	59
January 1–May 31, 1900	17
Total	191

naturally gathers." Indeed, it was "a matter of constant surprise" to the society "to see how many excellent free homes are open to such little children, whose tender age makes impossible the thought of their rendering for years to come any adequate return in service to their caretakers."[2]

Of the 191 cases examined, 13 children were legally adopted (see Table 2). An additional 49 cases might be classified as "adoption-like" (see below), since an exclusive parent–child relationship existed. Often in these situations the child did not know that it was not the family's biological child. And always in these cases, the child's personal and public identity was as a member of the family. Seventy-seven children were either too sick to be placed in adoptive homes or ineligible for permanent placement because the society expected to return them to their biological parents sometime in the future. For example, of the 115 children who entered care from 1882 to April 21, 1890, only 16 were classified as temporary. In 1895, however, 34 of the 59 children who entered custody were there on a temporary basis. By 1900, the CAS served primarily as a stopping place for children whose parents were temporarily unable to care for them. In 15 cases, there was not enough evidence to classify the children. Thus, in only 37 cases did children who were available for adoption or an adoption-like home not find one.

Criteria for Adoption-like Classification

I made the adoption-like determinations by applying criteria that Bruce Bellingham, a sociological historian, developed to code and analyze the records of the New York CAS from the early 1850s.[3] After reading a number of the case histories of Pennsylvania's CAS, I adapted Bellingham's design to reflect the conditions of the late nineteenth century.

In determining whether a relationship was adoption-like, I made a qualitative interpretation based on the irregular, uneven, and often anecdotal information contained in the case histories. Each case was, of course, unique; within

Table 2. Classification of Children Aged Five and Under

Legally adopted	13
Adoption-like	49
Insufficient evidence to make a determination	15
Temporary care	62
Too ill to be placed or died before finding a permanent home	15
Were not adopted and did not find an "adoption-like" home	37
Total	191

the welter of idiosyncratic relations I encountered, no one circumstance emerged as the prime indicator of an adoption-like situation. I do not have a statistical breakdown of how often each of my criteria occurred. Nor was it necessary for a certain number of the criteria to be met before I classified a case as adoption-like. Instead, a variety of factors played into my subjective determination that a genuine and enduring familial bond had been established between the foster parent and the child. My primary purpose was not to determine the number of adoptions but rather to use these cases to explore the meaning of adoption at this time and the types of relationships that adults created with these children. The criteria were as follows.

Was "adoption" mentioned? The first problem encountered in using the case histories was trying to gain an understanding of the intentions and feelings of the foster parents through the words, interpretations, and values of the caseworker who kept the records. Consequently, it was critical to be vigilant for the smallest clue. Who, for example, brought up adoption—the CAS agent or the foster family? Although a caseworker's notation that a child was "treated as own" could provide a first clue, these descriptions were never taken at face value or used as a determining factor.

Was the home free or did CAS pay the foster parents board? CAS generally paid board to foster parents who cared for infants, and many of these situations developed into adoption-like situations. The age of the child when CAS payment stopped was considered to ensure that board did not stop when a child could work for his or her keep. Also, did the foster parents expend more money on the child's welfare than the child could realistically contribute to the family economy? In the early 1890s, the CAS routinely began to pay board to foster parents regardless of a child's age to ensure that the child would not be overworked and would have the opportunity to attend school. Given this philosophy, the significance of a free home increased at this time.[4]

How long had the child been in the foster home? Records generally indicate that a child went to a foster family at age five or younger and remained there until he or she reached the age of majority or could command wages in the community's economy. Some relationships that the CAS agent called "as their own" ended as soon as the child misbehaved or showed signs of illness. It had to be apparent that the foster family willingly weathered the trials and illnesses of childhood and adolescence. Evidence of contact with the foster family after adulthood was also considered.[5]

Was there contact with birth parents? Any contact with a natural parent before a child attained majority excluded a case from being classified as adoption-like. Cases in which a child approached the CAS about finding his or her birth parents after reaching adulthood were evaluated on a case-by-case basis.

Were the foster parents concerned with the child's future? One of the most important factors in classifying a case as adoption-like was whether a foster parent provided for the child's future. Did the foster parent provide the training, education, or financial resources or support necessary for the child to succeed as an independent adult?[6]

Did the foster parents have a sense of obligation to the foster child? This criterion speaks to the child's relationship to the rest of the foster family and the degree to which the child was incorporated into the family structure. For example, did a foster parent keep the child if his or her spouse died, if finances became strained, or if the family moved? Did a relative of the foster parents, such as a son or daughter, brother or sister, assume responsibility for the child in the event of the foster parents' death? Was the foster family's home a place where the child felt that he or she would always be taken in?[7]

Did the foster parents resent the CAS's supervisory visits? The CAS was well aware that a foster family's resentment of or displeasure over its visits could indicate a sign of abuse. Agents seemed quite conscious of the dangers suggested by a less than warm reception. Consequently, it seems that if the agent noted some resentment but did not remove the child and instead continued to give satisfactory reports, it could be an adoption-like situation. Because many young foster children did not know that their foster parents were not their natural parents, a foster parent might understandably fear and possibly resent the agent's visits.[8]

Was there community identification? How was the child known in the community? Did he or she take the name of the foster parents? Did the child think that he or she was the foster parents' natural child? Did members of the community, such as schoolteachers, think that the child was the birth child of the foster parents? In many cases, this criterion was inapplicable because the adoptive parents were not a married couple of childbearing age. Often the adoptive parents were older, with grown children of their own. In other cases, a single woman was the primary caregiver, or the family consisted of an assortment of relatives.[9]

Reasons for Nonadoption

There were a number of reasons that the thirty-seven children did not find adoptive homes, ranging from continued contact with biological family members to plain bad luck. Often the initial placement did not work out and by the time the CAS removed the child he or she was older and had lost "adoptability" status. Following are some specific examples.

History of Cases No. 4. The CAS placed this five-year-old boy with a family with whom he remained until the age of seventeen. However, adoption was never mentioned, and the case record reported problems between the child and the family. There is no evidence to suggest that the young man maintained contact with the family after he left.

History of Cases No. 143. The society placed this five-year-old girl with a family and noted that the girl did not know that she was not their child. At the age of twelve or so, the girl began to steal, and the family returned her to the society. The CAS boarded the girl with another family, but after six months, the first family requested her return. When the society refused to return the girl, the family contacted the boarding family and continued to contact them for the next two years, at which time the CAS's record ends. It is unclear from the record whether or to what degree the first family actually saw or interacted with the girl while she lived with the other family. However, the case history noted that the girl's husband approached the society upon learning that the first foster father had died, wondering if the girl would be entitled to any part of his estate.

Notes

Introduction

1. During the period of this study, "foster" often was used interchangeably with "adoptive."

2. Avis Carlson, "To Test a Baby," *Atlantic Monthly* 165 (June 1940): 829–32.

3. Not all social workers were convinced of the predictive value of the new developmental tests. The development of "matching" and social workers' thoughts on the reliability of the new tests are discussed further in chapter 5.

4. In 1917, Minnesota passed a law that required a social investigation into the adoptive home before the adoption petition could be approved. In the next two decades, similar laws were passed in other states (E. Wayne Carp, *Family Matters: Secrecy and Disclosure in the History of Adoption* [Cambridge, Mass.: Harvard University Press, 1998], 21, 44). On social workers and the development of "matching," see Brian Gill, "The Jurisprudence of Good Parenting: The Selection of Adoptive Parents, 1894–1964" (Ph.D. diss., University of California–Berkeley, 1997), chaps. 4, 5; on placement practices in the late nineteenth and early twentieth centuries, see Patricia Susan Hart, "A Home for Every Child, a Child for Every Home: Relinquishment and Adoption at Washington Children's Home Society, 1896–1915" (Ph.D. diss., Washington State University, 1997), chap. 4.

5. Rayna Rapp discusses the increasing politicization of the family in "Toward a Nuclear Freeze? The Gender Politics of Euro-American Kinship Analysis," in *Gender and Kinship: Essays toward a Unified Analysis,* ed. Jane Fishburne Collier and Sylvia Junko Yanagisako (Stanford, Calif.: Stanford University Press, 1987), 119–31.

6. The federal government only began to collect national statistics on adoption in 1951. In 1975, it stopped gathering this information. On the relationship between adoption and infertility for the period before 1951, see Jamil Zainaldin, "The Origins of Modern Legal Adoption: Child Exchange in Boston, 1851–1893" (Ph.D. diss., University of Chicago, 1976), chap. 5, esp. 152. One study that analyzed the adoptions of 2,414 illegitimate children in Minnesota from 1918 to 1928 showed that 89 percent of the adopters were childless married couples (Alice Leahy, "Some Characteristics of Adoptive Parents," *American Journal of Sociology* 38 [January 1933]: 548). A study of adoptions completed between 1931 and 1940 showed that approximately 85 percent of people adopted because of infertility (Benson Jaffee and David Fanshel, *How They Fared in Adoption: A Follow-up Study* [New York: Columbia University Press, 1970], 62–64).

7. Judith Modell, *Kinship with Strangers: Adoption and Interpretations of Kinship in American Culture* (Berkeley: University of California Press, 1994), 3.

Numerous historians have documented the "family crisis" panic of the late nineteenth and early twentieth centuries and the rise of the democratic or companionate family in the early twentieth century. See especially Margaret Marsh, *Suburban Lives* (New Brunswick, N.J.: Rutgers University Press, 1990); Robert Griswold, *Fatherhood in America: A History* (New York: Basic Books, 1993); Steven Mintz and Susan Kellogg, *Domestic Revolutions: A Social History of American Family Life* (New York: Free Press, 1988), chap. 6.

8. Josephine Baker, M.D., "Choosing a Child," *Ladies' Home Journal,* February 1924, 81; Elizabeth Frazer, "The Baby Market," *Saturday Evening Post* 202 (February 1, 1930): 25; Constance Rathbun, "The Adoptive Foster Parent," *Child Welfare League of America (CWLA) Bulletin* 23 (November 1944): 5.

9. "Store Gets Nine Babies Adopted," *Dry Goods Economist* 78 (May 24, 1924): 41; L. H. to Grace Abbott, April 28, 1931, Children's Bureau Records, Central Files 1929–1932, File 7-3-3-4, Box 406.

10. Margaret Emery to Hazel Morrison, July 16, 1948, CBR, Central Files 1945–1948, File 7-3-3-4, Box 157.

11. Sybil Foster, "Fees for Adoption Service," in *Proceedings of the National Conference of Social Work, 1947* (New York: Columbia University, 1948), 345–46. For a fuller discussion of the changing social and economic value of children, see Viviana Zelizer, *Pricing the Priceless Child* (New York: Basic Books, 1985), 15, 169–207.

12. "Child Study Association Extension Report, 1934–1937," as quoted in Julia Grant, *Raising Baby by the Book: The Education of American Mothers* (New Haven, Conn: Yale University Press, 1998), 162.

13. Mary Frances Smith, "Adoption as the Community Sees It," *Journal of Social Work Process* 3 (December 1939): 6–8.

14. Mr. C. B. to Children Bureau, ca. January 24, 1935, CBR, Central Files 1933–1936, File 7-3-3-4, Box 548.

15. G. S. to My dear first lady, February 21, 1943, CBR, Central Files 1941–1944, File 7-3-3-4-1, Box 171.

16. Although my aim is to document the experience of adoptive parents, at no point do I offer a statistical analysis of adoption practices, nor do I seek to quantify the types of adoptive parents (their age, marital status, economic level, and so forth). Rather, I explore their experiences in the hope of expanding our understanding of the various meanings of family during the period under consideration.

17. There is an immense body of scholarship on the nineteenth-century conflation of woman with mother and the romanticization of motherhood during that period. See, for example, Barbara Welter, "The Cult of True Womanhood: 1820–1860," *American Quarterly* 18 (summer 1966): 151–74; Ruth Bloch, "American Feminine Ideals in Transition: The Rise of the Moral Mother, 1785–1815," *Feminist Studies* 4 (June 1978): 101–26; Kathryn Kish Sklar, *Catharine Beecher: A Study*

in American Domesticity (New Haven, Conn.: Yale University Press, 1973); Mary Ryan, *Cradle of the Middle Class: The Family in Oneida County, New York, 1790–1865* (New York: Cambridge University Press, 1981); Carl Degler, *At Odds: Women and the Family in America from the Revolution to the Present* (New York: Oxford University Press, 1980).

On women and infertility, see Margaret Marsh and Wanda Ronner, *The Empty Cradle: Infertility in America from Colonial Times to the Present* (Baltimore: Johns Hopkins University Press, 1996), 4–5, 154; Elaine Tyler May, *Barren in the Promised Land: Childless Americans and the Pursuit of Happiness* (New York: Basic Books, 1995), 4, 11. On the courts and the development of the maternal standard, see Modell, *Kinship with Strangers*, 28–32, and Michael Grossberg, *Governing the Hearth: Law and the Family in Nineteenth-Century America* (Chapel Hill: University of North Carolina Press, 1985), 284.

18. Agnes Sligh Turnbull, "The Great Adventure of Adopting a Baby," *American Magazine*, May 1929, 180; "Adopted Mother by Herself," *Scribner's Magazine*, January 1935, 59; Dorothy Hutchinson, *In Quest of Foster Parents, a Point of View on Homefinding* (New York: Published for the New York School of Social Work by Columbia University Press, 1943), 2, 8; Barbara Melosh, "Adoption Autobiography and the Construction of Identity," paper presented at annual convention of the Organization of American Historians, Atlanta, April 1994; Betsy Smith, Janet Surrey, and Mary Watkins, "'Real' Mothers: Adoptive Mothers Resisting Marginalization and Re-creating Motherhood," in *Mothering against the Odds: Diverse Voices of Contemporary Mothers*, ed. Cynthia Garcia Coll et al. (New York: Guilford Press, 1998), 194.

Other scholars also have noted the centrality of women in adoption; see Hart, "A Home for Every Child," 176; Katarina Wegar, *Adoption, Identity, and Kinship: The Debate over Sealed Birth Records* (New Haven, Conn.: Yale University Press, 1997), 55, 91–92.

19. Marsh and Ronner, *The Empty Cradle*, and May, *Barren in the Promised Land*, discuss the cultural stigma of childlessness. For the history of childbirth, see Judith Walzer Leavitt, *Brought to Bed: Childbearing in America, 1750–1950* (New York: Oxford University Press, 1986).

20. Herbert Gutman, *The Black Family in Slavery and Freedom, 1750–1925* (New York: Vintage Books, 1976), 221–29; Peter Holloran, *Boston's Wayward Children: Social Services for Homeless Children, 1830–1930* (Cranbury, N.J.: Associated University Presses, 1989), 144–48, 280 n. 26. According to Holloran, informal adoption of black children was very common in 1930s Boston.

21. The children's records of the Board of Children's Guardians begin in 1893. However, the records are incomplete (no records exist for a number of years) and stop completely in 1913. In Board of Children's Guardians adoptions, it appears that the adoptions were by persons unrelated to the children. Zainaldin found in his study of adoption in Boston in the last half of the nineteenth century that African

Americans adopted at roughly the same rate as whites relative to their proportion of the total population; however, the adoptions Zainaldin found were by relatives (Zainaldin, "Origins of Modern Legal Adoption," 120; May, *Barren in the Promised Land*, 75).

22. Mrs. H. B. C. to Mrs. Roosevelt, December 14, 1943, CBR,Central Files 1941–1944, File 7-3-3-4-1, Box 171.

23. Andrew Billingsley and Jeanne M. Giovannoni, *Children of the Storm* (New York: Harcourt Brace Jovanovich, 1972), 45–47, 66–68, chaps. 6, 7; Rickie Solinger, *Wake up Little Susie: Single Pregnancy and Race before* Roe v. Wade (New York: Routledge, 1992), 195–99; "Why Negroes Don't Adopt Children," *Ebony* 7 (July 1952): 31. Solinger notes that social workers' restrictive policies meant limited choices for African American women who wished to place their infants for adoption. Often agencies would not accept black infants because they said they could not find homes for the children. The majority of African American unwed mothers in the postwar period wanted to keep their children. Nevertheless, knowing that their children would likely remain in institutions or foster homes for extended periods made adoption an even more difficult decision.

24. Linda Gordon, *The Great Arizona Orphan Abduction* (Cambridge, Mass: Harvard University Press, 1999).

25. Rollin Lynde Hartt to Miss Sumner, May 10, 1915, CBR, Central Files 1914–1920, File 7-3-4-6, Box 60; Last Name H ———— , First Name A ———— , Sheltering Arms Collection, Group I, Series I, Children's Files (1928).

26. Susan Tiffen, *In Whose Best Interest? Child Welfare Reform in the Progressive Era* (Westport, Conn.: Greenwood Press, 1982); Michael Katz, *In the Shadow of the Poorhouse: A Social History of Welfare in America* (New York: Basic Books, 1986); LeRoy Ashby, *Saving the Waifs: Reformers and Dependent Children, 1890–1917* (Philadelphia, Temple University Press, 1984).

27. Peter Romanofsky, "The Early History of Adoption Practices, 1870–1930" (Ph.D. diss., University of Missouri–Columbia, 1969); Carp, *Family Matters*. Articles and books on institutions that sometimes placed children are too numerous to mention. The following have the most relevance to adoption specifically: Paula Pfeffer, "Homeless Children, Childless Homes," *Chicago History* (spring 1987): 51–65; Peter Romanofsky, "Professionals versus Volunteers: A Case Study of Adoption Workers in the 1920s," *Journal of Voluntary Action Research* 2 (April 1973): 95–101; Jamil Zainaldin and Peter Tyor, "Asylum and Society: An Approach to Institutional Change," *Journal of Social History* 13 (fall 1979): 23–48. For the history of adoption laws, see Grossberg, *Governing the Hearth*, and Jamil Zainaldin, "The Emergence of a Modern American Family Law: Child Custody, Adoption, and the Courts, 1796–1851," *Northwestern University Law Review* 73 (1979): 1038–89. In addition to histories of adoption written by historians, there is a vast literature on adoption, much of which contains historical summary, written by social workers.

28. Kathy S. Stolley, "Statistics on Adoption in the United States," *Future of Chil-*

dren 3 (spring 1993): 30–31; Helen Witmer et al., *Independent Adoptions* (New York: Russell Sage Foundation, 1963), 93–95.

29. Witmer, *Independent Adoptions,* 92–93.

30. Carp has documented the shift toward confidentiality in *Family Matters* and is one of the few historians to have access to adoption case records for the period after 1920.

31. Henry Morgenthau, "Cradles Instead of Divorces," *Literary Digest* 77 (April 14, 1923): 35. In 1907, Morgenthau was a founder and first president of the Free Synagogue in New York City, created to provide a forum for the reform-minded rabbi Stephen Wise. In 1916, Wise's wife, Louise, established one of the first private adoption agencies in the country (Robert Heilbroner, "Henry Morgenthau," *Dictionary of American Biography,* Supplement 4, 1946–1950, ed. John Garraty and Edward James [New York: Charles Scribner's Sons, 1974], 602–4).

32. Elizabeth Harral to Miss Mary Ruth Colby, July 15, 1942, CBR, Central Files 1941–1944, File 7-3-3-4, Box 170; on the Children's Bureau recommending popular magazine articles, see Mary Milburn to Mr. M. M., June 9, 1930, CBR, Central Files 1929–1932, File 7-3-3-4, Box 406.

33. For an example of the Children's Bureau's monitoring of the press, see Katharine Lenroot to Pearl Buck, August 20, 1946, CBR, Central Files 1945–1948, File 7-3-3-4, Box 158. Winifred Smith, "The Use of Popular Literature as a Medium for the Interpretation of Professional Standards of Adoption" (Master's thesis, Smith College School for Social Work, 1940), 1–2, 59.

34. Unrelated adoptions grew from 33,800 in 1951 to a peak of 89,200 in 1970, rapidly falling from that peak in the early 1970s. Since the mid-1970s, unrelated adoptions have remained relatively constant at about 50,000 per year. By 1950, the number of independent and agency (public and private) adoptions were roughly equal. In the period after 1955, the number of agency adoptions rose dramatically (William Pierce, *1989 Adoption Factbook* [Washington, D.C.: National Committee for Adoption, 1989], 69–70, 99–100; Melosh, "Adoption Autobiography").

1. Fear, Fulfillment, and Defining "Family"

As is customary when using case records that contain information of an extremely personal nature, names of individuals have been changed to preserve their anonymity.

1. Letter to WCOA, January 31, 1913, Cont. 3, File 255, Records of the Hillcrest Children's Center, Manuscript Division, Library of Congress (hereafter Hillcrest Collection, LC); emphasis in original.

2. The institution was originally called the Washington Female Orphan Asylum, but an act of Congress on May 24, 1828, changed the name to the Washington City Orphan Asylum.

3. Walter Trattner, *From Poor Law to Welfare State* (New York: Free Press, 1974), 52–55; Minutes of the Board of Lady Managers, 21, Cont. 45, Hillcrest Collection, LC. A study of the WCOA intake records from January 1887 through December 1893 shows that of the 221 children admitted, only 8 (4 percent) were full orphans (Partial Records of Admissions, 1881–97, Item 214, Cont. 36, Hillcrest Collection, LC).

4. Annual Report, 1865, 1, Cont. 35, Hillcrest Collection, LC.

5. Susan Tiffen, *In Whose Best Interest?* (Westport, Conn.: Greenwood Press, 1982), chap. 4.

6. Margaret Marsh and Wanda Ronner, *The Empty Cradle* (Baltimore: Johns Hopkins University Press, 1996), 17–20; John Demos, *A Little Commonwealth: Family Life in Plymouth Colony* (New York: Oxford University Press, 1970), 71–75; Yasuhide Kawashima, "Adoption in Early America," *Journal of Family Law* 20 (1981–1982): 677–96.

7. Michael Grossberg, *Governing the Hearth* (Chapel Hill: University of North Carolina Press, 1985), 268–70; Edward A. Hoyt, "Adoption and the Law in Vermont, 1804–1863: An Introductory Essay," *Vermont History* 64 (summer 1996): 159–73.

8. Grossberg, *Governing the Hearth*, 271–73; "An Act to Provide for the Adoption of Children," *Massachusetts Acts and Resolves, 1851* (Boston, 1851), reprinted in Robert Bremner, ed., *Children and Youth in America: A Documentary History*, vol. 1 (Cambridge, Mass.: Harvard University Press, 1970), 369–70.

9. The literature on the transformation of the family is extensive. See, for example, Grossberg, *Governing the Hearth*, 4–12; John D'Emilio and Estelle Freedman, *Intimate Matters: A History of Sexuality in America* (New York: Harper and Row, 1988), chap. 3; Mary Beth Norton, *Liberty's Daughters: The Revolutionary Experiences of American Women, 1750–1800* (Boston: Little, Brown, 1980); Linda Kerber, *Women of the Republic: Intellect and Ideology in Revolutionary America* (Chapel Hill: University of North Carolina Press, 1980); Nancy Cott, *The Bonds of Womanhood: "Woman's Sphere" in New England, 1780–1835* (New Haven, Conn.: Yale University Press, 1977); Demos, *A Little Commonwealth*; Mary Ryan, *Cradle of the Middle Class* (New York: Cambridge University Press, 1981); Steven Mintz and Susan Kellogg, *Domestic Revolutions* (New York: Free Press, 1988).

10. Grossberg, *Governing the Hearth*, chap. 7; Judith Modell, *Kinship with Strangers* (Berkeley: University of California Press, 1994), 29–33; Jamil Zainaldin, "The Emergence of a Modern American Family Law: Child Custody, Adoption, and the Courts, 1796–1851," *Northwestern University Law Review* 73 (1979); 1038–89.

11. Grossberg, *Governing the Hearth*, 257–59; Zainaldin, "Emergence of Modern American Family Law," 1081; Jamil Zainaldin, "The Origins of Modern Legal Adoption: Child Exchange in Boston, 1851–1893," (Ph.D. diss., University of Chicago, 1976), 102–6; Modell, *Kinship with Strangers*, 28.

12. Zainaldin, "Emergence of Modern American Family Law," 1042–43.

13. *An Act to Authorize the Adoption of Children in the District of Columbia,*

U.S. Statutes at Large 28 (1895); "Indentures for binding-out children, 1851–54," Cont. 3, File 250, Hillcrest Collection, LC.

14. For new policy, see Annual Report, 1882, 8, Cont. 35; for an example of rejection, see Minutes, March 1901, 547, Cont. 45, Hillcrest Collection, LC.

15. Cont. 38, Hillcrest Collection, LC. Orphanages and placing-out organizations nationwide responded to the call to keep families together. Hastings Hart, a well-known reformer, noted in 1910 that the majority of institutions across the country had become temporary care facilities (*Preventive Treatment of Neglected and Dependent Children* [1910; reprint, New York: Arno Press, 1971] 70).

16. Statistics are for the period 1893 to 1906, based on a random sample of 130 BCG wards from a total of 3,042. Records of the District of Columbia, Board of Children's Guardians, Record of Children Received, Item 152, Record Group (RG) 351, National Archives (hereafter NA).

17. Roy Lubove, *The Professional Altruist: The Emergence of Social Work as a Career, 1880–1930* (New York: Atheneum, 1972); House, *Care of Delinquent and Dependent Children in the District of Columbia*, 58th Cong. 2d sess., 1903–1904, H. Doc. 355.

18. These figures are rough estimates compiled from BCG annual reports and H. Doc. 355, 4.

19. *Thirteenth Annual Report of the Board of Children's Guardians for the Year 1906* (Washington, D.C.: GPO, 1907), 24.

20. Hastings Hart, *Child Welfare in the District of Columbia* (New York: Russell Sage Foundation, 1924), 60.

21. Hart, *Preventive Treatment*, 223–24.

22. *Fourteenth Annual Report of the Board of Children's Guardians for the Year 1907* (Washington, D.C.: GPO, 1908); in 1907, 651 wards were in homes in Washington, 244 in Virginia, and 102 in Maryland. Superintendent of Charities, *Report on Charitable and Reformatory Institutions of the District of Columbia* (Washington, D.C.: GPO, 1899), 209. Beginning in 1907, the annual reports of the Board of Children's Guardians give a racial breakdown of the wards on trial for adoption. A sample of fifteen adoptions of black or mulatto children shows their median age at the time of placement in an adoptive home to be slightly over two years. A sample of eleven white adoptions shows their median age to be about three and a half years at the time of placement.

23. Charles Rosenberg, "The Bitter Fruit: Heredity, Disease, and Social Thought in Nineteenth-Century America," *Perspectives in American History* 8 (1974): 189–235; William H. Whitmore, *The Law of Adoption* (1876), as quoted in Grossberg, *Governing the Hearth*, 272–73.

24. Henry H. Goddard, *The Kallikak Family: A Study in the Heredity of Feeble-mindedness* (New York: Macmillan, 1912); Henry H. Goddard, "Wanted: A Child to Adopt," *Survey* 27 (October 14, 1911): 1003–6; "Communications," *Survey* 27 (November 11, 1911): 1187.

25. Paul Boyer, *Urban Masses and Moral Order in America, 1820–1920* (Cambridge, Mass.: Harvard University Press, 1978), chap. 15.

26. Children's History, 1564, 1696, 1658, Item 153, RG 351, NA.

27. *Proceedings of the National Conference of Charities and Correction, 1899* (Boston: George H. Ellis, 1900), 169.

28. Children's History, 1064, RG 351, NA.

29. "Child-Rescue Campaign," *Delineator,* November 1907, 715. In the three months after the *Delineator* offered the BCG children, the BCG received at least thirteen inquiries about adopting in response to the campaign. The records do not indicate how many of these requests resulted in adoptions. See, for example, Letters Sent by the Agent of the Board, January 28, March 3, 1908, Item 150, RG 351, NA.

30. "Child-Rescue Campaign," *Delineator,* January 1908, 98; Children's History, 1743, RG 351, NA; "Child-Rescue Campaign," *Delineator,* April 1908, 607–8.

31. Letter to WCOA, April 9, 1901, Cont. 4, File 296, Hillcrest Collection, LC.

32. Regina Kunzel, *Fallen Women, Problem Girls: Unmarried Mothers and the Professionalization of Social Work, 1890–1945* (New Haven, Conn.: Yale University Press, 1993), chap. 1; E. Wayne Carp, "Professional Social Workers, Adoption, and the Problem of Illegitimacy, 1915–1945," *Journal of Policy History* 6 (1994): 161–83; Hart, *Preventive Treatment,* 73–74; Peter Romanofsky, "The Early History of Adoption Practices, 1870–1930" (Ph.D. diss., University of Missouri–Columbia, 1969), 84–90; LeRoy Ashby, *Endangered Children: Dependency, Neglect, and Abuse in American History* (New York: Twayne, 1997), 89.

33. Romanofsky, "Early History of Adoption," 92–93; Carp, "Professional Social Workers," 167–68; Tiffen, *In Whose Best Interest?* 170.

34. Viviana Zelizer, *Pricing the Priceless Child* (New York: Basic Books, 1985), 173–77, 196–98. The "milk" quote is from New York Society for the Prevention of Cruelty to Children, *15th Annual Report* (1890), 31, as quoted in ibid., 176. Charlotte Abbey, "Women in Social Service," *Transactions of the Alumni Association of the Women's Medical College of Pennsylvania* (1909): 122.

35. Martin Wolins and Irving Piliavin, *Institution or Foster Family? A Century of Debate* (New York: Child Welfare League of America, 1964), 14.

36. Zainaldin, "Origins of Modern Legal Adoption," 324, 332–44.

37. Senate, *Joint Select Committee to Investigate the Charities and Reformatory Institutions in the District of Columbia,* July 21, 1897, 55th Cong., 1st sess., doc. 185 (Washington, D.C.: GPO, 1897), 123, 134–37; "Sheltering Arms—A Noble Institution's Great Work for Friendless Women," *Philadelphia Times,* July 24, 1893.

38. The twenty-two adoptions came from Children's History, vol. 4, BCG, RG 351, NA. The racial breakdown of illegitimate infants was seven African American (two foundlings), three mulatto, and two white foundlings. "Child-Rescue Campaign," *Delineator,* April 1908, 608; Children's History, vol. 5, no. 2130, BCG, Item 153, RG 351, NA.

The records of the Children's Aid Society (CAS) of Pennsylvania also indicate that legitimacy was not a primary concern for the majority of adopters. Of nineteen legal adoptions of CAS wards, at least eight of the children were illegitimate. In the 200-plus case histories I examined, only one family expressed concern regarding the legitimacy of a foster child. This family, although acknowledging that the child was "a fine looking boy," decided that they could not keep him permanently because he was a foundling. Soon after his removal from this home, the boy was legally adopted by another family. See History of Cases, no. 2153, Records of the Children's Aid Society of Pennsylvania, Historical Society of Pennsylvania, Philadelphia (hereafter CAS/HSP).

Joan Jacobs Brumberg, in her study of a maternity home in upstate New York, also found that when unwed mothers gave up their children, the infants easily found adoptive homes (" 'Ruined' Girls: Changing Community Responses to Illegitimacy in Upstate New York, 1890–1920," *Journal of Social History* 18 [winter 1984]: 247–72).

39. Agent Letters, 1895, 56, RG 351, NA; Arno Dosch Fleurot, "Not Enough Babies to Go Around," *Cosmopolitan*, September 1910, 431; Zelizer, *Pricing the Priceless Child*, 195–200.

40. ——— to WCOA, March 1908, Cont. 3, File 263, Hillcrest Collection, LC; Children's History, 1039, RG 351, NA.

41. LeRoy Ashby, *Saving the Waifs* (Philadelphia: Temple University Press, 1984), 232–33 n. 92. A random sample of 130 BCG wards showed only 7 percent to be full orphans.

42. *Thirteenth Annual Report of the Board of Children's Guardians, 1906* (Washington, D.C.: GPO, 1907), 6.

43. Children's History, 91, RG 351, NA.

44. Agent Letter, March 11, 1895, RG 351, NA.

45. Agent Letter, March 19, 1895, RG 351, NA.

46. Board of Children's Guardians, Minutes, December 18, 1918, January 19, 1919, RG 351, NA.

47. "Was It Well or Ill Chosen?" *Harper's Weekly*, March 15, 1902, 325.

48. Michael Katz, *In the Shadow of the Poorhouse* (New York: Basic Books, 1986), chap. 5, esp. 124–30; Romanofsky, "Early History of Adoption," chap. 4.

49. Relinquishment of Children, 1876–1922, Cont. 38, Hillcrest Collection, LC; Minutes, February 1899, 496, April 1878, 9–10, August 1882, 153, Cont. 45, Hillcrest Collection, LC; Annual Report, 1877, 6, Hillcrest Collection, LC.

50. Minutes, June 1901, 555; December 1901, 566; January 1902, 570, Cont. 45, Hillcrest Collection, LC.

51. Agreement, Cont. 43, File 260, Hillcrest Collection, LC.

52. See, for example, Letter to WCOA, March 1908, Cont. 3, File 263; Minutes, 1908, 69, Cont. 45, Hillcrest Collection, LC.

53. Minutes, February 1889, 286–87, Hillcrest Collection, LC; Treasurer to Mrs. Sue Bradley, February 5, 1921, Cont. 3, File 255, Hillcrest Collection, LC.

54. Agent Letter, February 1, 1908, RG 351, NA.

55. Agent Letter, January 28, 1908, RG 351, NA.

56. Of the 500 children who entered BCG custody between October 26, 1903, and January 25, 1906, 21 were ultimately adopted. The legal adoption did not necessarily occur between October 1903 and January 1906. Rather, those dates are simply the period in which the children entered BCG Custody. Children's History, vol. 4, RG 351, NA.

57. Children's History, 1923, RG 351, NA.

58. Children's History, 1680, RG 351, NA.

59. Based on the adoptions listed in the Adoptions Register, 1877–1915 (which is incomplete), Cont. 43, Item 260, Hillcrest Collection, LC. After adoptions by relatives were removed (when known), the register shows the adoptions of seventy girls and thirty-three boys.

60. Letters to WCOA, October 11, 1899, November 14, 1899, Cont. 3, File 255; Minutes, November 1899, 511, Cont. 45, Hillcrest Collection, LC.

61. See, for example, Letter to WCOA, May 13, 1913, Cont. 3, File 255, Hillcrest Collection, LC.

62. Minutes, August 1888, 278, Cont. 45, Hillcrest Collection, LC.

63. Letter to WCOA, April 9, 1901, Cont. 4, File 296, Hillcrest Collection, LC.

64. Burton Bledstein, *The Culture of Professionalism* (New York: W. W. Norton, 1976), 98–99, 190, 282; Robert Wiebe, *The Search for Order 1877–1920* (New York: Hill and Wang, 1967), 116; Sophie van Senden Theis, *How Foster Children Turn Out* (New York: State Charities Aid Association, 1924), 127. For evidence suggesting that the confusion about adoption laws expressed by the Widmans was not uncommon, see Patricia Susan Hart, "A Home for Every Child, a Child for Every Home: Relinquishment and Adoption at Washington Children's Home Society, 1896–1915" (Ph.D. diss., Washington State University, 1997), 218; Marilyn Irvin Holt, *The Orphan Trains: Placing Out in America* (Lincoln: University of Nebraska Press, 1992), 141–42; History of Cases, no. 289, CAS/HSP.

65. Letter to WCOA, April 30, 1901, Cont. 4, File 296, Hillcrest Collection, LC.

66. *First Annual Report of the Children's Aid Society of Pennsylvania* (1882), 7.

67. Ashby, *Endangered Children*, chap. 3; Mary Ann Mason, *From Father's Property to Children's Rights* (New York: Columbia University Press, 1994), 79.

68. Priscilla Ferguson Clement, "Families and Foster Care: Philadelphia in the Late Nineteenth Century," in *Growing Up in America*, ed. N. Ray Hiner and Joseph Hawes (Chicago: University of Illinois Press, 1985), 139; Homer Folks, *The Care of Destitute, Neglected, and Delinquent Children* (New York: Arno Press Reprints, 1971), 49–50. Folks was at the CAS from August 1890 to January 1893, when he left for a position at the New York State Charities Aid Association (Walter Trattner, *Homer Folks: Pioneer in Social Welfare* [New York: Columbia University Press, 1968]).

69. *Twelfth Annual Report of the Children's Aid Society of Pennsylvania*, 1893, 11–13. For a discussion of standards for adoptive parents in the late nineteenth and early twentieth centuries, see Brian Gill, "The Jurisprudence of Good Parenting: The

Selection of Adoptive Parents, 1894–1964" (Ph.D. diss., University of California–Berkeley, 1997), chap. 3.

70. Zainaldin, "Emergence of Modern American Family Law," 1043–45 nn. 13, 14; Lawrence Friedman, *A History of American Law,* 2d ed. (New York: Simon and Schuster, 1985), 211–12.

71. History of Cases, no. 158, CAS/HSP. For other cases in which foster families expressed concern over the cost of adoption, see History of Cases, nos. 2307 and 1071.

72. History of Cases, no. 184, CAS/HSP; Hart, "A Home for Every Child," 218.

73. History of Cases, no. 35, CAS/HSP.

74. History of Cases, no. 3, CAS/HSP.

75. Stephanie Coontz, *The Way We Never Were: American Families and the Nostalgia Trap* (New York: Basic Books, 1992), chap. 6; Jane Collier et al., "Is There a Family? New Anthropological Views," in *Rethinking the Family: Some Feminist Questions,* ed. Barrie Thorne (New York: Longman, 1982), 34.

76. History of Cases, no. 10, CAS/HSP.

77. The CAS attorney drew up the act in 1886, and the state legislature passed it the next year (*Fourth Annual Report of the Children's Aid Society of Pennsylvania* [1886], 20).

78. Clement, "Families and Foster Care," 139, 144; Mrs. J. H. Evans, "Child Placing by Volunteers," in *Proceedings of the National Conference of Charities and Correction, 1910* (Fort Wayne, Ind.: Archer, 1910), 132.

79. *Sixth Annual Report of the Children's Aid Society of Pennsylvania* (1887), 7. The CAS of Pennsylvania was not the only organization to forgo any legal documentation when it placed a child. The CAS of New York also placed its children without an indenture (Holt, *The Orphan Trains,* 62), as did Boston's Temporary Home for the Destitute, an organization that was more specifically concerned with adoption placement (Zainaldin, "Origins of Modern Legal Adoption," 326). Boston's Temporary Home for the Destitute, in language almost identical to that used later by the CAS of Pennsylvania, noted in 1860, "We have found that the freer the *formal bond* that connects the guardian and child, the stronger the intertwining of the growth of affections, which after all are the only ties favorable to the best conditions of both parties."

80. History of Cases, no. 161, CAS/HSP.

81. Grossberg, *Governing the Hearth,* 272; History of Cases, no. 61; History of Cases, nos. 179 and 220, CAS/HSP.

82. See, for example, History of Cases, nos. 204, 980, 1035, and 1052, CAS/HSP; David Dudley Field, New York (State) Commissioners of the Code, *The Civil Code of the State of New York: Reported Complete* 36 (1865), as cited in Zainaldin, "Emergence of Modern American Family Law," 1044.

83. E. Wayne Carp, *Family Matters* (Cambridge, Mass.: Harvard University Press, 1998), 87–97, 124; Ada Patterson, "Giving Babies Away," *Cosmopolitan,* August 1905, 408.

84. Clement, "Families and Foster Care," 141–42.
85. Carp, *Family Matters*, 40–44, chaps. 3, 4; History of Cases, no. 237, CAS/HSP.
86. Agent Letter, April 4, 1900, RG 351, NA.
87. Agent Letter, April 10, 1900, RG 351, NA.
88. Ashby, *Endangered Children*, 90.

2. Rescue a Child and Save the Nation

1. Wilder told this story about the inspiration behind the "Child-Rescue Campaign" in a newspaper interview in 1909 (*Delineator* Scrapbook, Box 421, Papers of Theodore Dreiser, Special Collections, Van Pelt–Dietrich Library, University of Pennsylvania [hereafter Dreiser Papers]). It is difficult to determine the exact number of children who found adoptive homes as a direct result of the *Delineator*'s campaign. The magazine claimed a direct link between the campaign and the adoption of at least 2,000 children; however, it is possible that the campaign inspired even more people to adopt (Folder 6585 Dreiser Papers).

The *Delineator* began in 1873 as a ladies' fashion magazine promoting Butterick dress patterns. By 1907, it had expanded to include articles on homemaking and occasionally featured stories on social issues. By 1912, the mail circulation had almost reached the million mark (Frank L. Mott, *A History of American Magazines, 1865–1885*, vol. 3 [Cambridge, Mass.: Harvard University Press, 1938], 481–90.

2. Peter Romanofsky, "The Early History of Adoption Practices, 1870–1930" (Ph.D. diss., University of Missouri–Columbia, 1969); Harold A. Jambor, "Theodore Dreiser, the *Delineator* Magazine, and Dependent Children: A Background Note on the Calling of the 1909 White House Conference," *Social Service Review* 32 (1958): 33–40; Elvena Bage Tillman, "The Rights of Childhood: The National Child Welfare Movement, 1890–1919" (Ph.D. diss., University of Wisconsin, 1968); LeRoy Ashby, *Saving the Waifs* (Philadelphia: Temple University Press, 1984), 53–55.

3. Viviana Zelizer, *Pricing the Priceless Child* (New York: Basic Books, 1985), 169–207; Michael Grossberg, *Governing the Hearth* (Chapel Hill: University of North Carolina Press, 1985), 268–85; Jamil Zainaldin, "The Origins of Modern Legal Adoption: Child Exchange in Boston, 1851–1893" (Ph.D. diss., University of Chicago, 1976).

4. Mabel Potter Daggett, "The Child without a Home," *Delineator*, October 1907, 505–10; Lydia Kingsmill Commander, "The Home without a Child," *Delineator*, November 1907, 720–23, 830.

5. *Delineator*, November 1907, 715. The honorary committee included, among others, Mrs. Ellen M. Henrotin, honorary president of the General Federation of Women's Clubs; Mrs. Robert M. LaFollette, wife of the governor of Wisconsin; Miss Mary McDowell, head worker of the University of Chicago Settlement; and Mrs. Florence Pullman Lowden, founder of the Florence Ward of St. Luke's Hospital in Chicago. The *Delineator* never specifically indicated what this committee actually did.

6. *Delineator*, March 1908, 337, 425.

7. Mabel Potter Daggett, "Where 100,000 Children Wait," *Delineator*, November 1908, 860; January 1910, 54, 68. Other examples of lead articles include W. B. Sherrard, "Does It Pay?" July 1908, 115–116; Mabel P. Daggett, "A Father to Forty," December 1910, 464, 530–32; Charles R. Henderson, "Home-Finding: An Idea that Grew," April 1908, 609–11; and Lucy Huffaker, "Waifs Who Have Become Famous," June 1908, 1005–6.

8. *Delineator*, January 1908, 100–3; it is unclear which letters came spontaneously and which Dreiser solicited.

9. *Charities and the Commons* 19 (February 22, 1908): 1612–13.

10. Scrapbook, "Printing News," New York, December 1907, Box 421, Dreiser Papers. Still others, such as sociologist Robert Hunter, refused to write for the *Delineator* because of the magazine's antilabor practices. Ben Lindsay, the well-known juvenile court judge of Denver, also noted the need to protect the children's parents in his letter that supported the campaign (*Delineator*, January 1908, 101).

11. Mary Ellen Waller, "Popular Women's Magazines, 1890–1917" (Ph.D. diss., Columbia University, 1987), 47–48; *Delineator* Correspondence, December 24, 1910, Folder 1465, Dreiser Papers; *Delineator*, February 1908, 253–54.

12. Charles Hanson Towne, *Adventures in Editing* (New York: n.p., 1926), 123–25. Towne had been an editor at both the *Delineator* and *Designer* magazine.

13. See, for example, Julia Ward Howe, "The Joys of Motherhood," *Delineator*, May 1908, 806, and "What My Children Mean to Me," *Delineator*, September 1909, 212. Interestingly, Boston society had criticized Howe as a poor mother and housekeeper (Paul Boyer, "Julia Ward Howe," in *Notable American Women, 1607–1950*, ed. Edward T. James [Cambridge, Mass.: Belknap Press, 1971], 226).

Ellen Hoekstra notes that women's magazine fiction of this time presents mother's love as superior to marital love ("The Pedestal Myth Reinforced: Women's Magazine Fiction, 1900–1920," in *New Dimensions in Popular Culture*, ed. Russell Nye [Bowling Green, Ohio: Bowling Green University Popular Press, 1972], 43–58).

14. *Delineator*, August 1908, 263; *Delineator*, August 1909, 134.

15. Howe, "Joys of Motherhood"; Helen Christine Bennett, "The Gift of Life," *Delineator*, August 1908, 260–63; *Delineator*, March 1908, 424.

16. *Delineator*, March 1908, 425; *Delineator*, December 1909, 566; Bennett, "The Gift of Life," 263; *Delineator*, February 1909, 249.

17. Mark Haller, *Eugenics* (New Brunswick, N.J.: Rutgers University Press, 1963), 170–71; Henry H. Goddard, "Wanted: A Child to Adopt," *Survey* 27 (October 14, 1911): 1004.

18. *Delineator*, August 1909, 134; *Delineator*, November 1907, 719; *Delineator*, July 1908, 113; Jacob Riis, "God's Children, Give Them a Chance: A Comparison of the Influence of Heredity and Environment," *Delineator*, May 1908, 809; Lucy Huffaker, "Waifs Who Have Become Famous," *Delineator*, June 1908, 1005.

19. Elaine Tyler May, *Barren in the Promised Land* (New York: Basic Books, 1995),

62–63, 72. The term "race suicide" was actually coined by sociologist E. A. Ross, but Roosevelt popularized the term in a 1903 speech. Margaret Marsh and Wanda Ronner, *The Empty Cradle* (Baltimore: Johns Hopkins University Press, 1996), 113.

20. *Delineator*, November 1907, 719; Jambor, "Theodore Dreiser," 35 n. 9.

21. *Delineator*, October 1908, 576, 578; May 1909, 696.

22. George Wilder to Dreiser, ca. October 1908, Folder 882, Dreiser Papers.

23. For fears of ethnic difference, see, for example, *Delineator*, April 1908, 611. For the movement to "Americanize" immigrants during the Progressive Era, see John Higham, *Strangers in the Land: Patterns of American Nativism, 1860–1925* (New Brunswick, N.J.: Rutgers University Press, 1955).

24. James West correspondence, April 27, 1918, Folder 6585, Dreiser Papers. John had been abandoned by his birth parents at the age of eleven months. He was four years old when the *Delineator* profiled him in the January 1908 issue. He was adopted by a couple whose only son had died. His adoptive mother's ancestors had arrived on the *Mayflower*. John was a BCG ward. Details of his background appeared in chapter 1, where he was referred to as "James."

25. Scholars of language have noted that every narrative, even one claiming to be nonfiction, is constructed, because reality does not "present itself to perception in the form of well-made stories, with central subjects, proper beginnings, middles and ends" (Hayden White, "The Value of Narrativity in the Representation of Reality," in *On Narrative*, ed. W. J. T. Mitchell [Chicago: University of Chicago Press, 1981], 23).

The power of the *Delineator*'s narrative formula can best be seen when contrasted with a typical example of a dispassionate, theoretically objective case record of the time. The following example appears in Michael Katz, *In the Shadow of the Poorhouse* (New York: Basic Books, 1986), 126: "Mr. G., who was a driver, died of stomach trouble in 1908, leaving no insurance and but small savings. For six months before his death the family had been aided by the C.O.S. and the widow turned immediately to that Society for help and advice. Her father and mother were living with her, both being at that time without employment. . . , [Mrs. G.] secured work in a factory. Her father also secured work. . . . Nine months later, when the father lost his position and Mrs. G.'s work was very slack, she decided to commit the children to an institution." Following is part of a profile that appeared in the *Delineator*, September 1908, 444: "Five-year-old Ted has known in his baby life what sorrow and trouble mean. . . . Once Ted remembers, he had a father and mother. Then his father went away. The neighbors called it a harsh word—'deserted.' Ted does not know what this means. . . . After a time there was very little to eat and sometimes nothing at all. Then one day he . . . took a journey—there was a hurried kiss—he remembers his mother cried."

26. Diana Reep, *The Rescue and Romance: Popular Novels before World War I* (Bowling Green, Ohio: Bowling Green State University Press, 1982).

27. Julie Berebitsky, "'To Raise as Your Own': The Growth of Legal Adoption in Washington," *Washington History* 6 (spring/summer 1994): 4–26.

28. *Delineator*, November 1907, 718; Rev. Simeon R. Reno, "The First Child-Rescue Mission," *Delineator*, February 1909, 252.

29. *Delineator*, January 1908, 98; Board of Children's Guardians (BCG), Children's History, 2130, Records of the District of Columbia, RG 351, NA; BCG Agent Letters, 1908, 10, RG 351, NA; *Delineator*, April 1908, 608.

30. Robert H. Elias, *Theodore Dreiser, Apostle of Nature* (New York: Knopf, 1949), 29–30; Jambor, "Theodore Dreiser," 34.

31. See, for example, *Delineator*, March 1908, 486–87, and December 1908, 996; Roland Marchand, *Advertising the American Dream: Making Way for Modernity, 1920–1940* (Berkeley: University of California Press, 1985).

32. *Delineator*, June 1908, 1003, and January 1909, 133. The "Child-Rescue Campaign" coincided with the period sociologist Viviana Zelizer (*Pricing the Priceless Child*) has described as moving away from an understanding of children in terms of their economic potential and toward a construction of children as emotionally priceless and vital to the happiness and completion of a family.

33. *Delineator*, August 1909, 134. Also see *Delineator*, January 1909, 103.

34. *Delineator*, December 1910, 515.

35. *Delineator*, May 1908, 808.

36. For a discussion of the move toward what Zelizer terms "sentimental adoptions," see Zelizer, *Pricing the Priceless Child*, 169–207; Marsh and Ronner, *The Empty Cradle*, 106–10, 126–28.

37. Richard Lingeman, *Theodore Dreiser: An American Journey, 1908–1945* (New York: G. P. Putnam's Sons, 1990). Dreiser's biographers grapple with the contradictions in his life; some, like R. N. Mookerjee, believe that he alternated between fatalism and idealism (*Theodore Dreiser: His Thought and Social Criticism* [Delhi, India: National, 1974], 33–34).

Dreiser would later be critical of his efforts at the *Delineator*. In 1913, he told a newspaper that "an orphan asylum can bring up a child better than the average mother" (Lingeman, *Theodore Dreiser*, 90). On another occasion, he assessed his time at the magazine thus: "It was pathetic, as I look at it now, the things we were trying to do and the conditions under which we trying to do them—the raw commercial force and theory which underlay the whole thing, the necessity of explaining and fighting for so much that one should not, as I saw it then, have to argue over at all" (F. O. Matthiessen, *Theodore Dreiser* [New York: William Sloane, 1951], 107–8).

38. Letter from George Wilder to Dreiser, ca. October 1908, Folder 882 (Butterick Correspondence), Dreiser Papers. Wilder was quite opinionated about what sort of articles should appear in the magazine and how they should be presented. Some letters hint that Dreiser did not always appreciate Wilder's heavy-handed input. Wilder seemed to believe that one of the main problems facing America was that women were bad mothers and that it was his duty to provide them with the scientific information (some of it based on his own knowledge gained as the father of four) to be better mothers. See Correspondence with H. L. Mencken, July 16, 1908, Folder 4082,

Box 75, Dreiser Papers. Wilder was also the impetus behind the short-lived child-care series that preceded the "Child-Rescue Campaign."

39. Letter from George Wilder to Dreiser, ca. October 1908, Folder 882 (Butterick Correspondence), Dreiser Papers.

40. Folder 1465, December 24, 1910, Dreiser Papers.

41. *Delineator*, February 1909, 250; June 1909.

42. See *Delineator*, June 1909, for a description of how the magazine handled readers' requests. Because of state law, many of the profiles stated that the child could be placed only in a home in the state in which the child resided. Supposedly the first qualified reader who wrote got the child.

Even before the *Delineator* announced that it would accept general applications and forward them to the proper authorities, it had often forwarded requests for specific children to agencies in the readers' states if they were not the lucky one to get the child. See, for example, December 1908, 995. For an example of a reader requesting the *Delineator*'s assistance, see August 1909, 134.

43. For a discussion of the antagonism between advocates of placing out and proponents of institutional care, see Ashby, *Saving the Waifs*. Ashby cites a study of one institution in which in the mid-1890s only 2 of the 138 children in its care qualified for home placement (32). Ashby also cites a study in New York, Minnesota, Michigan, and Missouri that concluded that by 1912, over 80 percent of dependent children had at least one parent alive (232–33 n. 92). For more information on the shortage of adoptable children, see Berebitsky, "To Raise as Your Own"; Jamil Zainaldin and Peter Tyor, "Asylum and Society: An Approach to Institutional Change," *Journal of Social History* 13 (fall 1979): 31–32; Arno Dosch Fleurot, "Not Enough Babies to Go Around," *Cosmopolitan*, September 1910; *Charities and the Commons* 19 (February 22, 1908): 1612–13. In the *Delineator*, see October 1908, May 1909, and June 1909.

44. *Delineator*, April 1910, 323.

45. *Delineator*, August 1909, 134; December 1910, 515.

46. For a thorough discussion of the *Delineator*'s and Theodore Dreiser's role in the 1909 White House Conference on the Care of Dependent Children, see Jambor, "Theodore Dresier," and Tillman, "The Rights of Childhood." For creation of the Child-Welfare League, see *Delineator*, November 1908, 710.

47. *Delineator*, November 1908, 862.

48. For the history of the shift from the nineteenth century's emphasis on saving the child to the twentieth century's focus on saving the family, see Susan Tiffen, *In Whose Best Interest?* (Westport, Conn.: Greenwood Press, 1982); Katz, *In the Shadow of the Poorhouse*, 125. For the *Delineator*'s growing focus on the need for mothers' pensions, see October 1909, December 1909, August 1910, and October 1910.

49. *Delineator*, August 1910, 128; Zelizer, *Pricing the Priceless Child*, 200.

50. Obviously, the majority of the *Delineator*'s readers did not need to adopt

because they would have children of their own. Others would not want to or would not be able to because of finances or other reasons. For these readers, the focus on mothers' pensions probably seemed natural, and, as the success of the specific campaign for mothers' pensions a few years later showed, the majority supported the idea. For this group of women, the *Delineator's* emphasis on the homeless children was simply misleading. For women who really wanted to adopt, however, the *Delineator's* focus on mothers' pensions betrayed their interests. It is impossible to know how large this group of women was. Infertility among married couples has remained constant for the last century, ranging from just under 10 to about 13 percent (Marsh and Ronner, *The Empty Cradle*, 1–2). Added to this group would be women whose birth children had died or had grown up who still wanted to mother.

51. Theda Skocpol, *Protecting Soldiers and Mothers: The Political Origins of Social Policy in the United States* (Cambridge, Mass.: Belknap Press, 1992), 432–42. Skocpol credits this series with preparing the "ideological ground" for the rapid passage of mothers' pensions nationwide.

52. Honore Willsie, "The Home He Should Have Had," *Delineator*, May 1919; Honore Willsie, "'Not a Boy, Please!'" *Delineator*, July 1919, 33; Judy Barrett Litoff, "Carolyn Conant Van Blarcom," in *Notable American Women—The Modern Period*, ed. Barbara Sicherman and Carol Hurd Green (Cambridge, Mass.: Belknap Press, 1980), 703–4.

53. For the rise of "scientific motherhood," see Rima Apple, *Mothers and Medicine: A Social History of Infant Feeding, 1890–1950* (Madison: University of Wisconsin Press, 1987), and Molly Ladd Taylor, *Raising a Baby the Government Way: Mothers' Letters to the Children's Bureau: 1915–32* (New Brunswick, N.J.: Rutgers University Press, 1986), 22–23.

54. The last issue of the series seems to have been March 1920.

55. *Delineator*, July 1908, 114.

56. *Delineator*, October 1909, 311.

3. Redefining "Real" Motherhood

1. "How It Feels to Have Been an Adopted Child," *American Magazine*, August 1920, 72.

2. Gayle Letherby, "Mother or Not, Mother or What? Problems of Definition and Identity," *Women's Studies International Forum* 17 (1994): 525–32. As discussed in the introduction, adoption has only recently been seen as a parenthood rather than a motherhood issue. After 1920, men occasionally appeared in stories about adoption, such as in Ruth Garver Gagliardo, "We Wanted Children," *Parents*, May 1937, 28–29, which reflected new standards of companionate marriage. Before 1920 (and still somewhat after 1920), articles emphasized that men generally consented to adoption only because their wives really wanted children.

Two recent books provide excellent detail on how women feel pressure to mother in our pro-natalist society and how infertile women especially felt as though they were failures as women. See Margaret Marsh and Wanda Ronner, *The Empty Cradle* (Baltimore: Johns Hopkins University Press, 1996), and Elaine Tyler May, *Barren in the Promised Land* (New York: Basic Books, 1995).

3. Mrs. C. R. M. to Mrs. F. D. Roosevelt, April 20, 1943, CBR, Central Files 1941–1944, File 7-3-3-4-1, Box 171.

4. Laurel Thatcher Ulrich, *Good Wives: Image and Reality in the Lives of Women in Northern New England, 1650–1750* (New York: Vintage Books, 1991); Nancy Cott, *The Bonds of Womanhood* (New Haven, Conn.: Yale University Press, 1977); Linda Kerber, *Women of the Republic* (Chapel Hill: University of North Carolina Press, 1980); Jan Lewis, "The Republican Wife: Virtue and Seduction in the Early Republic," *William and Mary Quarterly* 44 (October 1987): 689–721; Mary Ryan, *Cradle of the Middle Class* (New York: Cambridge University Press, 1981; Barbara Welter, "The Cult of True Womanhood, 1820–1860," *American Quarterly* 18 (summer 1966): 151–74.

5. Kathryn Kish Sklar, *Catharine Beecher* (New York: W. W. Norton, 1973). For Progressive Era women reformers, see Robyn Muncy, *Creating a Female Dominion in American Reform, 1890–1935* (New York: Oxford University Press, 1991).

6. Rev. John Todd, "Address to Mothers," *Mother's Magazine*, November 1839, 249, as quoted in Jan Lewis, "Mother's Love: The Construction of an Emotion in Nineteenth-Century America," in *Social History and Issues in Human Consciousness: Some Interdisciplinary Connections*, ed. Andrew E. Barnes and Peter N. Stearns (New York: New York University Press, 1989), 209; Eli Brown, *Sex and Life: The Physiology and Hygiene of the Sexual Organization* (Chicago: F. J. Schulte, 1891), 103, 106; E. Marea, *The Wife's Manual* (Cortland, N.Y.: n.p., 1896), 18.

7. S. Josephine Baker, M.D., "Choosing a Child," *Ladies' Home Journal*, February 1924, 81. For some of this chapter, I focus on the experience of married adoptive mothers who had never given birth. Since national statistics on adoption were not kept in the late nineteenth or early twentieth centuries, it is impossible to know how many adoptive parents also had biological children. However, before World War II, and especially in the late nineteenth and early twentieth centuries, adoptions by older couples whose biological children were grown, by married women who had given birth but whose children had died or who wanted a sibling for an only child, or by single women were not uncommon. Still, evidence suggests that even at this point, "childlessness was the general rule." See Jamil Zainaldin, "The Origins of Modern Legal Adoption: Child Exchange in Boston, 1851–1893" (Ph.D. diss., University of Chicago, 1976), chap. 5, esp. 152. After World War II, virtually everyone who adopted did so because of infertility (May, *Barren in the Promised Land*, 141–49).

8. Kerber, *Women of the Republic*; Lewis, "The Republican Wife."

9. Kerber, *Women of the Republic*; Linda Kerber, "A Constitutional Right to Be

Treated Like American Ladies: Women and the Obligations of Citizenship," in *U.S. History as Women's History*, ed. Linda Kerber, Alice Kessler-Harris, and Kathryn Kish Sklar (Chapel Hill: University of North Carolina Press, 1995), 17–35.

10. May, *Barren in the Promised Land*, 61–62; Elmer Gates, "The Homeless Child and Childless Home Movement," *American Motherhood*, February 1908, copy in *Delineator* Scrapbook, Box 4221, Dreiser Papers.

11. "Training Babies for the 'Golden Spoon,'" *Literary Digest*, April 8, 1916, 1020.

12. "A Plea for Adoption," *Good Housekeeping*, July 1911, 132.

13. "Child-Rescue Campaign," *Delineator*, August 1908, 263. Most of the articles written by adoptive mothers appear after 1920. Before that, articles used quotes from interviews with or letters from adoptive mothers. Consequently, it must be considered that the quotes were chosen because they represented the views of the author.

14. Zona Gale, "Adoption," in *Friendship Village Love Stories* (New York: Macmillan, 1909), 274–92.

15. John D'Emilio and Estelle Freedman, *Intimate Matters* (New York: Harper and Row, 1988), 233, 240–50; Steven Mintz and Susan Kellogg, *Domestic Revolutions* (New York: Free Press, 1988), esp. 114–16; Sheila Rothman, *Woman's Proper Place: A History of Changing Ideals and Practices, 1870 to the Present* (New York: Basic Books, 1978), chaps. 3, 5; Molly Ladd Taylor, *Raising a Baby the Government Way* (New Brunswick, N.J.: Rutgers University Press, 1986), 22–23; Ronald L. Howard, *A Social History of American Family Sociology, 1865–1940* (Westport, Conn.: Greenwood Press, 1981), 63–70.

16. "An Adopted Mother Speaks," *Survey* 47 (March 18, 1922): 962–63; "Foster Parents Speak for Themselves," *Child Welfare League of America Bulletin* 9 (April 1930): 4.

17. "Adopted Mother by Herself," *Scribner's Magazine*, January 1935, 57; Kathleen Norris, "Adopt that Baby!" *Ladies' Home Journal*, April 1930, 8.

18. "Adopted Mother by Herself," 57.

19. Gagliardo, "We Wanted Children," 28–29; Dorothy Thompson, "Fit for Adoption," *Ladies' Home Journal*, May 1939, 4; Rothman, *Woman's Proper Place*, 194.

20. Lillian Gatlin, "Adopting a Baby: The Stork Gives Blindly, but Only the Fittest Qualify as Parents by Proxy," *Sunset, the Pacific Monthly*, February 1921, 85; E. Wayne Carp, *Family Matters* (Cambridge, Mass.: Harvard University Press, 1998), 90–96; "How It Feels to Have Been an Adopted Child," *American Magazine*, August 1920, 114, 116.

21. Julia Grant, *Raising Baby by the Book* (New Haven, Conn.: Yale University Press, 1998), introduction, 60; Rothman, *Woman's Proper Place*, chap. 3; Robert Griswold, *Fatherhood in America* (New York: Basic Books, 1993), 126–32, 301–2; Barbara Ehrenreich and Deirdre English, *For Her Own Good: 150 Years of the Experts' Advice to Women* (New York: Anchor Books, 1979), 189; Steven L. Schlossman, "Before Home Start: Notes toward a History of Parent Education in America, 1897–1929," *Harvard Educational Review* 46 (August 1976): 436–67.

22. "Adopting a Baby," *Woman's Journal* 14 (July 1929): 9.

23. Honore Willsie, "The Adopted Mother," *Century Magazine*, September 1922, 666.

24. Jessie Taft, "What It Means to Be a Foster Parent," *Progressive Education* 3 (October 1926): 352–53.

25. Bertha Van Hoosen, M.D., "The Adopted Mother," *Medical Woman's Journal* 34 (December 1927): 361.

26. Lee M. Brooks and Evelyn C. Brooks, *Adventuring in Adoption* (Chapel Hill: University of North Carolina Press, 1939), 7.

27. Mrs. J. C. N. to Mrs. Katherine Lenroot, January 5, 1948, CBR, Central Files 1945–1948, File 7-3-3-4, Box 158.

28. Regina Markell Morantz-Sanchez, *Sympathy and Science: Women Physicians in American Medicine* (New York: Oxford University Press, 1985), 132; Dorothy M. Brown, *Mabel Walker Willebrandt: A Study of Power, Loyalty, and Law* (Knoxville: University of Tennessee Press, 1984), 123; Mrs. Eldridge (pseudonym), Records of the Good Samaritan Home, Case 272 (1926), Letter to Mrs. Atwood, May 3, 1927.

29. O'Ryan Rickard, *A Just Verdict: The Life of Caroline Bartlett Crane* (Kalamazoo: Western Michigan University, New Issues Press, 1994), 162, 219, 224, 247.

30. H. David Kirk, *Shared Fate: A Theory of Adoption and Mental Health* (New York: Free Press, 1964), chap. 2.

31. For a discussion of how an assumption of difference has influenced today's attitudes toward adoption, see Katarina Wegar, *Adoption, Identity, and Kinship* (New Haven, Conn.: Yale University Press, 1997).

32. Records of the Good Samaritan Home, Case 260 (1934), Letters to Mrs. Atwood, n.d. (ca. September 1934) and August 25, 1937.

33. LeRoy Ashby, *Endangered Children* (New York: Twayne, 1997), 108–9; Mrs. L. A. P. to Child Welfare Department, September 6, 1919, CBR, Central Files 1914–1920, File 7-3-4-3, Box 67; Alfred Toombs, "War Babies," *Woman's Home Companion* 71 (April 1944): 32; Mrs. W. S. to Dear Sir, November 4, 1942, CBR, Central Files 1941–1944, File 7-3-3-4-1, Box 171.

34. Taylor, *Raising a Baby the Government Way,* 2; Kriste Lindenmeyer, *"A Right to Childhood": The U.S. Children's Bureau and Child Welfare, 1912–1946* (Urbana and Chicago: University of Illinois Press, 1997); Emelyn Foster Peck, *Adoption Laws in the United States,* U.S. Children's Bureau Publication No. 148 (Washington, D.C.: GPO, 1925).

35. CBR, Central Files 1914–1920, File 7-3-4-3, Box 67; CBR, Central Files 1921–1924, File 7-3-4-3, Box 211; S. Josephine Baker, M.D., "A Home for Every Child," *Ladies' Home Journal*, May 1926, 29. This article encouraged prospective parents to write to the bureau and at least fifteen did. CBR, Central Files 1925–1928, File 7-3-4-3, Box 294; Folders: "Appeals from People Wishing for Children to Adopt," CBR, Central Files 1941–1944, File 7-3-3-4-1, Box 171.

36. Mrs. R. A. to Mr. Heisterman, October 28, 1935, CBR, Central Files 1933–1936, File 7-3-3-4, Box 549; Mrs. B. L. to the Children's Bureau, August 25, 1932, CBR, Central Files 1929–1932, File 7-3-3-4, Box 406. Men wrote 8.4 percent of the letters in a sample that looked at the first four months of every fourth year beginning in 1921 and ending in 1948. Because the letters do not constitute a scientific sample of adoptive parents, and because each letter contains different types of information (for example, not all include the writer's age, occupation, or ethnic background or the reason why he or she is seeking to adopt), I have not tried to quantify any of the information I found. Rather, I tried to identify recurring patterns or themes in the letters, interpreting reoccurrence as a sign that the experience or emotion described was common to many adoptive parents.

37. Adrienne Rich, *Of Woman Born: Motherhood as Experience and Institution* (New York: W. W. Norton, 1976; reprint, New York: Bantam Books, 1981), chaps. 1, 2. My argument is informed by the work of Regina Kunzel and other cultural historians who have examined the relationship between individual experience and cultural meanings of that experience (Regina Kunzel, "Pulp Fictions and Problem Girls: Reading and Rewriting Single Pregnancy in the Postwar United States," *American Historical Review* 100 (December 1995): 1465–87.

38. In addition to the connection between women's education and sterility in the nineteenth century, in the 1930s, psychoanalytically influenced physicians suggested that a woman's infertility could be the result of her failure to accept her female role. This topic is discussed in more detail in chap. 5. More recently, career women who have chosen to postpone childbearing into their thirties have been blamed for any fertility problems they may face (Margarete Sandelowski, "Failures of Volition: Female Agency and Infertility in Historical Perspective," *Signs* 15 [Spring 1990]: 476–77; Marsh and Ronner, *The Empty Cradle*, 247).

39. Mrs. N. R. to President Roosevelt, December 6, 1940, CBR, Central Files 1941–1944, File 7-3-3-4-1, Box 171.

40. Marsh and Ronner, *The Empty Cradle*, 154–57, 198–200; May, *Barren in the Promised Land*, 156–66, quote on 160.

41. Mrs. M. S. to Mrs. Roosevelt, December 23, 1942, CBR, Central Files 1941–1944, File 7-3-3-4-1, Box 171.

42. Mrs. H. W. R., Jr., to Mrs. E. Rosevelt, CBR, Central Files 1941–1944, File 7-3-3-4-1, Box 171; Mr. and Mrs. L. H. to Mrs. Roosevelt, February 16, 1944, CBR, Central Files 1941–1944, File 7-3-3-4-1, Box 171; Mrs. C. O. D. to Mr. and Mrs. Franklin D. Roosevelt, July 29, 1939, CBR, Central Files 1937–1940, File 7-3-3-4, Box 822.

43. Mrs. M. B. R. to Federal Children's Bureau, June 20, 1923, CBR, Central Files 1921–1924, File 7-3-4-3, Box 211.

44. Mrs. W. K. to Julia Lathrop, June 8, 1928, CBR, Central Files 1925–1928, File 7-3-4-3, Box 294; Mr. and Mrs. L. H. to Mrs. Roosevelt, February 16, 1944, CBR, Central Files 1941–1944, File 7-3-3-4-1, Box 171; Patricia Susan Hart, "A Home for Every

Child, a Child for Every Home: Relinquishment and Adoption at Washington Children's Home Society, 1896–1915" (Ph.D. diss., Washington State University, 1997), 230–47.

45. Mrs. J. M. B. to the Children's Bureau, April 26, 1921, and Mrs. J. M. B. to Dear Madam, April 27, 1921, CBR, Central Files 1921–1924, File 7-3-4-3, Box 211.

46. Mrs. W. C. to Mrs. Eleanore Roosevelt, November 20, 1941, CBR, Central Files 1941–1944, File 7-3-3-4, Box 170; Mrs. B. G. to Mrs. Roosevelt, January 10, 1944, CBR, Central Files 1941–1944, File 7-3-3-4-1, Box 171. Scholars Margarete Sandelowski and Elaine Tyler May have found strikingly similar attitudes expressed by contemporary infertile women who are seeking children through adoption or reproductive technology (Margarete Sandelowski, "Fault Lines: Infertility and Imperiled Sisterhood," *Feminist Studies* 16 [Spring 1990]: 34; May, *Barren in the Promised Land*, 224–31).

47. Mrs. G. R. to The Children's Bureau, September 30, 1935, CBR, Central Files 1933–1936, File 7-3-3-4, Box 548.

48. Records of the Good Samaritan Home, Case 256 (1925), Letter to Gertrude Atwood, January 28, 1929. The adoptive parents retained custody of the child, although the adoption was not finalized until 1940.

49. It is impossible to accurately determine correspondents' socioeconomic background. However, clues ranging from spelling and grammar to a listing of occupation, income, or education suggest that a wide variety of Americans looked to the Roosevelts. The letters discussed later in this section are from people who felt that their income was responsible for their inability to find a child.

50. Lizabeth Cohen, *Making a New Deal: Industrial Workers in Chicago, 1919–1939* (Cambridge: Cambridge University Press, 1990), 285; Mrs. H. L. to Franklin Roosevelt, November 1938, CBR, Central Files 1937–1940, File 7-3-3-4, Box 822; G. S. to My dear first lady, February 23, 1943, CBR, Central Files 1941–1944, File 7-3-3-4-1, Box 171; Mrs. E. M. N. to Mrs. F. D. Roosevelt, January 16, 1944, CBR, Central Files 1941–1944, File 7-3-3-4-1, Box 171.

51. Marsh and Ronner, *The Empty Cradle*, 143–44, 153. For increased applications during the war see Mrs. Edward Gresham to Mary Ruth Colby, June 19, 1942, CBR, Central Files 1941–1944, File 7-3-3-4, Box 170; Jessie Condit to Mary Ruth Colby, November 6, 1942, CBR, Central Files 1941–1944, File 7-3-3-4, Box 170.

52. Mrs. I. K. to Mrs. Roosevelt, December 5, 1936, CBR, Central Files 1933–1936, File 7-3-3-4, Box 549; Mrs. H. E .D. to Mrs. Roosevelt, November 9, 1943, CBR, Central Files 1941–1944, File 7-3-3-4-1, Box 171.

53. Mrs. C. O. D. to Mr. and Mrs. Franklin D. Roosevelt, July 29, 1939, and Emily Brown to Mary Ruth Colby, August 28, 1939, CBR, Central Files 1937–1940, File 7-3-3-4, Box 822.

54. Mrs. B. G. to Mrs. Roosevelt, June 10, 1944, CBR, Central Files 1941–1944, File 7-3-3-4-1, Box 171.

55. "The Epidemic of Adoption," *Living Age* 294 (September 8, 1917): 632.

56. Mary Havor, "And After Adoption—What Then?" *Woman's Day*, November 1947, 35.

57. Jessie Taft, "Concerning Adopted Children," *Child Study* 6 (January 1929): 85–87.

4. *"Mother-Women" or "Man-Haters"?*

1. Carol S. Prentice, *An Adopted Child Looks at Adoption* (New York: D. Appleton-Century, 1940), x, 30–32, 38–39, 41–42, 36.

2. A number of contemporary social commentators noted that adoption seemed to achieve a new level of cultural acceptance in the 1920s. This topic is explored more fully in the next chapter.

3. Alice Kunz Ray, "A Good Adoption Program: Can Standards Be Maintained without Sacrificing Flexibility?" in *Proceedings of the National Conference of Social Work* (New York: Columbia University Press, 1945), 299.

4. According to historian Elaine Tyler May, 11 percent of women born in the decade following the Civil War never married. Among women born around 1900, 8 percent remained single. Less than 5 percent of women born in the 1910s and 1920s never married (*Barren in the Promised Land* [New York: Basic Books, 1995], 51, 276 n. 83). In addition, although divorce rates were rising during this period, they were still quite low.

National statistics on adoption were not kept until after World War II, so there is no way of telling exactly how many single women adopted. To provide readers with a sense of how many unmarried women adopted, the following evidence, admittedly scant, is given. In his study of nineteenth-century adoptions in Boston, Jamil Zainaldin found that in the period 1851 to 1875, 8.4 percent of adoptive parents were either single or widowed. In the period 1880 to 1893, 13.8 percent were single or widowed. Unfortunately, Zainaldin does not specify what percentage of these adoptions were adoptions by relatives. Also, these figures include some single men, such as a grandfather who adopted his orphaned grandchild ("The Origins of Modern Legal Adoption: Child Exchange in Boston, 1851–1893" [Ph.D. diss., University of Chicago, 1976], 145). Also for this early period, political scientist George James Bayles noted, "By far the greater number of legal adoptions of children throughout the United States are undertaken by married and single women" (*American Women's Legal Status* [New York: P. F. Collier and Son, 1905], 102).

A study of 100 legal adoptions prior to 1920 in Massachusetts showed that one divorced woman, five widows, and four unmarried women were included among the adoptive parents (Ida Parker, *"Fit and Proper"? A Study of Legal Adoption in Massachusetts* [Boston: Church Home Society, 1927], 97). Of 472 unrelated adoptions known to social agencies in Cook County, Illinois, in 1925, four widows and one divorced woman were included. Although the study's author stated that there was no fixed policy among child-placing agencies regarding single women, a number of child-placing agencies had already come out against allowing single women to adopt (Elinor Nims, *The Illinois Adoption Law and Its Administration* [Chicago: University of Chicago Press, 1928], 68). In addition, a study of this sort might not be representative, since most single women probably would not have gone through an agency to find a child. Instead, they would have adopted a child they had encountered through their professional or personal relationships.

Another study from the Midwest also showed a small percentage of single women adopting. Less than 1 percent of the adoptive parents of 2,414 illegitimate children adopted in Minnesota from 1918 to 1928 were unmarried (Alice Leahy, "Some Characteristics of Adoptive Parents," *American Journal of Sociology* 38 [January 1933]: 555). In 1927, sociologist Ernest Groves noted, "Of late there has been a slight tendency among middle-aged single women to adopt very young children, two or three women sometimes living together to form a home circle" (*Social Problems of the Family* [Philadelphia: J. B. Lippincott, 1927], 63). A study of sixty adoptions completed prior to 1939 included four single women. Their average age at the time of the adoption was forty, compared with thirty-four for married adoptive mothers. All four women adopted children under the age of five (Lee M. Brooks and Evelyn C. Brooks, *Adventuring in Adoption* [Chapel Hill: University of North Carolina Press, 1939], 180–81).

5. Constance Kirby, "Bargains in Babies," *Harper's Bazaar*, June 1912, 280; Henry Dwight Chapin, M. D., "Finding Babies for Folks to Adopt," *American Magazine*, November 1919, 42–44. For other examples of articles that approved of single women adopting, see the *Delineator's* "Child-Rescue Campaign," March, August, and December 1908; Judd Mortimer Lewis, "Dealing in Babies," *Good Housekeeping*, February 1914, 194–98; Honore Willsie, "Our Child-Helping Department," *Delineator*, October 1919, 33.

6. "I Want to Be Really a Woman," *Delineator*, July 1913, 10.

7. Although magazine articles noted that single women were adopting, they rarely gave names or demographic information about those women. I have identified a number of single women who adopted, but these women were, of course, women who were in some way visible to the public and so have been remembered. The majority of these women were reformers and physicians, and many lived in New York or other large cities. It must be considered that the lives of other single women who adopted were not the same as the lives of the women about whom I was able to gather information. Sources show that wealthy widows, for example, often adopted, but I was unable to locate their accounts. I believe, however, that after 1920, when single women fell out of favor, most single adoptive mothers would have lived lives similar to what I am describing, that is, urban professional women with a large support network of women like themselves.

8. Joanne Passet, *Cultural Crusaders: Women Librarians in the American West, 1900–1917* (Albuquerque: University of New Mexico Press, 1994), 33; "How It Feels to Have Been an Adopted Child," *American Magazine*, August 1920, 114; Estelle B.

Freedman, *Maternal Justice: Miriam Van Waters and the Female Reform Tradition* (Chicago: University of Chicago Press, 1996), 152.

9. The 1910 adoption application form of a child-placing agency in Illinois, for example, suggests that single women would be considered. With regard to income, the form queried female applicants, "If she is the support of the family, what is her occupation?" (Brian Gill, "The Jurisprudence of Good Parenting: The Selection of Adoptive Parents, 1894–1964," [Ph.D. diss., University of California–Berkeley, 1997], 224). However, a study of adoptions at the Washington (State) Children's Home Society from 1896 to 1915 found that adoptions by single persons were extremely rare (Patricia Susan Hart, "A Home for Every Child, a Child for Every Home: Relinquishment and Adoption at Washington Children's Home Society, 1896–1915," [Ph.D. diss., Washington State University, 1997], 198).

Betty Hannah Hoffman, "Gertrude Battles Lane," in *Notable American Women, 1607–1950,* ed. Edward T. James (Cambridge, Mass.: Belknap Press, 1971), 363–65. Doris Fielding Reid, *Edith Hamilton: An Intimate Portrait* (New York: W. W. Norton, 1967), 58, 64, 86; Helen Bacon, "Edith Hamilton," in *Notable American Women— The Modern Period,* ed. Barbara Sicherman and Carol Hurd Green (Cambridge, Mass.: Belknap Press, 1980), 306–8.

10. As late as 1939, the average age of adoptive parents was forty, and people over fifty routinely requested infants (Brooks and Brooks, *Adventuring in Adoption,* 31); Kirby, "Bargains in Babies," 280.

11. Biographical information on Irwin and Anthony is sketchy. It is unclear, for example, exactly how many children Irwin adopted. It appears that she might have adopted only one child legally but informally adopted at least two others. Other members of the New York City reform community who adopted include Clara Spence and Charlotte Baker, who opened the Spence Adoption Agency. For information on Spence and Baker, see Charles Gilmore Kerley, M.D., "The Adoption of Children," *Outlook,* January 12, 1916, 107.

In *Pitied but Not Entitled: Single Mothers and the History of Welfare, 1890–1935* (New York: Free Press, 1994), 78–79, Linda Gordon estimates that approximately one-quarter of the female reformers she examined had female life partners. Josephine Nelson, "Would You 'Bootleg' a Baby?" *Independent Woman,* February 1936, 42; Patricia Albjerg Graham, "Elisabeth Antoinette Irwin," in James, *Notable American Women,* 255–57; Judith Schwarz, *Radical Feminists of Heterodoxy: Greenwich Village 1912–1940,* rev. ed. (Norwich, Conn.: New Victoria Publishers, 1986), 86–87, 116, 119; Caroline F. Ware, *Greenwich Village, 1920–1930: A Comment on American Civilization in the Post-War Years* (Boston: Houghton Mifflin, 1935). For information on Johnson and Forbes, see Joyce Antler, *The Making of a Modern Woman* (New Haven, Conn.: Yale University Press, 1987), 209–10.

12. Freedman, *Maternal Justice,* 154–55. Van Waters legally adopted Sarah in 1932.

13. M. B. to Dear Sir, October 28, 1941, CBR, Central Files 1941–1944, File 7-3-3-4, Box 170.

14. Julia Grant, *Raising Baby by the Book* (New Haven, Conn.: Yale University Press, 1998), 206, 214–15.

15. M. E. G. to Miss Grace Abbott, May 17, 1929, CBR, Central Files 1929–1932, File 7-3-3-4, Box 406.

16. Alice S. Rossi, *The Feminist Papers* (New York: Bantam Books, 1973), 336–37; Elizabeth Putnam Gordon, *The Story of the Life and Work of Cordelia A. Greene, M.D.* (Castile, N.Y.: Castilian, 1925), 20–22.

17. Bertha Van Hoosen, M.D., "The Adopted Mother," *Medical Woman's Journal* 34 (December 1927): 361.

18. Clare Beck, "Adelaide Hasse: The New Woman as Librarian," in *Reclaiming the American Library Past: Writing the Women In*, ed. Suzanne Hildenbrand (Norwood, N.J.: Ablex, 1996), 99–120; author's correspondence with Clare Beck, August 9, 1998.

19. Annelise Orleck, *Common Sense and a Little Fire* (Chapel Hill: University of North Carolina Press, 1995), 136–37, 144–46.

20. Diana Reep, *The Rescue and Romance* (Bowling Green, Ohio: Bowling Green State University Press, 1982), 4.

21. Mary E. Wilkins Freeman, "A Gatherer of Simples," in *A Humble Romance and Other Stories* (New York: Harper and Brothers, 1887), 280–95. For other stories in which single women either raise or adopt (legally or informally) children, see Alyn Yates Keith, *A Spinster's Leaflets* (Boston: Lee and Shepard, 1894); Grace Ellery Channing, "The Children of the Barren," *Harper's Monthly Magazine*, March 1907, 511–19; Kathleen Norris, "Mothering Cecelia," *Good Housekeeping*, March 1913, 304–15.

22. Margaret Deland, "The Child's Mother," in *Old Chester Tales* (New York: Harper and Brothers, 1898), 135–74.

23. Margaret Deland, *The Awakening of Helena Ritchie* (New York: Harper and Brothers, 1906); Diana Reep, *Margaret Deland* (Boston: Twayne, 1985), 15.

24. Deland, *Helena Ritchie*, 282; Regina Kunzel, *Fallen Women, Problem Girls* (New Haven, Conn.: Yale University Press, 1993), 32–33; Reep, *Margaret Deland*, 6.

25. Deland, *Helena Ritchie*, 337–57. Interestingly, this is a sort of twist on the notion of rescuing a child. In this case, adoption rescues the adoptive mother from an immoral life.

26. Olivia Howard Dunbar, "Miss Hildreth: 'Mother of Ten,' " *Harper's Bazaar*, September 1912, 443–44.

27. For the Women's Political Union, see Diva Daims, *Toward a Feminist Tradition: An Annotated Bibliography of Novels in English by Women, 1891–1920* (New York: Garland, 1982), in the description of *The Supplanter*; Grace Duffie Boylan, *The Supplanter* (Boston: Lothrop, Lee, Shepard, 1913), 70.

28. Boylan, *Supplanter*, 91, 143.

29. Ibid., 279, 357, 175–78.

30. Dunbar, "Miss Hildreth," 443–44.

31. Linda Gordon, *Woman's Body, Woman's Right* (New York: Penguin Books, 1977), 19–22.

32. Boylan, *Supplanter*, 143, 175–78. The Annunciation is the holiday celebrating the announcement of the Incarnation to the Virgin Mary.

33. Ellen Hoekstra, "The Pedestal Myth Reinforced: Women's Magazine Fiction, 1900–1920," in *New Dimensions in Popular Culture*, ed. Russell Nye (Bowling Green, Ohio: University of Bowling Green Popular Press, 1972), 50.

34. "I Want to Be Really a Woman," 10.

35. Dunbar, "Miss Hildreth," 444.

36. Nancy Cott, *The Grounding of Modern Feminism* (New Haven, Conn.: Yale University Press, 1987), 158; Lillian Faderman, *Odd Girls and Twilight Lovers* (New York: Penguin Books, 1991), 48–54; Carroll Smith-Rosenberg, *Disorderly Conduct: Visions of Gender in Victorian America*, (New York: Oxford University Press, 1985), 53–76.

37. Nelson, "Would You 'Bootleg' a Baby?" 42; "How It Feels to Have Been an Adopted Child," 72–73. Holt and Hardy sought to legally adopt children; other single women might have avoided the legal hassle by not going through the formality of legally adopting, although by the 1930s, social workers were fairly insistent that foster parents adopt. Harriet Hardy Oral History, interview by Regina Morantz-Sanchez, Women in Medicine Archives, Medical College of Pennsylvania, Philadelphia; see pp. 38–39. I am grateful to Allison Hepler for sharing this information with me.

38. Records of the Good Samaritan Home, *Superintendent's Report* (summer 1940).

39. Brooks and Brooks, *Adventuring in Adoption*, 34–35, 185–86.

40. Robert Griswold, *Fatherhood in America* (New York: Basic Books 1993), 91–97; Groves, *Social Problems of the Family*, 63.

41. Elizabeth Frazer, "The Baby Market," *Saturday Evening Post*, February 1, 1930, 88.

42. Ibid., 88; Sheila Rothman, *Woman's Proper Place* (New York: Basic Books, 1978), 210–11.

43. June Axinn, "Jessie Taft," in Sicherman and Green, *Notable American Women*, 674.

44. Nelson, "Would You 'Bootleg' a Baby?" 44. Taft also discussed the issue of single women adopting in an article in 1933. Taft believed that single women should be allowed to adopt only if a "normal" home could not be found or in exceptional cases. She maintained that "every child needs a father, and every child needs more than one parent." To this end, Taft felt that two women, a father and daughter, or a mother and son were preferable to a lone woman (Jessie Taft, "The Adopted Child," *Delineator*, September 1933, 12).

45. Elsa Castendyck to Miss Charlotte Whitton, July 21, 1938, and Lenroot to Miss Charlotte Whitton, July 6, 1938, CBR, Central Files 1937–1940, File 7-3-3-2, Box 820.

46. Elsa Castendyck to Miss Charlotte Whitton, July 21, 1938, CBR, Central Files 1937–1940, File 7-3-3-2, Box 820.

47. Freedman, *Maternal Justice*, 107–8, 178–79. Unmarried women reformers in the Children's Bureau, for example, found their sexuality challenged in Congress in acrimonious debates over the Sheppard-Towner Act in the 1920s (Gordon, *Pitied but Not Entitled*, 81).

48. "I Just Adopted a Baby," *Ladies' Home Journal*, August 1937, 14; Records of the Good Samaritan Home, Case 260 (1934), Letter to Mrs. William Atwood, August 25, 1937.

49. Florence Clothier, "Placing the Child for Adoption," *Mental Hygiene* 26 (1942): 267; Helene Deutsch, *The Psychology of Women: A Psychoanalytic Interpretation*, vol. 2 (New York: Grune and Stratton, 1945), 396–97.

50. Dorothy M. Brown, *Mabel Walker Willebrandt* (Knoxville: University of Tennessee Press, 1984), 120–31.

51. Ibid., 124–26; Mabel Walker Willebrandt, "First Impressions," *Good Housekeeping*, May 1928, 38–39.

52. Brown, *Willebrandt*, 134–36.

53. Letter to the Walkers, April 21, 1926, Box 3, Mabel Walker Willebrandt Papers, Manuscript Division, Library of Congress, Washington, D.C.

54. "Travailogue," *Time* 47 (April 29, 1946): 31; Ann Barley, *Patrick Calls Me Mother* (New York: Harper and Brothers, 1948), 184–95; "Barley, Ann L.," *Book Review Digest* (New York: H. W. Wilson, 1949), 44.

55. "Travailogue."

56. Barley, *Patrick Calls Me Mother*, 1–5.

57. Ibid., 5–7.

58. Ibid., 210–12.

59. Pamela Taylor, "Son without Stork," *Saturday Review of Literature* 31 (July 31, 1948): 17; "Barley, Ann L."; Virginia Rowe Terrett, "Un Petit Homme d'Affaires," *New York Times Book Review*, July 11, 1948, 15; Barley, *Patrick Calls Me Mother*, 226.

60. Gill, "Jurisprudence of Good Parenting," 225; Michael Schapiro, *A Study of Adoption Practice*, vol. 1, *Adoption Agencies and the Children They Serve* (New York: Child Welfare League of America, 1956), 75.

5. "The Best" or "Good Enough"?

1. Helen D. Sargent, "Is It Safe to Adopt a Child?" *Parents' Magazine*, October 1935, 26.

2. Carol S. Prentice, *An Adopted Child Looks at Adoption* (New York: D. Appleton-Century, 1940), xi. For the popularity of adoption and the shortage of adoptable children, see Arthur Joyce, "Chronicle of a Search for a Homeless Waif in Philadelphia—Where There Aren't Any," *Philadelphia Record*, June 30, 1929, 1; "Cradles instead of Divorces," *Literary Digest* 77 (April 14, 1923): 35–36; Dorothy Dunbar Bromley, "Demand for Babies Outruns the Supply," *New York Times Magazine*,

March 3, 1935, 9. Agnes Hanna, "The Interrelationship between Illegitimacy and Adoption," *Child Welfare League of America (CWLA) Bulletin* 16 (September 1937): 5; Agnes Hanna to Mrs. R. D. W., February 24, 1942, CBR, Central Files 1941–1944, File 7-3-3-4, Box 170.

3. "Adopted Waifs Often Grow to Resemble New Parents," *Kansas City Star,* January 24, 1943.

4. Mary Ruth Colby, *Problems and Procedures in Adoption,* U.S. Children's Bureau Publication No. 262 (Washington, D.C.: GPO, 1941), 21. National statistics were not kept during the period under consideration, so it is difficult to determine the exact number of adoptions in which social workers were involved. Still, scattered evidence suggests that social workers significantly increased their involvement in placements between 1920 and 1945. Studies in New Jersey and Massachusetts in the 1920s, for example, showed that state-licensed child-placing institutions placed only one-quarter to one-third of children (E. Wayne Carp, *Family Matters* [Cambridge, Mass.: Harvard University Press, 1998], 20). Similar low rates were found in Pennsylvania and Ohio in the 1920s (Lawrence C. Cole, "A Study of Adoptions in Cuyahoga County," *Family* 6 [January 1926]: 261; "Adoption in Pennsylvania," *Medical Woman's Journal* 32 [January 1925]: 21).

5. On the twentieth century movement away from public life and toward private fulfillment, see Elaine Tyler May, *Barren in the Promised Land* (New York: Basic Books, 1995), 255–59.

6. Roy Lubove, *The Professional Altruist* (New York: Atheneum, 1972); Regina Kunzel, *Fallen Women, Problem Girls* (New Haven, Conn.: Yale University Press, 1993), 38–45.

7. Kunzel, *Fallen Women,* 52–54; E. Wayne Carp, "Professional Social Workers, Adoption, and the Problem of Illegitimacy, 1915–1945," *Journal of Policy History* 6 (1994): 170–72; Peter Romanofsky, "The Early History of Adoption Practices, 1870–1930," (Ph.D. diss., University of Missouri–Columbia, 1969), 74–80.

8. On early adoption agencies, see Romanofsky, "Early History," chap. 6; Peter Romanofsky, "Professionals versus Volunteers: A Case Study of Adoption Workers in the 1920s," *Journal of Voluntary Action Research* 2 (April 1973): 95–101; Henry Dwight Chapin, M.D., "Finding Babies for Folks to Adopt," *American Magazine,* November 1919, 42–44; Louise Waterman Wise, "Mothers in Name," *Survey* 43 (March 20, 1920): 779–80.

9. A. S. Chapman, "Homes for Babies; Babies for Homes," *Hygeia* 10 (December 1932): 1106–9; Milton MacKaye, "The Cradle," *Saturday Evening Post,* April 9, 1938, 12–13; Paula Pfeffer, "Homeless Children, Childless Homes," *Chicago History* (spring 1987): 51–65. On Judd Mortimer Lewis, see "A Humorist's 'Baby Bureau,' " *Literary Digest* 47 (July 19, 1913): 100–101; Judd Mortimer Lewis, "Dealing in Babies," *Good Housekeeping,* February 1914, 194–98; Ewing Galloway, "He Likes Babies," *Collier's,* June 20, 1914, 23.

10. For social workers' increased interest in adoption in the 1920s, see Edmond J.

Butler, "Standards of Child Placing and Supervision," in *Standards of Child Welfare. A Report of the Children's Bureau Conferences, May and June, 1919,* Children's Bureau Publication No. 60 (Washington, D.C.: U.S. Department of Labor, 1919), 353–62; Sophie van Senden Theis, *The Child in the Foster Home* (New York: New York School of Social Work, 1921); State Charities Aid Association, *How Foster Children Turn Out* (New York: State Charities Aid Association, 1924); Romanofsky, "Professionals versus Volunteers"; Ida Parker, *"Fit and Proper"?* (Boston: Church Home Society for the Care of the Children of the Protestant Church, 1927); Elinor Nims, *The Illinois Adoption Law and Its Administration* (Chicago: University of Chicago Press, 1928).

11. Carp, *Family Matters,* 21; Mary Ruth Colby, "Modern Safeguards in Adoption Legislation," *CWLA Bulletin* 20 (December 1941): 3.

12. Brian Gill, "The Jurisprudence of Good Parenting: The Selection of Adoptive Parents, 1894–1964" (Ph.D. diss., University of California–Berkeley, 1997), 79–87.

13. Agnes Hanna to J. C. Furnas, January 14, 1942, CBR, Central Files 1941–1944, File 7-3-3-4, Box 171; Katharine Lenroot to Dr. P. Poling, August 20, 1948, CBR, Central Files 1945–1948, File 7-3-3-4, Box 157; Agnes Hanna to Mrs. H. M. F., October 6, 1935, CBR, Central Files 1933–1936, File 7-3-3-4, Box 549.

14. A. H. Stoneman, "Safeguarding Adoptions, Legally and Socially," in *Proceedings of the National Conference of Social Work* (Chicago: University of Chicago Press, 1924), 144–45, 150.

15. Theis, *Child in the Foster Home,* 15, 33; Hyman S. Lippman, "Suitability of the Child for Adoption," *American Journal of Orthopsychiatry* 7 (1937): 270–73.

16. Lubove, *Professional Altruist;* Kunzel, *Fallen Women,* documents the process in work with unwed mothers. For a discussion of the antagonistic relationship between social-work professionals and adoption volunteers, see Pfeffer, "Homeless Children," and Romanofsky, "Professionals versus Volunteers." Mrs. J. H. Evans, "Child Placing by Volunteers," in *Proceedings of the National Conference of Charities and Corrections* (Fort Wayne, Ind.: Archer, 1910), 131–38.

17. Romanofsky, "Professionals versus Volunteers," 96–97; Eleanor G. Gallagher, *The Adopted Child* (New York: Reynal and Hitchcock, 1936), 12, chap. 10; for reviews of Gallagher, see Morris L. Bridgeman, "The Adopted Child" [book review] *CWLA Bulletin* 16 (January 1937): 5; *CWLA Bulletin* 16 (February 1937): 4; Sophie van Senden Theis, "Review," *Survey* 72 (October 1936).

18. Daniel J. Walkowitz, "The Making of a Feminine Professional Identity: Social Workers in the 1920s," *American Historical Review* 95 (October 1990): 1058; Dorothy Hutchinson, *In Quest of Foster Parents* (New York: Columbia University Press, 1943), 46–49.

19. Ruth Brenner, "The Selection of Adoptive Parents: A Casework Responsibility," *CWLA Bulletin* 25 (December 1946): 3; Ruth Brenner, *A Follow-up Study of Adoptive Families* (New York: Child Adoption Research Committee, 1951), 28–29, 98, 134; Hutchinson, *In Quest of Foster Parents,* 5.

20. Brenner, "Selection of Adoptive Parents," 1; Constance Rathbun, "The Adoptive Foster Parent: A Basis for Evaluation," *CWLA Bulletin* 23 (November 1944): 5.

21. Louisiana Department of Public Welfare, *How to Adopt a Child in Louisiana* (1950), 2, as quoted in H. David Kirk, *Shared Fate* (New York: Free Press, 1964), 23.

22. Florence Clothier, "Placing the Child for Adoption," *Mental Hygiene* 26 (April 1942): 257–74, reprinted in I. Evelyn Smith, *Readings in Adoption* (New York: Philosophical Library, 1963), 81; Pfeffer, "Homeless Children," 59.

23. Joseph Reid, "Principles, Values, and Assumptions Underlying Adoption Practice," *Social Work* 2 (January 1957), reprinted in Smith, *Readings in Adoption,* 30.

24. Winifred Cobbledick, "A Study of Adoption Agency Criteria in 'Matching' Children to Homes" (M.S.W. thesis, University of California, 1949), 40–41. For a fuller discussion of matching, see Gill, "Jurisprudence of Good Parenting."

25. Theis, *Child in the Foster Home,* 87. For an example of an agency that relied on testing in making placements in the 1920s, see the Children's Files of the Sheltering Arms Service, Special Collections, Rutgers University Library, New Brunswick, N.J. Carp, *Family Matters,* 28.

26. L. M. Terman, *The Measurement of Intelligence* (Boston: Houghton Mifflin, 1916), 115, as quoted in Stephen Jay Gould, *The Mismeasure of Man,* rev. ed. (New York: W. W. Norton, 1996), 213; this discussion of hereditarian thought is based on Gould, chap. 5. By the late 1930s, Terman, in the wake of a depression that toppled even the intelligent, backed off his position and acknowledged that environmental factors, as well as heredity, could contribute to an individual's station in life.

27. Arnold Gesell, M.D., "Reducing the Risks of Child Adoption," *CWLA Bulletin* 6 (May 15, 1927): 2.

28. Sophie van Senden Theis, *Social Aspects of Child Adoption* (New York: Child Welfare League of America, 1937); Florence Clothier, "Some Aspects of the Problem of Adoption," *American Journal of Orthopsychiatry* 9 (1939): 605; Child Welfare League of America, *Standards for Organizations Providing Foster Family Care* (New York: Child Welfare League of America, 1933), 18; Ora Pendleton, "New Aims in Adoption," *Annals of the American Academy of Political and Social Science* 151 (September 1930): 158–59.

29. C. C. Carstens, "Safeguards in Adoption," *CWLA Bulletin* 15 (April 1936): 4.

30. Michael Schapiro, *A Study of Adoption Practice,* vol. 1 (New York: Child Welfare League of America, 1956), 19.

31. Frances Lockridge, *Adopting a Child* (New York: Greenberg, 1948), 27.

32. Helen Witmer et al., *Independent Adoptions* (New York: Russell Sage Foundation, 1963), 90, 94.

33. It is unclear whether the policies of other private agencies mirrored those of the Cradle. Chapman, "Homes for Babies," 1107–8; Pfeffer, "Homeless Children," 59; MacKaye, "The Cradle," 95–96.

34. Gould, *Mismeasure of Man,* 188; William Healy et al., *Reconstructing Behavior in Youth: A Study of Problem Children in Foster Families,* Judge Baker Foundation

Publication No. 5 (New York: Alfred A. Knopf, 1931), 9; Kristin Elizabeth Gager, *Blood Ties and Fictive Ties: Adoption and Family Life in Early Modern France* (Princeton, N.J.: Princeton University Press, 1996), 7; Prentice, *An Adopted Child*, 171–73.

35. Rathbun, "Adoptive Foster Parent," 319.

36. Mrs. S. K. J. to Dear Friend, May 7, 1922, CBR, Central Files 1921–1924, File 7-3-4-3, Box 211; Mrs. V. L. L. to Mrs. Roosevelt, April 24, 1943,CBR, Central Files 1941–1944, File 7-3-3-4-1, Box 171.

37. Mrs. V. W. to Maud Morlock, November 24, 1944, CBR, Central Files 1941–1944, File 7-3-3-4, Box 171; Alice Kunz Ray, "A Good Adoption Program: Can Standards Be Maintained without Sacrificing Flexibility?" in *Proceedings of the National Conference of Social Work* (New York: Columbia University Press, 1945), 301.

38. Mrs. V. B. to Grace Abbott, October 22, 1929, CBR, Central Files 1929–1932, File 7-3-3-4, Box 406.

39. Mrs. L. E. C. to Dr. Ella Oppenheimer, June 5, 1934, CBR, Central Files 1933–1936, File 7-3-3-4, Box 548; Matthew Taback and Sidney Norton, "Adoption Practices in Baltimore, Maryland, 1938–1952," *Social Service Review* 29 (March 1955): 51.

40. The child was placed at six weeks of age. Infants needed to be at least three months old to take the standard developmental tests. Lockridge, *Adopting a Child*, 91.

41. Case History, application date April 17, 1934, Good Samaritan Home, Bangor, Maine.

42. This narrative came from a respondent to the Margaret Marsh/Wanda Ronner Infertility Survey conducted in 1994 for *The Empty Cradle* (Baltimore: Johns Hopkins University Press, 1996). Copy in author's possession; used with permission.

43. E. T. R. to Children's Bureau, September 19, 1935, CBR, Central Files 1933–1936, File 7-3-3-4, Box 548.

44. D. W. B. to Dear Sirs, November 18, 1944, CBR, Central Files 1941–1944, File 7-3-3-4-1, Box 171; Robert Griswold, *Fatherhood in America* (New York: Basic Books, 1993).

45. Mr. and Mrs. Jones are pseudonyms. Olive Wadlin to Julia Lathrop, March 19, 1921, and Mrs. J. S., Jr., to Julia Lathrop, April 19, 1921, CBR, Central Files 1921–1924, File 7-3-4-3, Box 211.

46. Historians disagree as to when social workers embraced psychoanalytic perspectives. Lubove, *Professional Altruist*, cites the 1920s as the key decade, although more recent scholarship argues that social workers were slow to adopt psychoanalytic casework methodology. Leslie Alexander, for example, argues that change began slowly in the late 1920s but was not complete until the postwar period ("Social Work's Freudian Deluge: Myth or Reality?" *Social Service Review* 46 [December 1972]: 517–38). Charlotte Towle, "The Evaluation of Homes in Preparation for Child Placements," *Mental Hygiene* 11 (1927): 463; Hutchinson, *In Quest of Foster Parents*, 3.

47. Theis, *Child in the Foster Home*, 31–35, 47–49.

48. Colby, *Problems and Procedures in Adoption*, 65; Hutchinson, *In Quest of Foster Parents*, 10–12.

49. Towle, "Evaluation of Homes," 466; Helene Deutsch, *The Psychology of Women* (New York: Grune and Stratton, 1945), 415, as quoted in Brenner, "Selection of Adoptive Parents," 5; Brenner, "Selection of Adoptive Parents," 4.

50. Clothier, "Placing the Child," 266–67; Elsa Castendyck to Mrs. B. A. S., March 1, 1944, CBR, Central Files 1941–1944, File 7-3-3-4-1, Box 171; Ernest Cady and Frances Cady, *How to Adopt a Child* (New York: Whiteside and William Morrow, 1956), chap. 9. The Cadys note that some agencies placed their age limit even lower, at thirty-five. At the 1951 CWLA conference, sixty-nine of seventy-nine agencies said that they would not place infants in homes where the parents were over forty (CWLA, *Adoption Practices, Procedures and Problems* [New York: CWLA, 1952], 33–34).

51. Hutchinson, *In Quest of Foster Parents*, 14–16, 63.

52. Clyde Getz (Children's Home Society of California) to Gay Shepperson, September 11, 1944, CBR, Central Files 1941–1944, File 7-3-3-4, Box 169.

53. Brenner, "Selection of Adoptive Parents," 4; Sargent, "Is It Safe," 26; Jessie Taft, "What It Means to Be a Foster Parent," *Progressive Education* 3 (October 1926): 352. Jane Collier et al., "Is There a Family? New Anthropological Views," in *Rethinking the Family: Some Feminist Questions*, ed. Barrie Thorne (New York: Longman, 1982), 25–39. The other reasons for adoption laws were, of course, to establish custody of the child and provide for a child's well-being (John Boswell, *The Kindness of Strangers* [New York: Pantheon Books, 1988], 66 n. 40, 115–16, 224; "Adoption among the Babylonians," *Biblical World* 30 [1907]: 228–29).

54. Children's Files, Group 1, Series 1, Box 1, Folder: Last Name "A_____", First Name "E_____" and "W_____" 1910, Sheltering Arms Collection; Tamara Hareven, *Family History at the Crossroads: A Journal of Family History Reader* (Princeton, N.J.: Princeton University Press, 1987), x; Hutchinson, *In Quest of Foster Parents*, 15.

55. Marsh and Ronner, *The Empty Cradle*, 168–69, 196–97, 204–6; Deutsch, *Psychology of Women*, 433; Brooks and Brooks, *Adventuring in Adoption*, 33; *New York Times*, May 31, 1953, 49.

56. Ruth Michaels, "Casework Considerations in Rejecting the Adoption Application," *Journal of Social Casework* 28 (1947): 371; "Personality in Dysmenorrhea and Sterility," *Journal of the American Medical Association*, January 18, 1941, 258.

57. Hutchinson, *In Quest of Foster Parents*, 16–18.

58. Ruth Carson, *So You Want to Adopt a Baby* (New York: CWLA, 1951), 10, 13–14; Clothier, "Placing the Child," 80; Rathbun, "Adoptive Foster Parent," 6; Hutchinson, *In Quest of Foster Parents*, 46. For infertility as a sign that a woman rejected her femininity, see Menninger and Orr, quoted in John Rock, "The Effect of Adoption on Fertility and Other Reproductive Functions," typescript (March 1949), John Rock Papers, Rare Books and Manuscripts Division, Countway Library of Medicine, Harvard University, Cambridge, Mass.

59. Kunzel, *Fallen Women*, 150–55; Rickie Solinger, *Wake up Little Susie* (New York: Routledge, 1992), chaps. 3, 5.

60. Margarete Sandelowski, "Fault Lines: Infertility and Imperiled Sisterhood," *Feminist Studies* 16 (spring 1990): 33–51.

61. Sophie van Senden Theis, "Some Aspects of Good Adoptive Practices," *CWLA Bulletin* 19 (November 1940): 1.

62. By 1944 in California, for example, the period between application and final action had stretched to two to three years. Clyde Getz to Gay Shepperson, September 11, 1944, CBR, Central Files 1941–1944, File 7-3-3-4, Box 169; MacKaye, "The Cradle," 95; "Adoption—An Integral Function," *CWLA Bulletin* 20 (February 1941): 9.

63. On case files, see Carp, *Family Matters*, 61–70.

64. Esther Stuart to Mary Ruth Colby, August 1, 1939, and Mary Ruth Colby to Esther Stuart, August 5, 1939, CBR, Central Files 1941–1944, File 7-3-3-4, Box 170.

65. Reid, "Principles, Values, and Assumptions," 35; Paul Beaven, M.D., "The Education of a Community," *CWLA Bulletin* 27 (Jan. 1948): 1; Judith Modell, *Kinship with Strangers* (Berkeley: University of California Press, 1994), 54–55, 104–8.

66. Reid, "Principles, Values, and Assumptions," 27; Gallagher, *The Adopted Child*, 45-46.

67. John Yunick's age was a point of contention in the trial. He had originally given his age as sixty-two, but subsequently said he had learned that he was much younger.

68. Michaels, "Casework Considerations," 370.

69. "Court Denies Plea for Tots," *Omaha World-Herald*, October 5, 1946; "I Won't Have to Give up my Babies," *Omaha World-Herald*, February 8, 1947; "Three Little Cakes Mark Birthday for Youngest of Yunicks' Children," *Omaha World-Herald* February 22, 1947; Dorothy Swisshelm to Edson Smith, February 10, 1947; Edson Smith to Dorothy Swisshelm, n.d.; Dorothy Swisshelm to Tom Wintersteen, February 24, 1947, CBR, Central Files 1945–1948, File 7-3-3-4, Box 158.

70. Dorothy Thompson, "Fit for Adoption," *Ladies' Home Journal*, May 1939, 4, 48.

71. Gesell, "Reducing the Risks," 2; "Adoption—An Integral Function"; Reid, "Principles, Values, and Assumptions," 26; Colby, *Problems and Procedures*, 28–29.

72. Nancy Schnog, "On Inventing the Psychological," in *Inventing the Psychological*, ed. Nancy Schnog and Joel Pfister (New Haven, Conn.: Yale University Press, 1997), 4–5; Nathan Hale, *The Rise and Crisis of Psychoanalysis in the United States* (New York: Oxford University Press, 1995), 98, chap. 16; Mrs. F. B. to Katharine Lenroot, June 9, 1944, CBR, Central Files 1941–1944, File 7-3-3-4-1, Box 171; Hutchinson, *In Quest of Foster Parents*, 14.

73. J. L. to Franklin D. Roosevelt, November 7, 1936, CBR, Central Files 1933–1936, File 7-3-3-4, Box 549; Gallagher, *The Adopted Child*, 55.

74. Towle, "Evaluation of Homes," 481; Gesell, "Reducing the Risks," 2.

75. Schapiro, *Study of Adoption Practice*, 18–20.

76. Sophie van Senden Theis, "Interpreting Adoption," *CWLA Bulletin* 27 (November 1948), 10–11.

77. *Berkeley Daily Gazette*, January 28, 1949, 3, as quoted in Cobbledick, "Study of Adoption Agency Criteria," 2.

78. Sophie van Senden Theis, "Adoption," in *Social Work Yearbook* (New York: Russell Sage Foundation, 1937), 23; Maud Morlock, "Relinquishment and Adoption," *CWLA Bulletin* 25 (November 1946), 1; Schapiro, *Study of Adoption Practice*, 109.

79. Schapiro, *Study of Adoption Practice*, 18–20; Benson Jaffee and David Fanshel, *How They Fared in Adoption: A Follow-up Study* (New York: Columbia University Press, 1970), 2; Kunzel, *Fallen Women*, chap. 6; Kathy S. Stolley, "Statistics on Adoption in the United States," *Future of Children* 3 (spring, 1993): 30–31.

80. Reid, "Principles, Values, and Assumptions," 30–33.

81. Ibid.

82. Schapiro, *Study of Adoption Practice*, 78–79

83. May, *Barren in the Promised Land*, 140–49.

84. Brenner, *Follow-up Study*, 51–53; Reid, "Principles, Values, and Assumptions," 31–33.

85. Schapiro, *Study of Adoption Practice*, 83–85.

86. Rathbun, "Adoptive Foster Parent," 315.

87. Mrs. D. V. F. to Dr. John Rock, January 15, 1954, Rock Papers.

Epilogue

1. For a summary of Mead's comments, see Miss Nutt to I. Evelyn Smith, December 18, 1947, CBR, Central Files 1945–1948, File 7-3-3-4, Box 158.

2. Howard Altstein and Rita J. Simon, introduction to *Intercountry Adoption: A Multinational Perspective* (New York: Praeger, 1990).

3. Dorothy Nelkin and M. Susan Lindee, *The DNA Mystique: The Gene as a Cultural Icon* (New York: W. H. Freeman, 1995), chap. 4; Elizabeth Bartholet, *Family Bonds: Adoption and the Politics of Parenting* (Boston: Houghton Mifflin, 1993).

4. Because national statistics on adoption did not specify whether an adoption was transracial, no one knows exactly how many transracial adoptions occurred in the 1960s and early 1970s, with estimates ranging from 12,000 to 20,000. Dawn Day, *The Adoption of Black Children* (Lexington, Mass.: Lexington Books/D. C. Heath, 1979), chap. 6; National Association of Black Social Workers (NABSW), "Position Statement on Trans-Racial Adoptions, September 1972," reprinted in *Children and Youth in America*, vol. 3, ed. Robert Bremner (Cambridge, Mass.: Harvard University Press, 1974), 777–78; Andrew Billingsley and Jeanne M. Giovannoni, *Children of the Storm* (New York: Harcourt Brace Jovanovich, 1972), 197–99; Patricia Collmeyer, "From 'Operation Brown Baby' to 'Opportunity': The Placement of Children of Color at the Boys and Girls Aid Society of Oregon," *Child Welfare* 74 (January/February 1995): 242–63.

5. NABSW, "Position Statement," 778–79 (emphasis added); Billingsley and Giovannoni, *Children of the Storm*, 198.

6. LeRoy Ashby, *Endangered Children* (New York: Twayne, 1997), 142, 168–70; Charisse Jones, "Debate on Race and Adoptions Is Being Reborn," *New York Times*, October 24, 1993, 1; "Adoption across the Color Line," *Washington Post*, April 9, 1992, editorial page; Rachel E. Stassen-Berger, "Return Girl to White Home, Doctors Say," *Philadelphia Inquirer*, July 12, 1995, 1; Martha Brant, "Storming the Color Barrier," *Newsweek*, March 20, 1995, 29; Bartholet, *Family Bonds*, 186, chap. 6.

7. Naomi Miller, *Single Parents by Choice: A Growing Trend in Family Life* (New York: Insight Books, 1992), 56; William Feigelman and Arnold R. Silverman, *Chosen Children: New Patterns of Adoptive Relationships* (New York: Praeger, 1983), 177.

8. National Council for Single Adoptive Parents, "Would You Rather Be Called Mommy or Daddy . . . Instead of Aunt or Uncle?" (May 1997) at www.adopting.org/ncsap.html; Lois Gilman, *The Adoption Resource Book*, 3d ed. (New York: Harper Perennial, 1992), 29.

9. Hope Marindin, *The Handbook for Single Adoptive Parents* (Chevy Chase, Md.: Committee for Single Adoptive Parents, 1987), 1; Mady Prowler, "Single Parent Adoption: What You Need to Know," *National Adoption Center* (1990), edited version at www.adopt.org/datacenter/bin/AQ_single1.htm (November 1999).

10. John Brinkerhoff, "Adopting Solo," *Family Matters* (March 1996), excerpt at "Strategies for Adopting 'Solo'," www.adopt.org/datacenter/bin/AQ_single3.htm (November 1999).

11. David Dunlap, "Support for Gay Adoptions Seems to Wane," *New York Times*, May 1, 1995, sec. A, p. 13; Ashby, *Endangered Children*, 172–73; "New York's Highest Court Rules that Unmarried Couples Can Adopt," *New York Times*, November 3, 1995; Carole S. Collum, "Co-Parent Adoptions: Lesbian and Gay Parenting," at www.adopt.org/datacenter/bin/AQ_gay2.htm (November 1999). For a first-person account of the difficulty lesbian couples have adopting and the cultural and psychological difficulties that can arise because one of the mothers is not a legal parent, see Carol Austin, "Latent Tendencies and Covert Acts," in *The Adoption Reader: Birth Mothers, Adoptive Mothers and Adopted Daughters Tell Their Stories*, ed. Susan Wadia-Ells (Seattle: Seal Press, 1995), 105–13.

12. Robert Hanley, "Court Allows Lesbian to Adopt Her Partner's Twins," *New York Times*, October 28, 1995, sec. 1, p. 26.

13. The concept of open adoption was first introduced by two social workers, Annette Baran and Reuben Pannor, and a psychiatrist, Arthur Sorosky. During the mid-1970s, the trio published their thoughts on open adoption in a number of academic journals and were often interviewed by the print media. They were (are) widely regarded as the experts on the effects of closed adoption and have served as the intellectual spokespeople for the adoption reform movement. In 1978, their work

was published in book form and was widely received (Arthur D. Sorosky, Annette Baran, and Reuben Pannor, *The Adoption Triangle* [New York: Anchor/Doubleday, 1978]). For a discussion of the development of the adoption reform movement, see E. Wayne Carp, *Family Matters* (Cambridge, Mass.: Harvard University Press, 1998), chap. 5.

14. There are no reliable statistics on how many white unwed mothers kept their children in the postwar period. Rickie Solinger, *Wake up Little Susie* (New York: Routledge, 1992), 33; Kathy S. Stolley, "Statistics on Adoption in the United States," *Future of Children* 3 (spring 1993): 30–33.

15. Ruth McRoy, Harold Grotevant, and Susan Ayers-Lopez, "Changing Practices in Adoption," AdoptINFO, Minnesota Children Youth and Family Consortium Electronic Clearinghouse, at www.cyfc.umn.edu/Adoptinfo/changing.html (May 1997); Lincoln Caplan, *An Open Adoption* (New York: Farrar, Straus, 1990), 49–51; Bruce Rappaport, *The Open Adoption Book: A Guide to Adoption without Tears* (New York: Macmillan, 1992), 165; Stolley, "Statistics on Adoption," 30–31. Because the government does not keep statistics on adoption, it is impossible to determine the percentage of adoptions arranged independently versus those arranged through an agency. The National Committee for Adoption, a lobbying organization for conventional agencies, estimates that one-third of the adoptions of unrelated children are independent, although others say that the numbers are much higher, even as many as four out of five. Not all independent adoptions are open.

16. Kathleen Silber and Phylis Speedlin, *Dear Birthmother: Thank You for Our Baby* (San Antonio, Tex.: Corona, 1983), 94–95.

17. McRoy et al., "Changing Practices"; Judith Modell, *Kinship with Strangers* (Berkeley: University of California Press, 1994), 202; Caplan, *Open Adoption*, 84; Gilman, *Adoption Resource Book*, 102; Rappaport, *Open Adoption Book*, 34.

18. Gilman, *Adoption Resource Book*, 107–9; Rappaport, *Open Adoption Book*, 40–41, 143–48; Ashby, *Endangered Children*, 172.

19. Silber and Speedlin, *Dear Birthmother*, 91, chap. 6.

20. Wadia-Ells, *Adoption Reader*, ix.

21. Arlie Hochschild, *The Second Shift: Working Parents and the Revolution at Home* (New York: Viking Press, 1989); Modell, *Kinship with Strangers*, 32; Katarina Wegar, *Adoption, Identity and Kinship* (New Haven, Conn.: Yale University Press, 1997), 123–27; Ashby, *Endangered Children*, 170–72; "Samantha's Choice," 48 Hours, CBS News, June 17, 1999, transcript 538.

22. Silber and Speedlin, *Dear Birthmother*, 144.

23. Gilman, *Adoption Resource Book*, 99–100, 108; Rappaport, *Open Adoption Book*, 146.

24. "The Politics of Adoption," *Newsweek*, March 21, 1994, 64–65; "Making a Baby, 10 Different Ways," *U.S. News and World Report*, April 12, 1999, 43.

Appendix

1. National Conference of Charities and Correction, *History of Child Saving in the United States* (1893; reprint, Montclair, N.J.: Patterson Smith, 1971), 57; Mrs. L. A. P. to Child Welfare Department, September 6, 1919, CBR, Central Files 1914–1920, File 7-3-4-3, Box 67. Also see National Conference of Charities and Correction, *Proceedings of the National Conference of Charities and Correction, 1899* (Boston: George H. Ellis, 1900), 184, which notes that children ages three and under were most often adopted. In 1909, a West Coast child-placing agency noted that of 111 applications, 80 were for children under the age of five (Patricia Susan Hart, "A Home for Every Child, a Child for Every Home: Relinquishment and Adoption at Washington Children's Home Society, 1896–1915" [Ph.D. diss., Washington State University, 1997], 175). For examples of adoptive parents who expressed concern about the child or a member of the community discovering that the child was adopted, see History of Cases, nos: 51, 52, 122, 294, 1071, CAS/HSP.

2. Susan Tiffin, *In Whose Best Interest?* (Westport, Conn: Greenwood Press, 1982), 98–99; *Seventh Annual Report of the Children's Aid Society of Pennsylvania* (1888), 6.

3. Bruce Bellingham, "Little Wanderers: A Socio-Historical Study of the Nineteenth-Century Origins of Child Fostering and Adoption Reform, Based on Early Records of the New York Children's Aid Society" (Ph.D. diss., University of Pennsylvania, 1984).

4. See, for example, History of Cases, no. 201, CAS/HSP, in which a two-week-old illegitimate boy was taken for free by a family with whom he remained forever. For an explanation of the CAS's new policy regarding boarding, see *Eleventh Annual Report of the Children's Aid Society* (1892), 5–6.

5. Bellingham, "Little Wanderers," 66, 68–69.

6. See, for example, History of Cases, nos. 25 and 966, CAS/HSP.

7. See, for example, History of Cases, nos. 49, 120, 122, and 1052, CAS/HSP.

8. For an example of a case in which the foster parents vehemently resented the society's visits but in which the CAS was confident of the safety of the child, see History of Cases, no. 52, CAS/HSP. Also see *Fourteenth Annual Report of the Children's Aid Society of Pennsylvania* (1895).

9. See, for example, History of Cases, 1882–1891, nos. 51 and 52, CAS/HSP. For examples of adoption-like situations with nontraditional adoptive parents, see History of Cases, nos. 5, 96, 122, and 1034, CAS/HSP.

Bibliography

Manuscript and Archival Collections

Countway Library of Medicine, Harvard University, Rare Books and Manuscripts Division, John Rock Papers
Good Samaritan Home, Bangor, Maine
Historical Society of Pennsylvania, Philadelphia, Pa., Records of the Children's Aid Society of Pennsylvania; Orphan Society of Philadelphia
Library of Congress, Manuscripts Division, Washington, D.C., Hillcrest Children's Center; Mabel Walker Willebrandt Papers
National Archives, Washington, D.C., Records of the District of Columbia, Record Group 351, Board of Children's Guardians; Children's Bureau Records, Record Group 102
Rutgers University Library, Special Collections, New Brunswick, N.J., Sheltering Arms Collection
University of Pennsylvania, Van Pelt–Dietrich Library, Special Collections, Theodore Dreiser Papers

Government Documents

An Act to Authorize the Adoption of Children in the District of Columbia. Statutes at Large 28 (1895).
Butler, Edmond J. "Standards of Child Placing and Supervision." In *Standards of Child Welfare. A Report of the Children's Bureau Conferences, May and June, 1919.* Children's Bureau Publication No. 60. Washington, D.C.: U.S. Department of Labor, 1919.
Colby, Mary Ruth. *Problems and Procedures in Adoption.* Children's Bureau Publication No. 262. Washington, D.C.: GPO, 1941.
Peck, Emelyn Foster. *Adoption Laws in the United States.* Children's Bureau Publication No. 148. Washington, D.C.: GPO, 1925.
U.S. Bureau of the Census. *Benevolent Institutions, 1904.* Washington, D.C.: GPO, 1905.
———. *Benevolent Institutions, 1910.* Washington, D.C.: GPO, 1913.
———. *Children under Institutional Care, 1923.* Washington, D.C.: GPO, 1927.
U.S. Congress. House. *Annual Report of the Superintendent of Charities of the District of Columbia, 1892.* 52d Cong., 2d sess., 1892–1893. H. Exdoc. 9.

————. *Care of Delinquent and Dependent Children in the District of Columbia.* 58th Cong., 2d sess., 1903–1904. H. Doc. 355.

U.S. Congress. Senate. *Proceedings of the Conference on the Care of Dependent Children, Held at Washington, D.C., January 25–29, 1909.* 60th Cong., 2d sess., 1909. S. Doc. 721.

————. *Providing for Dependent Children in the District of Columbia.* 52d Cong., 1st sess., 1891–1892. S. Rpt. 842.

Primary Sources

Abbey, Charlotte. "Women in Social Service." *Transactions of the Alumni Association of the Women's Medical College of Pennsylvania* (1909): 118–19.

"Adopted Mother by Herself." *Scribner's Magazine,* January 1935, 56.

"An Adopted Mother Speaks." *Survey* 47 (March 18, 1922): 962–63.

"Adopting a Baby." *Woman's Journal* 14 (July 1929): 9.

"Adoption among the Babylonians." *Biblical World* 30 (1907): 228–29.

"Adoption—An Integral Function." *Child Welfare League of America Bulletin* 20 (February 1941): 9.

"Adoption in Pennsylvania." *Medical Woman's Journal* 32 (January 1925): 21.

Antoine, Josephine, as told to Vera Connolly. "I Was an Adopted Child." *Woman's Home Companion,* February 1947, 36.

Baker, S. Josephine, M.D. "Choosing a Child." *Ladies' Home Journal,* February 1924, 36.

————. "A Home for Every Child." *Ladies' Home Journal,* May 1926, 29.

Barley, Ann. *Patrick Calls Me Mother.* New York: Harper and Brothers, 1948.

Beaven, Paul. "The Education of a Community." *Child Welfare League of America Bulletin* 27 (January 1948): 1.

Boylan, Grace Duffie. *The Supplanter.* Boston: Lothrop, Lee, Shepard, 1913.

Bradley, Trudy. *An Exploration of Caseworkers' Perceptions of Adoptive Applicants.* New York: Child Welfare League of America, 1967.

Brenner, Ruth. *A Follow-up Study of Adoptive Families.* New York: Child Adoption Research Committee, 1951.

————. "The Selection of Adoptive Parents: A Casework Responsibility." *Child Welfare League of America Bulletin* 25 (December 1946): 1–6.

"Brighter Day Dawns for Foundlings." *Literary Digest,* December 5, 1936, 31.

Bromley, Dorothy Dunbar. "Demand for Babies Outruns the Supply." *New York Times Magazine,* March 3, 1935, 9.

Brooks, Lee M., and Evelyn C. Brooks. *Adventuring in Adoption.* Chapel Hill: University of North Carolina Press, 1939.

Brown, Eli. *Sex and Life: The Physiology and Hygiene of the Sexual Organization.* Chicago: F. J. Schulte, 1891.

Brownell, Frederick. "Bottleneck for Babies." *Christian Herald Magazine,* August 1948, 27–29.

———. "Why You Can't Adopt a Baby!" *Christian Herald Magazine,* July 1948, 17–18.

Burgess, Ernest. "Family Tradition and Personality Development." In *Proceedings of the National Conference of Social Work.* Chicago: University of Chicago, 1928.

Cady, Ernest, and Frances Cady. *How to Adopt a Child.* New York: Whiteside and William Morrow, 1956.

Canfield, Dorothy. "Children without Parents." *Woman's Home Companion,* May 1939, 21.

Carlson, Avis. "To Test a Baby." *Atlantic Monthly* 165 (June 1940): 829.

Carson, Ruth. *So You Want to Adopt a Baby.* New York: Child Welfare League of America, 1951.

Carstens, C. C. "Safeguards in Adoption." *Child Welfare League of America Bulletin* 15 (April 1936): 4.

Channing, Grace Ellery. "The Children of the Barren." *Harper's Monthly Magazine,* March 1907, 511–19.

Chapin, Henry Dwight, M.D. "Finding Babies for Folks to Adopt." *American Magazine,* November 1919, 42.

Chapman, A. S. "Homes for Babies; Babies for Homes." *Hygeia* 10 (December 1932): 1106.

"Child-Rescue Campaign." *Delineator,* October 1907 through February 1911, January 1912.

Child Welfare League of America. *Adoption Practices, Procedures and Problems.* New York: Child Welfare League of America, 1952.

———. *Standards for Organizations Providing Foster Family Care.* New York: Child Welfare League of America, 1933.

"Childless." *Good Housekeeping,* April 1911, 532.

"The Childless Wife." *Good Housekeeping,* July 1911, 21.

"Chosen Children." *Time,* May 15, 1939, 39.

Clark, Thomas Arkle. "A Home without Children May Still Be a Home." *American Magazine,* August 1927, 44.

Clothier, Florence. "Placing the Child for Adoption." *Mental Hygiene* 26 (April 1942): 257–74.

———. "Some Aspects of the Problem of Adoption." *American Journal of Orthopsychiatry* 9 (1939): 598–615.

Colby, Mary Ruth. "Modern Safeguards in Adoption Legislation." *Child Welfare League of America Bulletin* 20 (December 1941): 3–6.

Cole, Lawrence C. "A Study of Adoptions in Cuyahoga County." *Family* 6 (January 1926): 259–64.

Comstock, Harriet. *Mam'selle Jo.* Garden City, N.Y.: Doubleday, Page, 1918.

"Cradles Instead of Divorces." *Literary Digest* 77 (April 14, 1923): 35.

Cranston, Claudia. "The Left-Over Baby." *Good Housekeeping*, April 1917, 39.

Deland, Margaret. *The Awakening of Helena Ritchie*. New York: Harper and Brothers, 1906.

———. *Old Chester Tales*. New York: Harper and Brothers, 1898.

Deutsch, Helene. *The Psychology of Women: A Psychoanalytic Interpretation*. New York: Grune and Stratton, 1945.

Doss, Carl, and Helen Doss. *If You Adopt a Child*. New York: Henry Holt, 1957.

Dow, Charles. "New Legal Ruling in Adoption Cases." *Child Welfare League of America Bulletin* 15 (September 1936): 2.

Dunbar, Olivia Howard. "Miss Hildreth: 'Mother of Ten.' " *Harper's Bazaar*, September 1912, 443–44.

"The Epidemic of Adoption." *Living Age* 294 (September 8, 1917): 632–34.

Evans, Mrs. J. H. "Child Placing by Volunteers." In *Proceedings of the National Conference of Charities and Correction*. Fort Wayne, Ind.: Archer, 1910.

Farmer, Robert A. *How to Adopt a Child*. New York: Arco, 1967.

Fisher, Dorothy Canfield. "Children without Parents." *Woman's Home Companion*, May 1939, 21.

Fleurot, Arno Dosch. "Not Enough Babies to Go Around." *Cosmopolitan*, September 1910, 431.

Folks, Homer. *The Care of Destitute, Neglected, and Delinquent Children*. Albany, N.Y.: Charities Review, 1900. Reprint, New York: Arno Press, 1971.

Foster, Sybil. "Fees for Adoption Service." In *Proceedings of the National Conference of Social Work, 1947*. New York: Columbia University, 1948.

"Foster Parents Speak for Themselves." *Child Welfare League of America Bulletin* 9 (April 1930): 4.

Fradkin, Helen. *The Adoption Home Study*. Trenton: New Jersey Department of Institutions and Agencies, Division of Public Welfare, Bureau of Children's Services, 1963.

Frazer, Elizabeth. "The Baby Market." *Saturday Evening Post*, February 1, 1930, 25.

Freeman, Mary E. Wilkins. *A Humble Romance and Other Stories*. New York: Harper and Brothers, 1887.

Gagliardo, Ruth Garver. "We Wanted Children." *Parents*, May 1937, 28–29.

Gale, Zona. *Friendship Village Love Stories*. New York: Macmillan, 1909.

Gallagher, Eleanor G. *The Adopted Child*. New York: Reynal and Hitchcock, 1936.

Galloway, Ewing. "He Likes Babies." *Collier's*, June 20, 1914, 23–24.

Gardner, Mona. "Traffic in Babies." *Collier's*, September 16, 1939, 14–15.

Gatlin, Lillian. "Adopting a Baby: The Stork Gives Blindly, but Only the Fittest Qualify as Parents by Proxy." *Sunset, the Pacific Monthly*, February 1921, 83–86.

Gesell, Arnold, M. D. "Reducing the Risks of Child Adoption." *Child Welfare League of America Bulletin* 6 (May 15, 1927): 2.

Gibson, Mrs. Charles Dana. "When a Child Adopts You." *Good Housekeeping,* July 1927, 79.

Goddard, Henry H. *The Kallikak Family: A Study in the Heredity of Feeblemindedness.* New York: Macmillan, 1912.

———. "Wanted: A Child to Adopt." *Survey* 27 (October 14, 1911): 1004.

Grant, Robert. "Domestic Relations and the Child." *Scribner's Magazine,* May 1919, 525–30.

Groves, Ernest. *The Drifting Home.* Cambridge: Riverside Press, Houghton-Mifflin, 1926.

———. *Social Problems of the Family.* Philadelphia: J. B. Lippincott, 1927.

Hanna, Agnes. "The Interrelationship between Illegitimacy and Adoption." *Child Welfare League of America Bulletin* 16 (September 1937): 1.

Harding, Allan. "'Aunt Sat' Davis Has Mothered More than Forty Children." *American Magazine,* February 1924, 18–20.

Hart, Hastings. *Child Welfare in the District of Columbia.* New York: Russell Sage Foundation, 1924.

———. *Preventive Treatment of Neglected and Dependent Children.* 1910. Reprint, New York: Arno Press, 1971.

Havor, Mary. "And After Adoption—What Then?" *Woman's Day,* November 1947, 35.

Heisterman, Carl. "A Summary of Legislation on Adoption." *Social Service Review* 9 (June 1935): 269–93.

Hohman, Leslie B., M.D. "All Parents Can Profit from Adoption's Story." *Ladies' Home Journal,* September 1942, 88–89.

Hollingworth, Leta S. "Social Devices for Impelling Women to Bear and Rear Children." *American Journal of Sociology* 22 (July 1916): 19–29.

"The Homeless Child and the Childless Home." *Charities and the Commons* 19 (February 22, 1908): 1612–13.

"How It Feels to Have Been an Adopted Child." *American Magazine,* August 1920, 72–73.

Howard, Carrington. "Adoption by Advertisement." *Survey* 35 (December 11, 1915): 285–86.

"A Humorist's 'Baby Bureau'." *The Literary Digest,* July 19, 1913, 100-101.

Hutchinson, Dorothy. *Cherish the Child: Dilemmas of Placement.* Edited by Maude von P. Kemp. Metuchen, N.J.: Scarecrow Press, 1972.

———. "Foster Home Care in Wartime." In *Proceedings of the National Conference of Social Work.* New York: Columbia University Press, 1944.

———. *In Quest of Foster Parents, a Point of View on Homefinding.* New York: Published for the New York School of Social Work by Columbia University Press, 1943.

———. "Re-examination of Some Aspects of Case Work Practice in Adoption." *Child Welfare League of America Bulletin* 25 (November 1946): 4–7.

"I Just Adopted a Baby." *Ladies' Home Journal*, August 1937, 14–15.

"I Want to Be Really a Woman." *Delineator*, July 1913, 10.

"Ideal Motherhood." *American Jewess*, September 1895, 279.

Jaffee, Benson, and David Fanshel. *How They Fared in Adoption: A Follow-up Study*. New York: Columbia University Press, 1970.

Jenkins, R. L. "On Adopting a Baby." *Hygeia* 13 (December 1935): 1066–68.

Joyce, Arthur. "Chronicle of a Search for a Homeless Waif in Philadelphia—Where There Aren't Any." *Philadelphia Record*, June 30, 1929, 1.

Kalins, Dorothy. "Baby Hunt: The Agony and the Ecstasy of Our Private Adoption." *New York*, July 26, 1993, 26–33.

Keith, Alyn Yates. *A Spinster's Leaflets*. Boston: Lee and Shepard, 1894.

Kerley, Charles Gilmore, M.D. "The Adoption of Children." *Outlook*, January 12, 1916, 104–7.

Kirby, Constance. "Bargains in Babies." *Harper's Bazaar*, June 1912, 280.

Lawder, Elizabeth A., et al. *A Followup Study of Adoptions: Post-Placement Functioning of Adoption Families*. New York: Child Welfare League of America, 1969.

Leahy, Alice. "Some Characteristics of Adoptive Parents." *American Journal of Sociology* 38 (January 1933): 548–63.

Levinson, A. "When Adopting a Baby." *Hygeia* 7 (February 1929): 135–38.

Lewis, Judd Mortimer. "Dealing in Babies." *Good Housekeeping*, February 1914, 196–98.

Liggett, Edith. "Red Tape and Runaround in Adoption." *Woman*, June 1946, 29–32.

Lippman, Hyman S. "Suitability of the Child for Adoption." *American Journal of Orthopsychiatry* 7 (1937): 270–73.

Lockridge, Frances. *Adopting a Child*. New York: Greenberg, 1948.

———. "How to Adopt." *Children, the Magazine for Parents*, October 1928, 14–15.

MacKaye, Milton. "The Cradle." *Saturday Evening Post*, April 9, 1938, 12–13.

Marea, E. *The Wife's Manual*. Cortland, N.Y.: n.p. 1896.

"Meet the Andreasons and Their Four Adopted Children of Eugene, Oregon." *Ladies' Home Journal*, September 1942, 83–86.

Michaels, Ruth. "Casework Considerations in Rejecting the Adoption Application." *Journal of Social Casework* 28 (1947): 370–76.

Mohr, George. "Adoption." *Child Welfare League of America Bulletin* 16 (October 1937): 1.

Morgenthau, Henry. "Cradles Instead of Divorces." *Literary Digest* 77 (April 14, 1923).

Morlock, Maud. "Relinquishment and Adoption." *Child Welfare League of America Bulletin* 25 (November 1946): 1.

National Conference of Charities and Correction. *History of Child Saving in the United States*. 1893. Reprint, Montclair, N.J.: Patterson Smith, 1971.

———. *Proceedings of the National Conference of Charities and Correction, 1899*. Boston: George H. Ellis, 1900.

Nelson, Josephine. "Would You 'Bootleg' a Baby?" *Independent Woman*, February 1936, 42–44.

Nims, Elinor. *The Illinois Adoption Law and Its Administration*. Chicago: University of Chicago Press, 1928.

Norris, Kathleen. "Adopt that Baby!" *Ladies' Home Journal*, April 1930, 8.

———. "Mothering Cecelia." *Good Housekeeping*, March 1913, 304–15.

O'Hagan, Anne. "The Biography of a Foundling." *Munsey's Magazine*, June 1901, 308–16.

"Our Adopted Son." *Ladies' Home Journal*, April 1924, 35.

"Our Greatest Experience." *Scribner's Magazine*, January 1938, 60.

Parker, Ida R. *"Fit and Proper"? A Study of Legal Adoption in Massachusetts*. Boston: Church Home Society for the Care of Children of the Protestant Church, 1927.

Patterson, Ada. "Giving Babies Away." *Cosmopolitan*, August 1905, 405–12.

Pendleton, Ora. "New Aims in Adoption." *Annals of the American Academy of Political and Social Science* 151 (September 1930): 154–61.

Perkins, H. F. "Adoption and Fertility." *Eugenical News* 21 (September–October 1936): 95–101.

"Personality in Dysmenorrhea and Sterility." *Journal of the American Medical Association*, January 18, 1941, 258.

"A Plea for Adoption." *Good Housekeeping*, July 1911, 132.

"Postponement of Motherhood." *Good Housekeeping*, January 1912, 84–89.

Prentice, Carol S. *An Adopted Child Looks at Adoption*. New York: D. Appleton-Century, 1940.

"A Program in Education." *Child Welfare League of America Bulletin* 17 (November 1938): 4–5.

Public Charities Association of Pennsylvania. *Adoptions in Pennsylvania*. Philadelphia: Family and Child Welfare Division, January 1939.

Rathbun, Constance. "The Adoptive Foster Parent: A Basis for Evaluation." *Child Welfare League of America Bulletin* 23 (November 1944): 5–7, 12–14.

Ray, Alice Kunz. "A Good Adoption Program: Can Standards Be Maintained without Sacrificing Flexibility?" In *Proceedings of the National Conference of Social Work*. New York: Columbia University Press, 1945.

Reid, Joseph. "Principles, Values, and Assumptions Underlying Adoption Practice." *Social Work* 2 (January 1957): 22–29.

Reynolds, Wilfred S. "Standards of Placing Out in Free Family Homes." In *Proceedings of the National Conference of Charities and Correction*. Fort Wayne, Ind.: Fort Wayne Printing Company, 1914.

Richardson, Charles. *A New Dictionary of the English Language*. Philadelphia: E. H. Butler, 1951.

Riis, Jacob. "A Christmas Reminder of the Noblest Work in the World." *Forum* 16 (January 1894): 624–33.

Robinson, Virginia P., ed. *Jessie Taft: Therapist and Social Work Educator.* Philadelphia: University of Pennsylvania Press, 1962.

Sants, H. J. "Genealogical Bewilderment in Children with Substitute Parents." *Child Adoption* 47 (summer 1965): 32–42.

Sargent, Helen D. "Is It Safe to Adopt a Child?" *Parents' Magazine,* October 1935, 26.

Sayles, Mary B. *Substitute Parents: A Study of Foster Families.* New York: Commonwealth Fund, 1936.

Schapiro, Michael. *A Study of Adoption Practice.* Vol. 1, *Adoption Agencies and the Children They Serve.* New York: Child Welfare League of America, 1956.

———. *A Study of Adoption Practice.* Vol. 2, *Selected Scientific Papers Presented at the National Conference on Adoption, January, 1955.* New York: Child Welfare League of America, 1956.

Seeley, Evelyn. "Adoptions: Maryland's Better Way." *Survey Graphic* 37 (May 1948): 255–58.

Shea, Alice Leahy. "Family Background and the Placement of Illegitimate Children." *American Journal of Sociology* 43 (July 1937): 103–4.

Slingerland, William. *Child-Placing in Families; a Manual for Students and Social Workers.* New York: Russell Sage Foundation, 1919.

Smith, I. Evelyn. *Readings in Adoption.* New York: Philosophical Library, 1963.

Smith, Mary Frances. "Adoption as the Community Sees It." *Journal of Social Work Process* 3 (December 1939): 6–8.

State Charities Aid Association. *How Foster Children Turn Out.* New York: State Charities Aid Association, 1924.

Stoneman, A. H. "Safeguarding Adoptions, Legally and Socially." In *Proceedings of the National Conference of Social Work.* Chicago: University of Chicago Press, 1924.

"Store Gets Nine Babies Adopted." *Dry Goods Economist* 78 (May 24, 1924): 41.

Taback, Matthew, and Sidney Norton. "Adoption Practices in Baltimore, Maryland, 1938–1952." *Social Service Review* 29 (March 1955): 43–52.

Taft, Jessie. "The Adopted Child." *Delineator,* September 1933, 12.

———. "Concerning Adopted Children." *Child Study* 6 (January 1929): 85–87.

———. "What It Means to Be a Foster Parent." *Progressive Education* 3 (October 1926): 350–54.

Taft, Ruth. "Adoptive Families for 'Unadoptable' Children." *Child Welfare* 32 (June 1953): 5–9.

Taylor, Pamela. "Son without Stork." *Saturday Review of Literature* 31 (July 31, 1948).

Terrett, Virginia Rowe. "Un Petit Homme d'Affaires." *New York Times Book Review,* July 11, 1948.

Thayer, Stuart. "Moppets on the Market: The Problem of Unregulated Adoptions." *Yale Law Journal* 59 (March 1950): 715–36.

Theis, Sophie van Senden. *The Child in the Foster Home.* New York: New York School of Social Work, 1921.

———. *How Foster Children Turn Out*. New York: State Charities Aid Association, 1924.

———. "Interpreting Adoption." *Child Welfare League of America Bulletin* 27 (November 1948): 10–11.

———. *Social Aspects of Child Adoption*. New York: Child Welfare League of America, 1937.

———. "Some Aspects of Good Adoptive Practices." *Child Welfare League of America Bulletin* 19 (November 1940): 1.

Thompson, Dorothy. "Fit for Adoption." *Ladies' Home Journal*, May 1939, 4.

Toombs, Alfred. "War Babies." *Woman's Home Companion* 71 (April 1944): 32.

Towle, Charlotte. "The Evaluation of Homes in Preparation for Child Placements." *Mental Hygiene* 11 (1927): 460–81.

Towne, Charles Hanson. *Adventures in Editing*. New York: n.p., 1926.

"Training Babies for the 'Golden Spoon.'" *Literary Digest*, April 8, 1916, 1020.

"Travailogue." *Time*, April 29, 1946, 31.

Turnbull, Agnes Sligh. "The Great Adventure of Adopting a Baby." *American Magazine*, May 1929, 44.

Van Blarcom, Carolyn Conant. "Our Child Helping Department—Shall We Tell the Truth to Adopted Children?" *Delineator*, February 1920, 29.

———. "Our Child Helping Service." *Delineator*, November 1919, 34.

Van Hoosen, Bertha, M.D. "The Adopted Child." *Medical Woman's Journal* 35 (April 1928): 95–96.

———. "The Adopted Mother." *Medical Woman's Journal* 34 (December 1927): 361–62.

Vansant, Martha. "The Life of the Adopted Child." *American Mercury*, February 1933, 214–22.

Ware, Caroline F. *Greenwich Village 1920–1930; a Comment on American Civilization in the Post-War Years*. Boston: Houghton Mifflin, 1935.

"Was It Well or Ill Chosen?" *Harper's Weekly*, March 15, 1902, 325.

Wilds, Sophie. "The Fosters Adopt a Child." *Rotarian* 53 (September 1938): 34–37.

Willebrandt, Mabel Walker. "First Impressions." *Good Housekeeping*, May 1928.

Willsie, Honore. "The Adopted Mother." *Century Magazine*, September 1922, 654–68.

———. "Are You Afraid to Adopt a Child!" *Delineator*, August 1919, 25.

———. "The Home He Should Have Had." *Delineator*, May 1919, 1.

———. "Not a Boy, Please!" *Delineator*, July 1919, 33.

———. "Our Child-Helping Department." *Delineator*, October 1919, 33.

———. "When Is a Child Adoptable?" *Delineator*, December 1919, 35.

Winter, Marjorie. *For Love of Martha*. New York: Julian Messner, 1956.

Wise, Louise Waterman. "Mothers in Name." *Survey* 43 (March 20, 1920): 779–80.

Witmer, Helen, et al. *Independent Adoptions*. New York: Russell Sage Foundation, 1963.

"A Woman's Reason." *Independent*, April 4, 1907, 782.

Secondary Sources

Adamac, Christine, and William Pierce. *The Encyclopedia of Adoption.* New York: Facts on File, 1991.

Alexander, Leslie. "Social Work's Freudian Deluge: Myth or Reality?" *Social Service Review* 46 (December 1972): 517–38.

Altstein, Howard, and Rita J. Simon. *Intercountry Adoption: A Multinational Perspective.* New York: Praeger, 1990.

Antler, Joyce. *The Making of a Modern Woman.* New Haven, Conn.: Yale University Press, 1987.

Apple, Rima. *Mothers and Medicine: A Social History of Infant Feeding, 1890–1950.* Madison: University of Wisconsin Press, 1987.

Ashby, LeRoy. *Endangered Children: Dependency, Neglect, and Abuse in American History.* New York: Twayne, 1997.

———. *Saving the Waifs: Reformers and Dependent Children, 1890–1917.* Philadelphia: Temple University Press, 1984.

Austin, Linda Tollett. *Babies for Sale: The Tennessee Children's Home Adoption Scandal.* Westport, Conn.: Praeger, 1993.

Bartholet, Elizabeth. *Family Bonds: Adoption and the Politics of Parenting.* Boston: Houghton Mifflin, 1993.

Bayles, George James. *American Women's Legal Status.* New York: P. F. Collier and Son, 1905.

Beck, Clare. "Adelaide Hasse: The New Woman as Librarian." In *Reclaiming the American Library Past: Writing the Women In,* edited by Suzanne Hildenbrand. Norwood, N.J.: Ablex, 1996.

Berebitsky, Julie. "'To Raise as Your Own': The Growth of Legal Adoption in Washington." *Washington History* 6 (spring/summer 1994): 4–26.

Berry, Marianne. "Parent Access after Adoption." In *Debating Children's Lives: Current Controversies on Children and Adolescents,* edited by Mary Ann Mason and Eileen Gambrill. Thousand Oaks, Calif.: Sage Publications, 1994.

Billingsley, Andrew, and Jeanne M. Giovannoni. *Children of the Storm.* New York: Harcourt Brace Jovanovich, 1972.

Bledstein, Burton. *The Culture of Professionalism.* New York: W. W. Norton, 1976.

Bloch, Ruth. "American Feminine Ideals in Transition: The Rise of the Moral Mother, 1785–1815." *Feminist Studies* 4 (June 1978): 101–26.

Bogan, Hyman. *The Luckiest Orphans: A History of the Hebrew Orphan Asylum of New York.* Urbana: University of Illinois Press, 1992.

Boswell, John. *The Kindness of Strangers.* New York: Pantheon Books, 1988.

Boyer, Paul. *Urban Masses and Moral Order in America, 1820–1920.* Cambridge, Mass.: Harvard University Press, 1978.

Brant, Martha. "Storming the Color Barrier." *Newsweek,* March 20, 1995, 29.

Bremner, Robert, ed. *Children and Youth in America: A Documentary History.* 3 vols. Cambridge, Mass.: Harvard University Press, 1970–1974.

Brown, Dorothy M. *Mabel Walker Willebrandt: A Study of Power, Loyalty, and Law.* Knoxville: University of Tennessee Press, 1984.

Brumberg, Joan Jacobs. "'Ruined' Girls: Changing Community Responses to Illegitimacy in Upstate New York, 1890–1920." *Journal of Social History* 18 (winter 1984): 247–72.

Burns, George. *Gracie: A Love Story.* New York: Putnam, 1988.

Caplan, Lincoln. *An Open Adoption.* New York: Farrar, Straus, 1990.

Carp, E. Wayne. "Adoption and Disclosure of Family Information: A Historical Perspective." *Child Welfare* 74 (January/February 1995): 217–41.

———. *Family Matters: Secrecy and Disclosure in the History of Adoption.* Cambridge, Mass.: Harvard University Press, 1998.

———. "The Myth of Sealed Adoption Records: The Case of the Children's Home Society of Washington, 1895–1988." *Locus* 4 (spring 1992): 153–67.

———. "Professional Social Workers, Adoption, and the Problem of Illegitimacy, 1915–1945." *Journal of Policy History* 6 (1994): 161–84.

———. "The Sealed Adoption Records Controversy in Historical Perspective: The Case of the Children's Home Society of Washington, 1895–1988." *Journal of Sociology and Social Welfare* 19 (June 1992): 27–58.

———. "Secrecy Attacked: Social Science, the Media, and the Ideology of the Adoption Rights Movement." Paper presented at the 1994 annual meeting of the Organization of American Historians, April 1994, Atlanta.

Chodorow, Nancy. *The Reproduction of Mothering: Psychoanalysis and the Sociology of Gender.* Berkeley: University of California Press, 1978.

Clement, Priscilla Ferguson. "Families and Foster Care: Philadelphia in the Late Nineteenth Century." In *Growing Up in America,* N. Ray Hiner and Joseph Hawes. Chicago: University of Illinois Press, 1985.

Cohen, Lizabeth. *Making a New Deal: Industrial Workers in Chicago, 1919–1939.* Cambridge: Cambridge University Press, 1990.

Collins, Patricia Hill. *Black Feminist Thought: Knowledge, Consciousness and the Politics of Empowerment.* New York: Routledge, 1991.

Collmeyer, Patricia. "From 'Operation Brown Baby' to 'Opportunity': The Placement of Children of Color at the Boys and Girls Aid Society of Oregon." *Child Welfare* 74 (January/February 1995): 242–63.

Collum, Carole S. "Co-Parent Adoptions: Lesbian and Gay Parenting." http://www.adopt.org/datacenter/bin/AQ_gay2.htm. November 1999.

Coontz, Stephanie. *The Way We Never Were: American Families and the Nostalgia Trap.* New York: Basic Books, 1992.

Cott, Nancy. *The Bonds of Womanhood: "Woman's Sphere" in New England, 1780–1835.* New Haven, Conn.: Yale University Press, 1977.

———. *The Grounding of Modern Feminism*. New Haven, Conn.: Yale University Press, 1987.

D'Emilio, John, and Estelle Freedman. *Intimate Matters: A History of Sexuality in America*. New York: Harper and Row, 1988.

Daims, Diva. *Toward a Feminist Tradition: An Annotated Bibliography of Novels in English by Women, 1891–1920*. New York: Garland, 1982.

Day, Dawn. *The Adoption of Black Children*. Lexington, Mass.: Lexington Books/ D. C. Heath, 1979.

Degler, Carl. *At Odds: Women and the Family in America from the Revolution to the Present*. New York: Oxford University Press, 1980.

———. *In Search of Human Nature: The Decline and Revival of Darwinism in American Social Thought*. New York: Oxford University Press, 1991.

Demos, John. *A Little Commonwealth: Family Life in Plymouth Colony*. New York: Oxford University Press, 1970.

Douglas, Ann. *The Feminization of American Culture*. New York: Anchor Press, 1988.

Duggan, Lisa. "The Trials of Alice Mitchell: Sensationalism, Sexology, and the Lesbian Subject in Turn-of-the-Century America." *Signs* 18 (summer 1993): 791–814.

Dye, Nancy Schrom, and Daniel Blake Smith. "Mother Love and Infant Death, 1750–1920." *Journal of American History* 73 (1986): 329–53.

Ehrenreich, Barbara, and Deirdre English. *For Her Own Good: 150 Years of the Experts' Advice to Women*. New York: Anchor Books, 1979.

Elias, Robert H. *Theodore Dreiser, Apostle of Nature*. New York: Knopf, 1949.

Faderman, Lillian. *Odd Girls and Twilight Lovers*. New York: Penguin Books, 1991.

Feigelman, William, and Arnold R. Silverman. *Chosen Children: New Patterns of Adoptive Relationships*. New York: Praeger, 1983.

Filene, Peter. *Him/Her/Self: Sex Roles in Modern America*. New York: New American Library, 1974.

Franzen, Trisha. *Spinsters and Lesbians*. New York: New York University Press, 1996.

Freedman, Estelle B. *Maternal Justice: Miriam Van Waters and the Female Reform Tradition*. Chicago: University of Chicago Press, 1996.

Friedman, Lawrence. *A History of American Law*. 2d ed. New York: Simon and Schuster, 1985.

Gager, Kristin Elizabeth. *Blood Ties and Fictive Ties: Adoption and Family Life in Early Modern France*. Princeton, N.J.: Princeton University Press, 1996.

Gilman, Lois. *The Adoption Resource Book*. 3d ed. New York: Harper Perennial, 1992.

Gordon, Elizabeth Putnam. *The Story of the Life and Work of Cordelia A. Greene, M.D.* Castile, N.Y.: Castilian, 1925.

Gordon, Linda. *The Great Arizona Orphan Abduction*. Cambridge, Mass.: Harvard University Press, 1999.

————. *Pitied but Not Entitled: Single Mothers and the History of Welfare, 1890–1935.* New York: Free Press, 1994.

————. *Woman's Body, Woman's Right.* New York: Penguin Books, 1977.

Gould, Steven Jay. *The Mismeasure of Man.* Rev. ed. New York: W. W. Norton, 1996.

Grant, Julia. *Raising Baby by the Book: The Education of American Mothers.* New Haven, Conn.: Yale University Press, 1998.

Griswold, Robert. *Fatherhood in America: A History.* New York: Basic Books, 1993.

Grossberg Michael. *Governing the Hearth: Law and the Family in Nineteenth-Century America.* Chapel Hill: University of North Carolina Press, 1985.

Gutman, Herbert. *The Black Family in Slavery and Freedom, 1750–1925.* New York: Vintage Books, 1976.

Hale, Nathan. *The Rise and Crisis of Psychoanalysis in the United States.* New York: Oxford University Press, 1995.

Haller, Mark. *Eugenics.* New Brunswick, N.J.: Rutgers University Press, 1963.

Hareven, Tamara. *Family History at the Crossroads: A Journal of Family History Reader.* Princeton, N.J.: Princeton University Press, 1987.

Healy, William, et al. *Reconstructing Behavior in Youth: A Study of Problem Children in Foster Families.* Judge Baker Foundation Publication No. 5. New York: Alfred A. Knopf, 1931.

Higham, John. *Strangers in the Land: Patterns of American Nativism, 1860–1925.* New Brunswick, N.J.: Rutgers University Press, 1955.

Hochschild, Arlie. *The Second Shift: Working Parents and the Revolution at Home.* New York: Viking Press, 1989.

Hoekstra, Ellen. "The Pedestal Myth Reinforced: Women's Magazine Fiction, 1900–1920." In *New Dimensions in Popular Culture,* edited by Russell Nye. Bowling Green, Ohio: Bowling Green University Popular Press, 1972.

Hoffert, Sylvia. *Private Matters: American Attitudes toward Childbearing and Infant Nurture in the Urban North, 1800–1860.* Urbana: University of Illinois Press, 1989.

Holloran, Peter. *Boston's Wayward Children: Social Services for Homeless Children, 1830–1930.* Cranbury, N.J.: Associated University Presses, 1989.

Holt, Marilyn Irvin. *The Orphan Trains: Placing Out in America.* Lincoln: University of Nebraska Press, 1992.

Howard, Ronald L. *A Social History of American Family Sociology, 1865–1940.* Westport, Conn.: Greenwood Press, 1981.

Hoyt, Edward A. "Adoption and the Law in Vermont, 1804–1863: An Introductory Essay." *Vermont History* 64 (summer 1996): 159–73.

Jambor, Harold A. "Theodore Dreiser, the *Delineator* Magazine, and Dependent Children: A Background Note on the Calling of the 1909 White House Conference." *Social Service Review* 32 (1958): 33–40.

James, Edward T., ed. *Notable American Women, 1607–1950.* Cambridge, Mass.: Belknap Press, 1971.

Katz, Michael. *Poverty and Policy in American History.* New York: Academic Press, 1983.

———. *In the Shadow of the Poorhouse: A Social History of Welfare in America.* New York: Basic Books, 1986.

Kawashima, Yasuhide. "Adoption in Early America." *Journal of Family Law* 20 (1981–1982): 677–96.

Kerber, Linda. "A Constitutional Right to Be Treated Like American Ladies: Women and the Obligations of Citizenship." In *U.S. History as Women's History,* edited by Linda Kerber, Alice Kessler-Harris, and Kathryn Kish Sklar. Chapel Hill: University of North Carolina Press, 1995.

———. *Women of the Republic: Intellect and Ideology in Revolutionary America.* Chapel Hill: University of North Carolina Press, 1980.

Kirk, H. David. *Adoptive Kinship: A Modern Institution in Need of Reform.* Toronto: Butterworths, 1981.

———. *Shared Fate: A Theory of Adoption and Mental Health.* New York: Free Press, 1964.

Kunzel, Regina. *Fallen Women, Problem Girls: Unmarried Mothers and the Professionalization of Social Work, 1890–1945.* New Haven, Conn.: Yale University Press, 1993.

———. "Pulp Fictions and Problem Girls: Reading and Rewriting Single Pregnancy in the Postwar United States." *American Historical Review* 100 (December 1995): 1465–87.

Langsam, Miriam. *Children West.* Madison: University of Wisconsin, 1964.

Lasch, Christopher. *Haven in a Heartless World: The Family Besieged.* New York: Basic Books, 1977.

Leavitt, Judith Walzer. *Brought to Bed: Childbearing in America, 1750–1950.* New York: Oxford University Press, 1986.

Letherby, Gayle. "Mother or Not, Mother or What? Problems of Definition and Identity." *Women's Studies International Forum* 17 (1994): 525–32.

Lewin, Ellen. *Lesbian Mothers: Accounts of Gender in American Culture.* Ithaca, N.Y.: Cornell University Press, 1993.

Lewis, Jan. "Mother's Love: The Construction of an Emotion in Nineteenth-Century America." In *Social History and Issues in Human Consciousness: Some Interdisciplinary Connections,* edited by Andrew E. Barnes and Peter N. Stearns. New York: New York University Press, 1989.

———. "The Republican Wife: Virtue and Seduction in the Early Republic." *William and Mary Quarterly* 44 (October 1987): 689–719.

Lindenmeyer, Kriste. *"A Right to Childhood": The U.S. Children's Bureau and Child Welfare, 1912–1946.* Urbana and Chicago: University of Illinois Press, 1997.

Lingeman, Richard. *Theodore Dreiser: An American Journey, 1908–1945.* New York: G. P. Putnam's Sons, 1990.

Lubove, Roy. *The Professional Altruist: The Emergence of Social Work as a Career, 1880–1930.* New York: Atheneum, 1972.

McRoy, Ruth, Harold Grotevant, and Susan Ayers-Lopez. "Changing Practices in Adoption." *AdoptINFO*. www.cyfc.umn.edu/Adoptinfo/changing.html. May 1997.

Marchand, Roland. *Advertising the American Dream: Making Way for Modernity, 1920–1940*. Berkeley: University of California Press, 1985.

Marindin, Hope. *The Handbook for Single Adoptive Parents*. Chevy Chase, Md.: Committee for Single Adoptive Parents, 1987.

Marsh, Margaret. *Suburban Lives*. New Brunswick, N.J.: Rutgers University Press, 1990.

Marsh, Margaret, and Wanda Ronner. *The Empty Cradle: Infertility in America from Colonial Times to the Present*. Baltimore: Johns Hopkins University Press, 1996.

Mason, Mary Ann. *From Father's Property to Children's Rights*. New York: Columbia University Press, 1994.

Mason, Mary Ann, and Eileen Gambrill. *Debating Children's Lives: Current Controversies on Children and Adolescents*. Thousand Oaks, Calif.: Sage Publications, 1994.

Matthiessen, F. O. *Theodore Dreiser*. New York: William Sloane, 1951.

May, Elaine Tyler. *Barren in the Promised Land: Childless Americans and the Pursuit of Happiness*. New York: Basic Books, 1995.

———. *Homeward Bound: American Families in the Cold War Era*. New York: Basic Books, 1988.

Melosh, Barbara. "Adoption Autobiography and the Construction of Identity." Paper presented at the annual convention of the Organization of American Historians, Atlanta, April 1994.

Miles, Susan, ed. *Adoption Literature for Children and Young Adults*. New York: Greenwood Press, 1986.

Miller, Naomi. *Single Parents by Choice: A Growing Trend in Family Life*. New York: Insight Books, 1992.

Mintz, Steven, and Susan Kellogg. *Domestic Revolutions*. New York: Free Press, 1988.

Modell, Judith. *Kinship with Strangers: Adoption and Interpretations of Kinship in American Culture*. Berkeley: University of California Press, 1994.

Mookerjee, R. N. *Theodore Dreiser: His Thought and Social Criticism*. Delhi, India: National, 1974.

Morantz-Sanchez, Regina Markell. *Sympathy and Science: Women Physicians in American Medicine*. New York: Oxford University Press, 1985.

Morawski, J. G. "Not Quite New Worlds: Psychologists' Conceptions of the Ideal Family in the Twenties." In *In the Shadow of the Past: Psychology Portrays the Sexes*, edited by Miriam Lewin. New York: Columbia University Press, 1984.

Morell, Carolyn M. *Unwomanly Conduct: The Challenges of Intentional Childlessness*. New York: Routledge, 1994.

Morton, Marian. *And Sin No More: Social Policy and Unwed Mothers in Cleveland, 1855–1990*. Columbus: Ohio State University Press, 1993.

Norton, Mary Beth. *Liberty's Daughters: The Revolutionary Experiences of American Women, 1750–1800.* Boston: Little, Brown, 1980.

Mott, Frank L. *A History of American Magazines, 1865–1885.* Vol. 3. Cambridge, Mass.: Harvard University Press, 1938.

Muncy, Robyn. *Creating a Female Dominion in American Reform, 1890–1935.* New York: Oxford University Press, 1991.

National Council for Single Adoptive Parents. "Would You Rather Be Called Mommy or Daddy . . . Instead of Aunt or Uncle?" http://www.adopting.org/ncsap.html. May 1997.

Nelkin, Dorothy, and M. Susan Lindee. *The DNA Mystique: The Gene as a Cultural Icon.* New York: W. H. Freeman, 1995.

Orleck, Annelise. *Common Sense and a Little Fire.* Chapel Hill: University of North Carolina Press, 1995.

Passet, Joanne. *Cultural Crusaders: Women Librarians in the American West, 1900–1917.* Albuquerque: University of New Mexico Press, 1994.

Pfeffer, Paula. "Homeless Children, Childless Homes," *Chicago History* (spring 1987): 51–65.

Pierce, William. *1989 Adoption Factbook.* Washington, D.C.: National Committee for Adoption, 1989.

Platt, Anthony. *The Child Savers: The Invention of Delinquency.* Chicago: University of Chicago Press, 1969.

Presser, Stephen. "Background of the American Law of Adoption." *Journal of Family Law* 11 (1971–1972): 443–516.

Prowler, Mady. "Single Parent Adoption: What You Need to Know." http://www.adopt.org/datacenter/bin/AQ_single1.htm. November 1999.

Rapp, Rayna. "Toward a Nuclear Freeze? The Gender Politics of Euro-American Kinship Analysis." In *Gender and Kinship: Essays toward a Unified Analysis,* edited by Jane Fishburne Collier and Sylvia Junko Yanagisako. Stanford, Calif.: Stanford University Press, 1987.

Rappaport, Bruce. *The Open Adoption Book: A Guide to Adoption without Tears.* New York: Macmillan, 1992.

Reep, Diana. *Margaret Deland.* Boston: Twayne, 1985.

———. *The Rescue and Romance: Popular Novels before World War I.* Bowling Green, Ohio: Bowling Green State University Press, 1982.

Reid, Doris Fielding. *Edith Hamilton: An Intimate Portrait.* New York: W. W. Norton, 1967.

Rich, Adrienne. *Of Woman Born: Motherhood as Experience and Institution.* New York: W. W. Norton, 1976. Reprint, New York: Bantam Books, 1981.

Rickard, O'Ryan. *A Just Verdict: The Life of Caroline Bartlett Crane.* Kalamazoo: Western Michigan University, New Issues Press, 1994.

Romanofsky, Peter. "Professionals versus Volunteers: A Case Study of Adoption Workers in the 1920s." *Journal of Voluntary Action Research* 2 (April 1973): 95–101.

———. "Saving the Lives of the City's Foundlings: The Joint Committee and New York City Child Care Methods, 1860–1907." *New York Historical Society Quarterly* 61 (1977): 49–68.

Rosenberg, Charles. "The Bitter Fruit: Heredity, Disease, and Social Thought in Nineteenth-Century America." *Perspectives in American History* 8 (1974): 189–235.

Rosenberg, Rosalind. *Beyond Separate Spheres.* New Haven, Conn.: Yale University Press, 1982.

Rossi, Alice S. *The Feminist Papers.* New York: Bantam Books, 1973.

Rothman, Barbara Katz. *Recreating Motherhood: Ideology and Technology in a Patriarchal Society.* New York: W. W. Norton, 1989.

Rothman, David. *The Discovery of the Asylum.* 1971. Reprint, Boston: Little, Brown, 1990.

Rothman, Sheila. *Woman's Proper Place: A History of Changing Ideals and Practices, 1870 to the Present.* New York: Basic Books, 1978.

Rupp, Leila. "'Imagine My Surprise': Women's Relationships in Mid-Twentieth Century America." In *Hidden from History: Reclaiming the Gay and Lesbian Past,* edited by Martin Duberman, Martha Vicinus, and George Chauncey, Jr. New York: New American Library, 1989.

Ryan, Mary. *Cradle of the Middle Class: The Family in Oneida County, New York, 1790–1865.* New York: Cambridge University Press, 1981.

Sandelowski, Margarete. "Failures of Volition: Female Agency and Infertility in Historical Perspective." *Signs* 15 (spring 1990): 475–99.

———. "Fault Lines: Infertility and Imperiled Sisterhood." *Feminist Studies* 16 (spring 1990): 33–51.

Schlossman, Steven L. "Before Home Start: Notes toward a History of Parent Education in America, 1897–1929." *Harvard Educational Review* 46 (August 1976): 436–67.

Schnog, Nancy, and Joel Pfister, eds. *Inventing the Psychological.* New Haven, Conn.: Yale University Press, 1997.

Schwarz, Judith. *Radical Feminists of Heterodoxy: Greenwich Village 1912–1940.* Rev. ed. Norwich, Conn.: New Victoria Publishers, 1986.

Sherraden, Michael, and Susan Whitelaw Downs. "The Orphan Asylum in the Nineteenth Century." *Social Service Review* 57 (June 1983): 272–90.

Shields, Stephanie A. "To Pet, Coddle, and 'Do for.'" In *In the Shadow of the Past: Psychology Portrays the Sexes,* edited by Miriam Lewin. New York: Columbia University Press, 1984.

Sicherman, Barbara, and Carol Hurd Green, eds. *Notable American Women—The Modern Period.* Cambridge, Mass.: Belknap Press, 1980.

Silber, Kathleen, and Phylis Speedlin. *Dear Birthmother: Thank You for Our Baby.* San Antonio, Tex.: Corona, 1983.

Sklar, Kathryn Kish. *Catharine Beecher: A Study in American Domesticity.* New Haven, Conn.: Yale University Press, 1973.

Skocpol, Theda. *Protecting Soldiers and Mothers: The Political Origins of Social Policy in the United States.* Cambridge, Mass.: Belknap Press, 1992.

Smith, Betsy, Janet Surrey, and Mary Watkins. "'Real' Mothers: Adoptive Mothers Resisting Marginalization and Re-creating Motherhood." In *Mothering against the Odds: Diverse Voices of Contemporary Mothers,* edited by Cynthia Garcia Coll et al. New York: Guilford Press, 1998.

Smith-Rosenberg, Carroll. "Discourses of Sexuality and Subjectivity: The New Woman, 1870–1936." In *Hidden from History: Reclaiming the Gay and Lesbian Past,* edited by Martin Duberman, Martha Vicinus, and George Chauncey. New York: New American Library, 1989.

———. *Disorderly Conduct: Visions of Gender in Victorian America.* New York: Oxford University Press, 1985.

Solinger, Rickie. *Wake up Little Susie: Single Pregnancy and Race before* Roe v. Wade. New York: Routledge, 1992.

Sorosky, Arthur D., Annette Baran, and Reuben Pannor. *The Adoption Triangle.* New York: Anchor/Doubleday, 1978.

Stack, Carol. *All Our Kin.* New York: Basic Books, 1974.

Stolley, Kathy S. "Statistics on Adoption in the United States." *Future of Children* 3 (spring 1993): 26–42.

"Strategies for Adopting 'Solo.'" http://www.adopt.org/datacenter/bin/AQ_single 3.htm. November 1999.

Taylor, Molly Ladd. *Raising a Baby the Government Way: Mothers' Letters to the Children's Bureau: 1915–32.* New Brunswick, N.J.: Rutgers University Press, 1986.

Thorne, Barrie. *Rethinking the Family: Some Feminist Questions.* New York: Longman, 1982.

Tiffin, Susan. *In Whose Best Interest? Child Welfare Reform in the Progressive Era.* Westport, Conn.: Greenwood Press, 1982.

Trattner, Walter. *From Poor Law to Welfare State.* New York: Free Press, 1974.

———. *Homer Folks: Pioneer in Social Welfare.* New York: Columbia University Press, 1968.

Ulrich, Laurel Thatcher. *Good Wives: Image and Reality in the Lives of Women in Northern New England, 1650–1750.* New York: Vintage Books, 1991.

Wadia-Ells, Susan, ed. *The Adoption Reader: Birth Mothers, Adoptive Mothers and Adopted Daughters Tell Their Stories.* Seattle: Seal Press, 1995.

Waldman, Steven, and Lincoln Caplan. "The Politics of Adoption." *Newsweek,* March 21, 1994, 64–65.

Walkowitz, Daniel J. "The Making of a Feminine Professional Identity: Social Workers in the 1920s." *American Historical Review* 95 (October 1990): 1051–75.

Wegar, Katarina. *Adoption, Identity, and Kinship: The Debate over Sealed Birth Records.* New Haven, Conn.: Yale University Press, 1997.

Welter, Barbara. "The Cult of True Womanhood: 1820-1860." *American Quarterly* 18 (summer 1966): 151–74.

Weston, Kath. *Families We Choose: Lesbians, Gays, Kinship.* New York: Columbia University Press, 1991.

White, Hayden. "The Value of Narrativity in the Representation of Reality." In *On Narrative,* edited by W. J. T. Mitchell. Chicago: University of Chicago Press, 1981.

"Why Negros Don't Adopt Children." *Ebony* 7 (July 1952).

Wiebe, Robert. *The Search for Order 1877–1920.* New York: Hill and Wang, 1967.

Wishy, Bernard. *The Child and the Republic: The Dawn of Modern American Child Nurture.* Philadelphia: University of Pennsylvania Press, 1968.

Wolins, Martin, and Irving Piliavin. *Institution or Foster Family? A Century of Debate.* New York: Child Welfare League of America, 1964.

Zainaldin, Jamil. "The Emergence of a Modern American Family Law: Child Custody, Adoption and the Courts, 1796–1851." *Northwestern University Law Review* 73 (1979): 1038–89.

Zainaldin, Jamil, and Peter Tyor. "Asylum and Society: An Approach to Institutional Change." *Journal of Social History* 13 (fall 1979): 23–48.

Zelizer, Viviana. *Pricing the Priceless Child.* New York: Basic Books, 1985.

Zmora, Nurith. *Orphanage Reconsidered.* Philadelphia: Temple University Press, 1994.

Dissertations

Bellingham, Bruce. "Little Wanderers: A Socio-Historical Study of the Nineteenth Century Origins of Child Fostering and Adoption Reform, based on Early Records of the New York Children's Aid Society." Ph.D. diss., University of Pennsylvania, 1984.

Brown, June. "Safeguarding Adoption in California, 1870–1969." D.S.W. diss., University of Southern California, 1970.

Cobbledick, Winifred. "A Study of Adoption Agency Criteria in 'Matching' Children to Homes." M.S.W. thesis, University of California, 1949.

Dulberger, Judith Ann. "Refuge or Repressor: The Role of the Orphan Asylum in the Lives of Poor Children and Their Families in Late-Nineteenth Century America." Ph.D. diss., Carnegie-Mellon University, 1988.

Gill, Brian. "The Jurisprudence of Good Parenting: The Selection of Adoptive Parents, 1894–1964." Ph.D. diss., University of California–Berkeley, 1997.

Hart, Patricia Susan. "A Home for Every Child, a Child for Every Home: Relinquishment and Adoption at Washington Children's Home Society, 1896–1915." Ph.D. diss., Washington State University, 1997.

Romanofsky, Peter. "The Early History of Adoption Practices, 1870–1930." Ph.D. diss., University of Missouri–Columbia, 1969.

Smith, Winifred. "The Use of Popular Literature as a Medium for the Interpretation of Professional Standards of Adoption." Master's thesis, Smith College School for Social Work, 1940.

Tillman, Elvena Bage. "The Rights of Childhood: The National Child Welfare Movement, 1890–1919." Ph.D. diss., University of Wisconsin, 1968.

Waller, Mary Ellen. "Popular Women's Magazines, 1890–1917." Ph.D. diss., Columbia University, 1987.

Zainaldin, Jamil. "The Origins of Modern Legal Adoption: Child Exchange in Boston, 1851–1893." Ph.D. diss., University of Chicago, 1976.

Index